50 YEARS

lonely

OF

GRE

Alexis Averbuck, Amber Charmei, Rebecca Hall, Helen Iatrou, Vangelis Koronakis, Anastasia Miari, Sarah Souli, Ryan Ver Berkmoes

Adriatic Sea
TIRANA
NORTH MACEDONIA
ALBANIA
GREECE
Serres
Thessaloniki & Northern Greece 74
Edessa
Florina
Kastoria
Athens 6 hrs
Halkidiki
Kozani
Katerini
Lake Aliakmonas
Mt Olympus
Athens 1 hr
Corfu Town
Ioannina
Kalambaka
Larissa
Igoumenitsa
Corfu
Karditsa
Volos
Paxi
Antipaxi
Arta
Preveza
Delphi & Central Greece 98
Lefkada Town
Lake Kremasta
Lefkada
Agrinio
Halkida
Ithaki
Nafpaktos
Kefallonia
Patras
Egio
Gulf of Corinth
Argostoli
Ionian Islands 140
Corinth
Ionian Sea
Zakynthos Town
Aegina
Zakynthos
Pirgos
Nafplio
Poros
Tripoli
Hydra
Peloponnese 116
Spetses
Myrtoö Sea
Kalamata
Sparta
Kythira
Mediterranean Sea
Libyan Sea
0 200 km
0 100 miles
N

Acropolis (p62), Athens

Anastasia Miari

Based between Athens and Corfu, journalist Anastasia freelances for *Monocle Magazine*, *Konfekt Magazine*, the *Guardian*, the *Sunday Times* and is *Courier* magazine's Greece correspondent.

Sarah Souli

Sarah is a US journalist based in Greece. Though she mostly lives between Athens and Tinos, she's a firm believer that the north is actually the country's best secret. She has a penchant for slow travel and wild swimming. (Photo credit: Marco Arguello)

Ryan Ver Berkmoes

@ryanverberkmoes

Ryan first visited Greece in 1985 and has lived on the idyllic island of Hydra part-time since 2012 – shortly after he met the love of his life, his wife Alexis Averbuck. He has written more than 130 books for Lonely Planet.

Contents

Symi (p228), Dodecanese

ESSAYS

VISUAL GUIDES

WIDE OPEN **SPACES**

Greece is a land of grand spaces, where towering mountains dominate the horizons and drama fills the windswept coasts – it's the stuff of Homerian tales. No matter your landscape preference, you can find a dose here. From the forested villages of Zagorohoria alongside Vikos Gorge, to the lush springs of Naxos and Santorini's insane crescent of sunken caldera, dazzle your mind and awe your soul.

→ NYMPH-SPOTTING

Greek nature is imbued with mythical creatures. Keep an eye out for Dryads (tree nymphs), Oreads (mountain nymphs), Naiads (freshwater nymphs) and Nereids (sea nymphs), among others.

JUSTIN FOULKES/LONELY PLANET ©

Left and right Vikos Gorge (p89)
Below Wild boar

MAGICAL PELION

Donkey trails zigzag over rolling, forested hills to quiet, sandy coves and quaint villages on the Pelion Peninsula, the reputed home of the Centaurs.

RIGHT: STANISLAV DUBEN/SHUTTERSTOCK ©
LEFT: JUSTIN FOULKES/LONELY PLANET ©

↑ HUNTING SEASON

Late August to late February is hunting season in Greece. When hitting the trails, look for signs saying Κυνηγετικός χώρος (hunting area) – many are handmade.

Best Outdoor Experiences

- **Thrill at the magnificent views of the Santorini crater festooned with white-cubed villages. (p190)**
- **Follow ancient trails up the thickly forested slopes of Mt Olympus, once the lair of the Ancient Greek pantheon. (p84)**
- **Hike Crete's gorges from spectacular Samaria Gorge to equally breathtaking Imbros and Aradena gorges. (p170)**

AZURE SEAS & **SANDY SHORES**

Greece is virtually synonymous with beaches – broad sweeps of white sand, grey or even red-pebble coves, and black volcanic shores. Summer season is a tradition here, when families return to home islands and holidays are a call for R&R. A siren song for travellers, too, summer means crowds but also the best swimming of your life.

ADRIENNE PITTS/LONELY PLANET ©

→ TAKE A DIVE

Greeks at work don't forego the sea. They head out for a *voutiá*, a quick dive. Early mornings and twilight are perfect for solo swims.

Left Antipaxi (p145)
Right Paros (p200)
Below Crete (p160)

ACCESSIBLE BEACHES

Increasingly, Greece is installing ramps and providing assistive devices and wheels at popular beaches for getting into the sea. Not ubiquitous, but on the rise (check extramilers.eu).

RIGHT: NASTYA22/SHUTTERSTOCK ©, LEFT: AERIAL-MOTION/SHUTTERSTOCK ©

↑ PINK SANDS

It's minute bits of coral that create the long pink-hued sand dunes on Crete's west coast from Falasarna to Elafonisi.

Best Beach Experiences

- **Surrender to sun and clear, blue water on Antipaxi, for some of Greece's best swimming. (p145)**
- **Sample beaches on Naxos, where one glossy strand merges right into the next. (p202)**
- **Discover Milos' surreal rock-formation-backed volcanic beaches. (p192)**
- **Stroll on foot from beach to glorious beach in the Small Cyclades. (p204)**

Many islands now rent fat-tyre or e-bikes, perfect for cruising by beaches without a belching motor. Rules vary on whether you can hire a boat with or without a licence. If you have one, bring it, as some places are sticklers.

TAKE TO THE **WAVES**

Cobalt seas and beaches backed by thyme-scented hills call for exploration. All across Greece you can find your favourite: from kitesurfing the wind-whipped channels of the Cyclades to kayaking over sunken villas. Landlubbers can opt for seafront biking and horse riding, and open-sea swimmers will be spoiled for choice.

Best Active Experiences

▶ **Get your adrenaline pumping while windsurfing or kitesurfing in the channel between Paros and Antiparos. (p200)**

▶ **Ride horses through olive groves to the beach, then swim in the sea bareback on the Pelion Peninsula. (p106)**

▶ **Boat to Halkidiki's Diaporos, an uninhabited island with impossibly clear turquoise water. (p93)**

▶ **Hike Hydra's serene coastal paths to reach glorious swimming rocks and hidden bays. (p138)**

The word *xenos* means both 'stranger' and 'guest'; Greeks see *filoxenia* (hospitality) almost as a matter of personal pride and honour.

You can still see older men in the villages playing with the *komboloï* – they may look like prayer beads, but are only used for relaxation.

POSNOV/GETTY IMAGES ©

VILLAGE **LIFE**

Greek life has always taken place in the public sphere, whether it's talking politics at the local *kafeneio* (coffee house) or families gathering in neighbourhood squares while the kids play into the evening. And Greek villages, from seashore to mountain valley, are a quintessential place to experience daily life.

Left Cyclades (p184)
Right Zagorohoria (p89)

Best Village Experiences

- **Tramp ancient paths between Zagorohoria's stone villages near Vikos Gorge. (p89)**
- **Sequester yourself in the quaint Arkadian villages in the Peloponnese. (p123)**
- **Delight in the sheer variety and beauty of Crete's mountain villages. (p176)**
- **Stroll the cobbled paths of Apiranthos, one of Naxos' many multifaceted villages. (p203)**
- **Snap selfies in Cycladic white-cube harbour villages on Paros and Antiparos. (p200)**

ISLANDS GALORE

Stereotypes don't work on Greek islands, and marquee names may not always be the best fit for you. Each island has its own character, its own culture. And many have vastly different terrains, weather patterns and, certainly, histories. So a trip in the islands is an incredible smorgasbord – sample widely.

Paxi & Antipaxi

Shimmering Ionian jewels

Explore beyond grand Corfu to diminutive Paxi and its even smaller friend, Antipaxi. Hidden in plain sight, they offer azure waters with some of the best swimming in Greece, peaceful harbours with bobbing yachts and pensions tucked into olive groves.

30mins from Corfu

▶ p145

Hydra

Fascinating car-free getaway

Escape from Athens to the brilliantly preserved, car-free island of Hydra for ebullient harbour life and swims off the rocks. A beacon for artists, writers and musicians for decades, the island's rich cultural landscape – from historic mansions to cutting-edge international art – easily fills days.

2hrs from Athens

▶ p138

Milos

Parade of sensations

Circle the array of beaches on volcanic Milos, a gentler option than busy Santorini. Sarakiniko is a star, with creamy rock formations and blue, blue water, as is the hamlet of Klima with its colourful seafront fishing dwellings.

4hrs from Santorini

▶ p192

Sea of Marmara
0 200 km
0 100 miles
ANKARA
TURKEY
Chios
Aegean Sea
Andros
Samos
Tinos
Ikaria
Syros
Ermoupoli
Patmos
CYCLADES
Paros
Naxos
Antiparos
Amorgos
Kos
Astypalea
Rhodes Town
Santorini
Rhodes
Sea of Crete
Karpathos
Kasos
Iraklio
Crete
Sitia
Mediterranean Sea

Paros & Antiparos

Traditional Cyclades and easy fun

Entertain the whole family in Paros and Antiparos, where you can mix village strolls with beach play and even nightclub crawls. Parikia and Naoussa harbours are resplendent with blooming bougainvillea draping over cubist, white lanes packed with cafes and boutiques.

1hr from Athens

▸ p200

Karpathos

Traditional island spirit

Journey the misty mountains and lovely beaches of Karpathos, the birthplace of Prometheus and his Titans, in search of tiny Olymbos village with its unique dialect, local dress and delicious regional cookery.

70mins from Athens

▸ p220

Crete

Something for everyone

Dive deep into all aspects of Greek life on its largest and most diverse island, Crete, almost a country unto itself. Discover its pink-sand western beaches, its vast gorges begging to be hiked and its vibrant cities and mountain villages with top cuisine.

1hr from Athens

▸ p160

CULINARY RICHES **& WINE**

Greek food has been exported across the world, but there is simply no way to recreate the delight of sampling it in the spot where it is produced. Cheeses are made fresh in the mountains and herbs and greens picked from their slopes. Goats and lambs graze free, while small fish and calamari are harvested from the seas. And, of course, there are the subtly brilliant creative variations on how each region and each chef prepares them.

Left Greek salad
Right Cretan honey
Below Local wines

→ HONEY, HONEY

Rich honey is a product of native flowers and trees. Many are only available in homemade batches sold locally – look for these in smaller markets.

SEAFOOD LUNCH & SIESTA

A summertime cultural mainstay is a seafront taverna lunch, with its parade of dips and dishes, followed by a decadent siesta. Embrace it.

↑ KNOW YOUR WINES

You'll find Greek wines at supermarkets, but know your regions to learn how to tell the solid sips from truly delightful treats.

Best Food & Drink Experiences

- **Village-hop on Tinos to discover some of Greece's best regional food. (p196)**
- **Tour volcanic vineyards, then taste top *asyrtiko* white wines on Santorini. (p190)**
- **Savour the Italian-inflected cuisine of the Ionian Islands in charming Corfu Town. (p154)**
- **Sip delicate ouzos in Plomari on Lesvos, the island of Sappho. (p234)**
- **Relish glorious Cretan meals in Hania's excellent restaurants. (p166)**

EPIC ANCIENT WONDERS

World-renowned ancient sites – some featuring in the greatest tales of all time, the Greek myths – carpet the country. With every layer excavated, another civilisation is revealed. And the architecture and artefacts created to honour the gods – Athena, Poseidon, Apollo, Zeus, to name just a few – remain ready for us to marvel at and explore.

Delphi

Centre of the Ancient Greek world

Listen for the oracle's whisper at majestic Delphi. Zeus released two eagles at opposite ends of the world and they met here, on the slopes of Mt Parnassos with the Gulf of Corinth shimmering below, thus making Delphi the centre of the world.

3hrs from Athens

▶ p102

Ancient Olympia

Birthplace of the Olympic Games

Sprint around the stadium at Ancient Olympia, a 3000-year-old World Heritage–listed sanctuary to sporting glory, which hosted the original Olympic Games.

4hrs from Athens

▶ p130

Ancient Mycenae

Mighty kingdom rich in gold

Climb to the citadel of Ancient Mycenae with its immense royal beehive tomb of the Treasury of Atreus. It was home to magnificent gold masks and jewellery now in Athens' National Archaeological Museum.

30mins from Nafplio

▶ p131

Ionian Sea
Lefkada Town
Lefkada
GREECE
Akheloös
Agrinio
Messolongi
Delphi
Halkida
Evia
Kefallonia
IONIAN ISLANDS
Patras
Egio
Gulf of Corinth
Corinth
ATHENS
Piraeus
Kyllini
Zakynthos
Pirgos
Olympia
Tripoli
Mycenae
Aegina
Megalopoli
Hydra
Spetses
Sparta
Kalamata
Pylos
Mediterranean Sea
Areopoli
Myrtoön Sea
Neapoli

Athens' Acropolis

Wonder of the Western world

Make the pilgrimage to Athens' beautifully preserved Acropolis with its temples to Athena, columns shining above the city. Looking down, you'll see the Ancient Agora – the civic, political and commercial centre – plus Roman ruins and Byzantine churches, legacies of rulers past.

6hrs from Thessaloniki

▶ p62

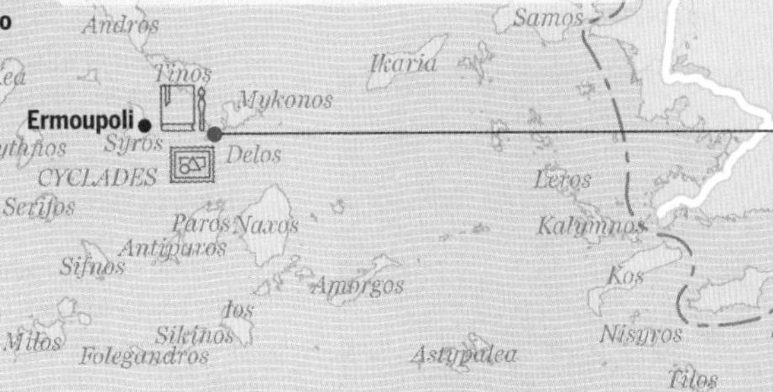

Delos

Centre of the Cyclades

Sail from party-hard Mykonos to the epic sanctuary at Delos, the centre of the Cyclades and birthplace of Apollo and Artemis. This uninhabited island is chockablock with ruined temples, treasuries and residences bedecked in mosaics; it also boasts a museum of priceless statuary.

30mins from Mykonos

▶ p199

Knossos

Palatial Minoan capital

Imagine the mysterious Minoan culture at Crete's marquee site, Knossos, as you ascend to monumental terraces with vibrant fresco restorations. It's ideally paired with the Heraklion Archaeological Museum, packed with elaborate finds from the site.

30mins from Iraklio

▶ p168

HIKING COASTS & MOUNTAINS

Whether you're just getting started or your boots are covered with the dust of a thousand hikes, Greece has a trail for everyone. Rove through the national parks to uncover roiling cascades or feel the salt on your skin as you ramble coastal trails. Islands are primo for exploring on foot, beckoning with well-marked pathways.

LEFT: JANA JANINA/SHUTTERSTOCK ©, BOTTOM: ERIC ISSELEE/SHUTTERSTOCK ©

EXPLORE WIDELY & GO DEEP

The social cooperative Paths of Greece (pathsofgreece.gr) creates new hiking routes across the country, many with cultural links.

Best Hiking Experiences

- Hike through Kefallonia's olive groves and vineyards. (p159)
- Walk the hilltops, hamlets and chapel-studded beaches of Sifnos. (p194)
- Drop out of time on Iraklia and follow well-marked trails over its small mountains. (p204)
- Stroll pine-covered dirt tracks to azure coves on Angistri. (p137)

← HIT THE E4 TRAIL

The long-distance route from Portugal to Cyprus encompasses ancient paths in Greece, like those from Livadi plateau (near Arahova) down to Delphi, or others near Mystras.

Above Mt Olympus (p84)
Left Sifnos (p194)

PALACES OF **CULTURE**

If there's one thing Greece has in spades, it's art and culture and the museums dedicated to their veneration. Any list of places to go is by definition incomplete. Grand city museums hold world-class treasures, and so do many humble village collections. Entry prices tend to be low, so explore widely.

Best Art & Culture Experiences

- **Admire ancient sculptures in the Acropolis Museum's spacious, superbly designed galleries. (p54)**
- **Browse the last several centuries of Greek painting at Athens' new National Gallery. (p54)**
- **Imagine the life of a great artist on Hydra at the Studio of Panayiotis Tetsis. (p138)**

← MUST SEE

Quietly filling a full block in Exarhia, the National Archaeological Museum is a treasure chest of ancient art from across Greece. Don't miss it.

JACKPOT

When visiting ancient sites – from Olympia and Delphi to Naxos' Temple of Demeter – leave time for their museums where countless prizes found on-site are protected.

Above National Archaeological Museum (p54)
Left Acropolis Museum (p54)

The *meltemi* ('north wind') is a summer wind whipping across the Aegean from the north, mainly between June and September.

→ Miaoulia Festival

In June, Hydra ignites in celebration of its contribution to the War of Independence with a spectacular boat burning, fireworks and folk dancing.

Hydra

← Athens Epidaurus Festival

The most prominent summer festival (June to August) features music, dance and drama at the ancient theatre on Athens' Acropolis and at Epidavros in the Peloponnese.

Athens and Epidavros

▶ aefestival.gr

Skopelos Rembetika Festival

Hit a musical jamboree in July at a three-day showcase for local folk-blues musicians.

Skopelos Town

▶ rembetikoskopelos festival.com

JUNE

Average daytime max: 29°C
Days of rainfall: 1

JULY

Greece in SUMMER

↓ Cool Pindos

Seek fewer crowds and cooler temperatures in Greece's northern mountains like the Pindos range.

Naxos Festivals

May to September concerts fill the Venetian *kastro* (castle), the Bazeos Tower hosts art exhibitions, and celebrations abound with food and music.

Naxos

Delphi Festival

In June and August, trip the light fantastic with musical and theatrical events in and around Delphi and Dorida.

Delphi

▸ delphifestival.gr

Demand for accommodation peaks during summer. View tours and overnight adventures in advance at lonelyplanet.com.

Average daytime max: 32°C
Days of rainfall: 0

AUGUST

Average daytime max: 32°C
Days of rainfall: 0

Packing Notes

A big hat and lots of sunscreen to protect against the fierce summer sun.

Autumn is tops for peaceful, late-season swims and excellent walking. Services begin closing on some islands, but those in popular locales remain open.

↘ Great Days of Nemea Wine Festival

Sample widely at this wine festival in September that celebrates Nemea's *agiorgitiko* grape with tastings, concerts and more.

Nemea

▸ nemeawineland.com

↖ Ohi Day

A simple 'no' (*ohi* in Greek) was the famous response when Mussolini demanded passage for his troops on 28 October 1940. Now, it's a national holiday with remembrance services and parades.

SEPTEMBER

Average daytime max: 28°C
Days of rainfall: 1

OCTOBER

Greece in AUTUMN

FROM LEFT: BARMALINI/SHUTTERSTOCK ©, MARIA CHOURDARI/NURPHOTO/ALAMY STOCK PHOTO ©, MATT MUNRO/LONELY PLANET ©, VERVERIDIS VASILIS/SHUTTERSTOCK ©; BOTTOM: GEORGE PAPAPOSTOLOU/500PX ©

↘ Thessaloniki International Film Festival

In November, around 150 films are crammed into 11 days of screenings, alongside concerts, exhibitions, talks and theatrical performances.

Thessaloniki

▶ filmfestival.gr

↖ Olive-picking

Autumn sees temperatures drop. Olive-picking is in full swing in places such as Crete and feta production picks up, giving you the opportunity to taste some seriously fresh cheese.

Average daytime max: 23°C
Days of rainfall: 3

NOVEMBER

Average daytime max: 18°C
Days of rainfall: 4

Packing Notes

Both bathing suit and light sweater or scarf, plus hiking boots for prime walking season.

The holiday season in Greece is understated and joyful, with Christmas bringing light-festooned harbours, honey cookies and good cheer on into the new year.

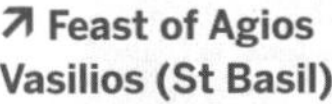

↗ Feast of Agios Vasilios (St Basil)

New Year's Day sees a church ceremony followed by gifts, singing, dancing and feasting. The *vasilopita* (golden glazed cake) is cut; if you get the slice with a coin, you'll have a lucky year.

↓ Snow in Athens

Greece sees snow in the north and on its mountaintops. Freak storms even occasionally powder Athens or the islands.

↘ Epiphany (Blessing of the Waters)

Christ's baptism is celebrated throughout Greece on 6 January, when seas, lakes and rivers are blessed, with the largest ceremony at Piraeus.

Piraeus

DECEMBER

JANUARY

Average daytime max: 15°C
Days of rainfall: 6

Greece in WINTER

↘ Thessaloniki Nightlife

The islands may be quiet but Thessaloniki (along with Athens) is in full swing. Nightlife there peaks during winter.

↓ Carnival

Carnival season culminates in a wild weekend (February/March) of costume parades, feasting and dancing. Patra's is the largest and Skyros' the most unusual.

📍 Patra and Skyros

↖ Quiet Acropolis

With fewer tourists, you won't have to push through crowds at the major sights like the Acropolis.

FEBRUARY

Average daytime max: 13°C
Days of rainfall: 5

Average daytime max: 14°C
Days of rainfall: 5

Packing Notes

Bring jumpers, a rain slicker and sturdy shoes for potential chilled rains and slippery marble cobbles.

Greece in SPRING

Spring is grand for hitting Greece's trails, when temperatures are mild and wildflowers splash colour across the land.

↘ Independence Day

The anniversary of the hoisting of the Greek flag is celebrated nationwide with parades and dancing on 25 March.

Prioritise islands that get overcrowded in summer since the droves haven't yet arrived: Santorini, Mykonos, Corfu, Rhodes and Hydra.

MARCH

Average daytime max: 16°C
Days of rainfall: 4

APRIL

↓ Easter

The Greek Orthodox calendar is chock-full of festivals and saints' namedays, but the biggest by far is Easter (April or May). Experience it on Patmos with fireworks, dancing in the streets, goats roasting and plenty of ouzo.

📍 Patmos

← Farmers Markets

Seek out farmers markets, known as *laïki agora* in Greek, which overflow with seasonal produce.

→ May Day

On 1 May, picnic in the country and gather wildflowers to make wreaths *(stefania)* to decorate houses.

Average daytime max: 20°C
Days of rainfall: 3

MAY

Average daytime max: 25°C
Days of rainfall: 2

Packing Notes

Layers, layers, layers – plus a swimsuit for variable weather.

ISLAND CRUSING
Trip Builder

TAKE YOUR PICK OF MUST-SEES AND HIDDEN GEMS

First trip to Greece and looking for island highlights? The Cyclades and Crete supply some of the country's top islands, most beautiful beaches, cultural highs and special villages. Mixing and matching is easy when island hopping, so a diversion anywhere along the way just adds to the fun.

Trip Notes

Hub islands Mykonos, Naxos, Santorini

How long Allow 10 days

Getting around Frequent ferries run between islands in summer, but decrease dramatically in winter. Some Cyclades islands as well as Crete have an airport.

Tips For larger islands where you need wheels, it's easier and cheaper to hire on each island than take a vehicle on ferries. Summer traffic is chaotic on popular islands like Santorini, Paros and Mykonos.

Paros
Stroll traditional Cycladic whitewashed lanes, then surf the waves between Paros and Antiparos or boat around their golden beaches.
1hr from Santorini

Sifnos
Walk, swim, eat...what's not to love? On this chic island with rainbow-prism waters, alternate between see-and-be-seen Apollonia with its excellent eateries and deep R&R.
2½hrs from Piraeus

Delos

Examine and imagine ancient sanctuaries at the sacred island of Delos, the treasury of the Delian League and reputed birthplace of twins Apollo and Artemis.

30mins from Mykonos

Mykonos

Slather on the sunscreen for see-and-be-seen lounging at fashionable bars and crowd-pleasing beaches on this world-famous island ideal for social butterflies and lovers of action.

45mins from Athens

Naxos

Hike to stone-topped peaks, mountain villages and ancient ruins, then recline on soft-white-sand beaches after a bountiful seafood taverna lunch.

45mins from Athens

Small Cyclades

Roam the teeny, tiny and out-of-the-way in this series of delectable islands hugging Naxos, each with its own vibe.

1hr from Naxos

Crete

Struggle with abundant choices: Minoan palace of Knossos and Iraklio wine country; charming Hania, a harbour city that's happily alive year-round; or gorgeous beaches and gorges beckoning to be hiked.

1hr from Athens

Santorini

Thrill in the awe of floating in the middle of a volcanic caldera, water sparkling and whitewashed villages perched above.

45mins from Athens

MAINLAND HISTORY
Trip Builder

TAKE YOUR PICK OF MUST-SEES AND HIDDEN GEMS

Greece's iconic ancient sites and thrilling multifaceted history are layered across the land. Trace the trail from Ancient Greece to more modern marauders while touring some of the country's most beautiful terrain.

Trip Notes

Hub towns Athens, Ioannina, Thessaloniki

How long Allow one week

Getting around It's best to tour with your own wheels and add extra days to hike or simply sip a drink on a shade-dappled terrace.

Tips Cultural sites are open year-round, so visiting outside summer will ensure quieter experiences. Always check ahead for winter hours, which can be significantly shorter than summer. See the Peloponnesian trip for more epic ancient ruins.

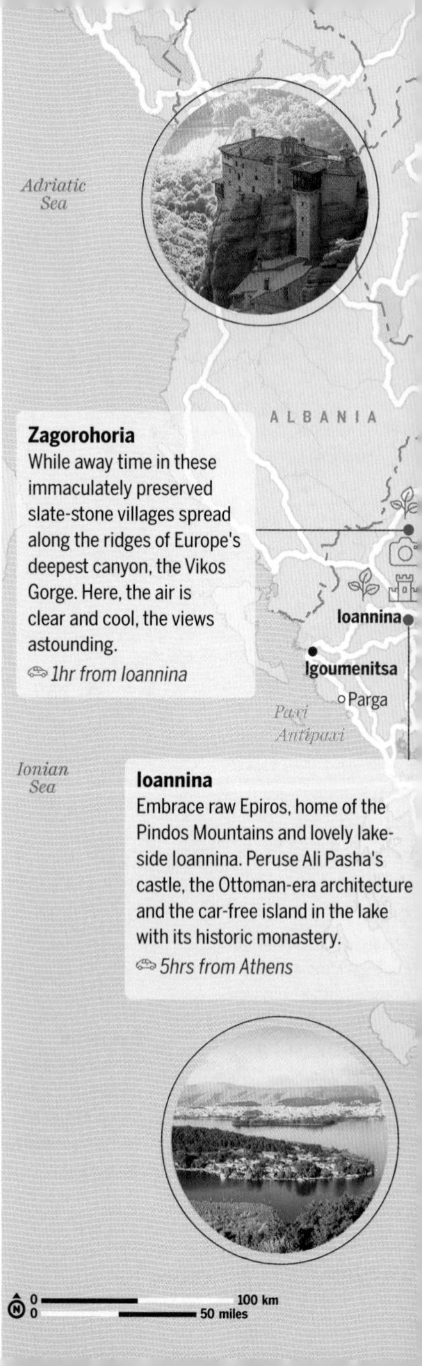

Zagorohoria
While away time in these immaculately preserved slate-stone villages spread along the ridges of Europe's deepest canyon, the Vikos Gorge. Here, the air is clear and cool, the views astounding.
1hr from Ioannina

Ioannina
Embrace raw Epiros, home of the Pindos Mountains and lovely lake-side Ioannina. Peruse Ali Pasha's castle, the Ottoman-era architecture and the car-free island in the lake with its historic monastery.
5hrs from Athens

Meteora
Clamber up stairs carved into soaring pillars of rock to reach magnificent 14th-century monasteries perched on their summits.
4½hrs from Athens

Thessaloniki
Enjoy a seaside sojourn in cultured Thessaloniki with its Ottoman-era architecture and vibrant arts scene, sipping coffee, dining in high style and sampling local sweets while you're there.
6hrs from Athens

Vergina
Have your mind blown at the Vergina Royal Tombs, where you descend to unspoiled royal Macedonian burials crammed with gobsmacking riches.
1hr from Thessaloniki

Athens
Pay homage at the grandest ancient sites like the Acropolis, Ancient Agora and Roman Agora. Dip into world-class museums, then emerge into modern life at markets and award-winning restaurants.
6hrs from Thessaloniki

Delphi
Seek advice at Ancient Delphi, the former home of the mysterious Delphic oracle. Gaze out over the Gulf of Corinth and understand why the ancient Greeks chose this as the centre of their world.
3hrs from Athens

IONIANS & PELOPONNESE Trip Builder

TAKE YOUR PICK OF MUST-SEES AND HIDDEN GEMS

If you have a hankering for island life along with beautiful towns, historic sights and dramatic scenery, tour the Ionian Islands - with their cooler climate and luxuriant olive and cypress trees - and the wonderful Peloponnese, with lofty, snowcapped mountains, vast gorges, sandy beaches and azure waters.

Trip Notes

Hub towns Corfu, Nafplio

How long Allow eight days

Getting around Ferries run between Ionian Islands (but plan ahead as schedules change) and Lefkada is connected to the mainland by a small bridge. Corfu has an airport with flights from European cities. In the Peloponnese, hire a car and cruise beautiful country lanes.

Tips The Peloponnese's west-coast highway has high crash rates. Stick to smaller roads when possible.

Adriatic Sea

Corfu
Wander through the amazing blend of Italian, French and British architecture in Corfu's Old Town, indulging in gourmet cuisine, exploring picturesque coastal villages and lounging on sandy beaches.
1hr from Athens

Ionian Sea

Ithaki
Hike through dramatic island scenery and past archaeological sites in Odysseus' homeland (aka Ithaca).
30mins from Kefallonia

0 100 km
0 50 miles

Lefkada

Investigate the little-known, thrillingly pure-white-pebble beaches backed by cliffs along Lefkada's west coast. Spend the night in charming Lefkada Town and zip into the mountainous interior for excellent taverna fare.

1hr from Kefallonia

Nemea Wine Region

Delight in the tipple from ancient vines of *agiorgitiko* grapes in the verdant rolling hills of Nemea, known for fine wines since the times when they supplied the royal court at nearby Mycenae.

50mins from Nafplio

Nafplio

Receive graceful Nafplio's embrace, with its Venetian-era mansions, interesting museums and lively port and cafe scene. A natural spot for romantics and families alike.

2hrs from Athens

Ancient Olympia

Stand in the 3000-year-old ruins of the stadium that hosted the first Olympic Games imagining the crowd roaring, then browse the site's excellent museums crammed with masterpieces.

4hrs from Athens

EASTERN ISLANDS
Trip Builder

TAKE YOUR PICK OF MUST-SEES AND HIDDEN GEMS

Strung along the Turkish coast, the Dodecanese and Northeastern Aegean Islands have endured a turbulent history that endowed them with a fascinating diversity. These far-flung islands harbour unspoilt scenery, and some remain relatively calm even when others are bulging with tourists at the height of summer.

Trip Notes

Hub towns Rhodes Town, Mytilini Town

How long Allow at least a week

Getting around The islands are interconnected by ferries and there are airports at several islands both in the Dodecanese and in the Northeastern Aegean with flights to Athens and some European cities.

Tips You can also ferry over from the Cyclades. Visiting Turkey's Aegean coastal resorts and historical sites from Samos, Chios and Lesvos is easy.

Lesvos
Bathe in thermal springs on Lesvos, birthplace of the poet Sappho and producer of some of Greece's finest olive oil and ouzo. Mytilini Town offers fantastic cultural life.
1hr from Athens

Patmos
Vibe out on Patmos' ethereal artistic and religious history and culture, and visit the cave where St John wrote the Book of Revelations. It holds a huge Easter celebration, too.
5½hrs from Rhodes

Kos
Dine on the day's catch at waterside seafood restaurants, then follow in the footsteps of Asclepius and Hippocrates, or stretch out on volcanic-sand beaches.
3¼hrs from Rhodes

Kalymnos
Test your mettle learning how to dive for sponges or down to wrecks and climbing the island's limestone cliffs.
40mins from Kos

Symi
Explore small Symi, one of Greece's great unknown gems. It's especially beautiful at dusk, when the setting sun turns the harbour's houses shades of pink, violet and gold.
1½hrs from Rhodes

Kastellorizo
Get lost in the labyrinth of neoclassical mansions in the harbour before gasping in awe at the colour in the most dramatic of blue caves in the Mediterranean.
3½hrs from Rhodes

Rhodes
While away a couple of days exploring the walled medieval Old Town and checking out its nightlife, plus diving in crystal-clear waters and touring its stunning Acropolis of Lindos.
1hr from Athens

Karpathos
Join in the island culture of feasting and traditional clothing in the village of Olymbos, then laze on isolated stretches of soft sand.
3¾hrs from Rhodes

ATHENS & CRETE Trip Builder

TAKE YOUR PICK OF MUST-SEES AND HIDDEN GEMS

Combine the bustle of Athens with Cretan landscape, which unfolds from sun-drenched beaches in the north to the rugged canyons and the cove-carved, cliff-lined southern coast. Trek through Europe's longest gorge, then dine in history-imbued Hania and Rethymno, whose lanes are lorded over by fortresses, Renaissance mansions and mosques.

Trip Notes

Hub towns Iraklio, Hania

How long Allow five to eight days

Getting around Buses crisscross Crete but having your own wheels definitely makes things more spontaneous.

Tips Get used to unusual driving – motorists may slow to a crawl, intending you to pass or, conversely, may zoom by you. If you want to hike a gorge, tour companies can drop you at one end and pick you up from the other.

Athens

Take in Athens' greatest hits, from the Acropolis to the National Gallery, stroll its chameleonic streets, then trip the light fantastic in its bars, restaurants and nightclubs.

6hrs from Thessaloniki

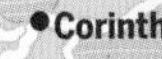

Western Beaches

Surrender to the shimmering turquoise waters lining the craggy Gramvousa Peninsula, the broad sweep of pink-cream Falasarna beach and Elafonisi, a symphony of fine pink sand and gentle rose dunes.

1hr from Hania

Rethymno

Bask along commanding bastions of a 15th-century fortress and the azure waters of the Mediterranean. The Venetian-Ottoman quarter is punctuated with graceful wood-balconied houses and the occasional minaret.

1¼hrs from Hania

Hania

Stroll the charming Venetian-style harbour and labyrinth of bougainvillea-draped pedestrian lanes, perfect for adjusting to a Greek rhythm, then enrich your Cretan culinary tour at the town's excellent restaurants.

2½hrs from Iraklio

Iraklio

Bounce between seafront tavernas and cultural sights like the superb archaeological museum in town before sampling fine vintages in Iraklio Wine Country, a mosaic of shapely hills, sun-baked slopes and lush valleys.

1hr from Athens

Knossos

Imagine the palaces filled with life at the captivating Minoan ruins of Knossos, with its vibrant frescoes and elaborate apartments and terraces.

25mins from Iraklio

Southwest Gorges

Discover Crete's wild side on a trek through the famous Samaria Gorge or one of its brethren, which spill out onto remote, attractive villages and beaches lapped by the crystal-clear Libyan Sea.

1½hrs from Hania

Amari

In the heart of pastoral Amari Valley, this village has an enchanting medley of Venetian buildings and a square filled with cafes and overflowing flowerpots.

1½hrs from Rethymno

GREECE BUILD YOUR TRIP

SLEEPER HITS
Trip Builder

TAKE YOUR PICK OF MUST-SEES AND HIDDEN GEMS

Slide a tad off the beaten track to find a combination of low-key islands featuring strong *filoxenia* (hospitality), some of Greece's best food, wild walking mountains and exceptional swimming waters. Throw in the ruins of multiple great civilisations and there's something for everyone.

Trip Notes

Hub towns Athens, Nafplio

How long Allow 10 days

Getting around This far-flung trip combines islands served by frequent ferries from Piraeus and a couple of Peloponnesian sights reachable from Hydra or by car from Athens. Kefallonia has an airport.

Tips You can hire wheels on each island (except Hydra, where all transit is on foot or by boat). Each spot beckons for a longer stay.

Paxi & Antipaxi
Dive into crystalline neon-blue waters at tiny, glorious Paxi and Antipaxi, where olive groves harbour boutique B&Bs and yachts bob in the harbours.
30mins from Corfu

Kefallonia
Roam this wild island's pretty villages surrounded by vineyards and olive groves, hike mountains spiralling into the sky, paddle kayaks between white-sand beaches, and sample local wines in colourful Fiskardo harbour.
1hr from Athens

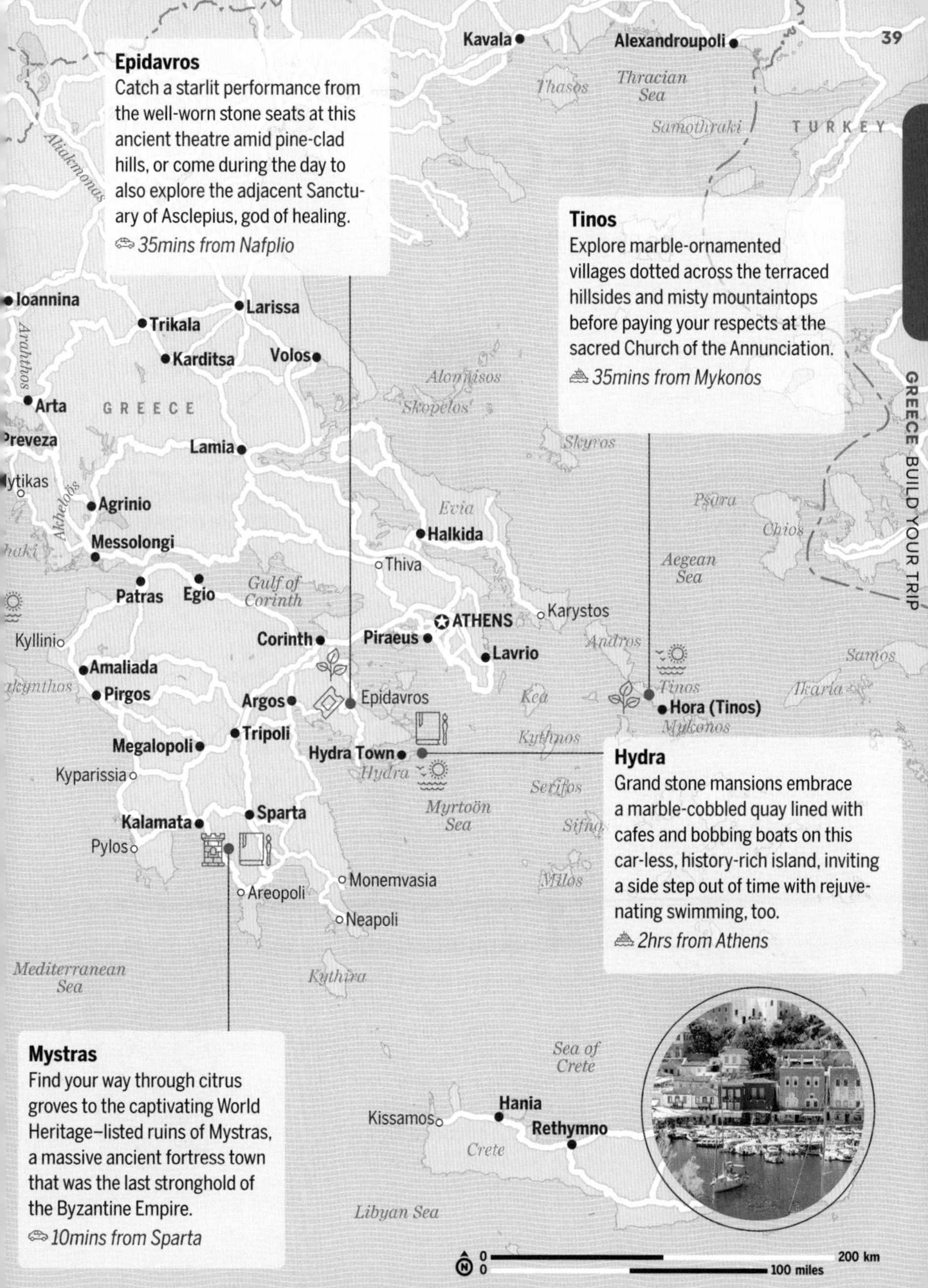

Epidavros

Catch a starlit performance from the well-worn stone seats at this ancient theatre amid pine-clad hills, or come during the day to also explore the adjacent Sanctuary of Asclepius, god of healing.

35mins from Nafplio

Tinos

Explore marble-ornamented villages dotted across the terraced hillsides and misty mountaintops before paying your respects at the sacred Church of the Annunciation.

35mins from Mykonos

Hydra

Grand stone mansions embrace a marble-cobbled quay lined with cafes and bobbing boats on this car-less, history-rich island, inviting a side step out of time with rejuvenating swimming, too.

2hrs from Athens

Mystras

Find your way through citrus groves to the captivating World Heritage–listed ruins of Mystras, a massive ancient fortress town that was the last stronghold of the Byzantine Empire.

10mins from Sparta

7 Things to Know about GREECE

INSIDER TIPS TO HIT THE GROUND RUNNING

1 Shopping Hours

Large shops are open from 9am to 9pm (Saturdays until 8pm), but many smaller businesses adhere to traditional shopping hours and close early (2.30pm or 3pm) for the time-honoured siesta, before reopening at 5pm on Tuesdays, Thursdays and Fridays (they remain closed on Monday, Wednesday and Saturday afternoons). On Sundays, all but the most essential stores and those in tourist areas are closed.

2 Coffee Culture

Greeks love spending hours outside, sipping coffee, conversing and watching the world go by. This leisurely pastime is one reason for the relatively high prices in popular cafes. Iced coffee is the preferred beverage, even in winter, although the famous frappé (shaken instant coffee served with ice) is no longer so popular. Instead, practically everyone drinks freddo (cold) espresso or cappuccino in myriad varieties.

3 Late Nights Out

Greeks go out late. They rarely have dinner before 9pm, and drinks usually begin after midnight. Many bars stay open till the wee hours of the morning.

4 Essential Summer Gear

Summers can be extremely hot, so never go out in the daytime without a bottle of water (available everywhere for €0.50), a hat and sunscreen. Sunglasses are also recommended during the day's bright hours.

5 Local Lingo

The Greek alphabet may look daunting, but once you know how to pronounce every letter and a few combinations of letters, you can actually read Greek.

Most Greeks speak at least some English, but they are always impressed by a visitor who makes the effort to say a few Greek words to them.

▶ See the Language chapter on p252.

6 Etiquette

Greeks like lively conversations and when they speak, it frequently sounds like they're arguing, but you'll know it when you witness a public squabble.

Drivers are not always considerate, and pedestrians must remain vigilant at all times.

If you go out to dinner with locals, it's very common to order an assortment of dishes, place them in the middle of the table and share everything. And, of course, when it's time to pay, your local hosts are highly unlikely to let you pay your share of the bill.

When you visit religious sites, avoid shorts and generally overly exposed attire.

Greeks enjoy discussing their rich history and the impact of Greek civilisation on the world. Politics is also a popular topic, but discussions can become heated – avoid discussing the civil war, and don't forget the full name when you mention neighbouring North Macedonia. Plain 'Macedonia' is a Greek region and a sensitive issue for many Greeks.

7 Stray Dogs

Many stray dogs and cats roam the streets, although the majority are not abandoned pets. They are actually born and raised on the streets, where they are cared for and fed by concerned citizens. Authorities run vaccination and sterilisation programmes for them, and the majority are safe and friendly.

Read, Listen, Watch & Follow

READ

Mani/Roumeli (Patrick Leigh Fermor; 1958/1966) Classics by one of the best travel writers of all time.

Austerity Measures (Ed Karen Van Dyck; 2016) Contemporary Greek poetry inspired by the economic crisis.

Cartes Postales from Greece (Victoria Hislop; 2016) A fond look at the country through a collection of short stories.

Greeks Bearing Gifts (Philip Kerr; 2018) Hard-boiled mystery in Athens 60 years ago.

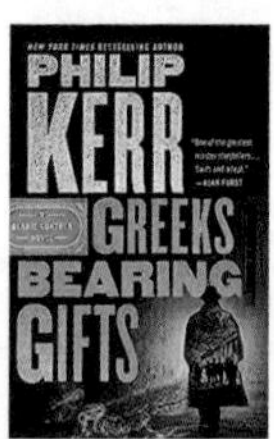

LISTEN

Gioconda's Smile (Manos Hadjidakis; 1965) A timeless instrumental masterpiece by one of the greatest Greek composers of all time.

Greece Goes Modern (Mimis Plessas; 1967) Traditional songs from around Greece conducted in a wonderful jazzy and bossa-nova style. Recently reissued.

2XXX (Lex; 2019) Stadium-filling Greek hip-hop with strong social and political concerns.

Anime (Fivos Delivorias; 2022) One of the hottest names on today's Greek music scene.

Athens Unpacked (sofkazinovieff.com/podcast) Writer Sofka Zinovieff tries to make sense of Athens' complexities.

WATCH

Never on Sunday (1960, pictured top right) An American's efforts to pull a kind-hearted prostitute out of her immoral lifestyle.

Summer Lovers (1982) A ménage à trois on glorious '80s Santorini, before the hordes.

The Big Blue (1988) Sublime cinematography of Amorgos and the Aegean Sea.

The Two Faces of January (2014, pictured bottom right) Film adaptation of Patricia Highsmith's atmospheric thriller novel.

The Durrells (2016–19) A family resettles from England in 1935 to a simple but fulfilling life on Corfu.

FOLLOW

eKathimerini
(ekathimerini.com) News and analysis by the leading Greek broadsheet.

Visitgreece
(visitgreece.gr) The official Greek National Tourism Organisation website.

Greece Is
(greece-is.com) All about Greece in English.

Discover Greece
(discovergreece.com) A complete guide by the Greek tourism industry.

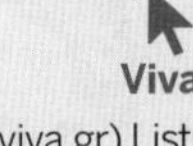

Viva
(viva.gr) Listings and tickets for all events.

ATHENS

CITY LIFE | CULTURE | HISTORY

ATHENS
Trip Builder

A city with millennia-long history, the capital of Greece is a modern metropolis that attracts throngs of visitors with the abundance of cultural sights, the blessed climate and the laid-back, fun-loving lifestyle. There's plenty to experience for the lovers of the outdoors, food and nightlife alike.

Spend a day by the sea in the bustling port of **Piraeus** (p70)
20mins from central Athens

Delve into Athens' glorious past at the **Acropolis** and the surrounding sites (p63)
15mins from Plateia Syntagmatos

Escape the city buzz in the stunning **Stavros Niarchos Park** (p56)
30mins from Plateia Syntagmatos

Enjoy the sunset with a panoramic view of the city from **Lykavittos Hill** (p50)
20mins from Plateia Syntagmatos

Browse international and local brands on the **Ermou** shopping strip (p73)
5mins from Plateia Syntagmatos

Tour Attica's ancient wine-producing region of **Mesogeia** (p58)
1hr from central Athens

See world-class modern art in **Basil & Elise Goulandris Foundation** (p68)
10mins from the Panathenaic Stadium

Visit a solemn open-air sculpture museum in **Athens' First Cemetery** (p52)
20mins from Plateia Syntagmatos

Practicalities

IRYNA BUDANOVA/SHUTTERSTOCK ©

ARRIVING

Eleftherios Venizelos International Airport Located 33km from the city centre. The metro runs half-hourly until 11.30pm, and it takes approximately 40 minutes to get to Plateia Syntagmatos (€10 single, €18 return). Bus X95 (€6) takes about 60 minutes and runs 24 hours. A taxi takes 30 to 40 minutes (flat rate €40/55 day/night). Several car rental companies, as well as private transfer companies, operate inside the airport building.

HOW MUCH FOR A

Souvlaki €3

Water bottle €0.50

5-day sites pass €30

WHEN TO GO

JUN–AUG
High and hot season; the city is packed with visitors.

SEP–NOV
Still pleasantly warm, mainly sunny and less crowded.

DEC–FEB
Mild winter, perfect to see the city's true colours.

MAR–MAY
Glorious spring, when Athens is at its best.

GETTING AROUND

Public transport The quickest and easiest way to move around the city is by metro and tram, operating between 5am and midnight with an extra hour on Fridays and Saturdays. There's also an extensive bus and trolleybus network – a decent mode of transport, traffic permitting.

Tickets (oasa.gr) A single 90-minute trip costs €1.20 but you can buy a five-day pass for €8.20 or a three-day pass including a return ride to the airport for €20.

Taxi You can hail a taxi in the street or use one of several apps: Free Now, Ikaros, Taxiplon, Uber (only professional drivers). The cost is €0.90 per kilometre (€1.25 midnight to 5am); minimum charge is €4.

EATING & DRINKING

Greek food is generally healthy and nutritious and Athens is full of street-food joints – souvlaki, of course, being the king among them. Every neighbourhood has its own *souvlatzidiko* and the vast majority are above par. The restaurants run the full range for all budgets and tastes, from ethnic and traditional Greek eateries to Michelin-starred establishments. Booking is usually required in most upmarket restaurants. For a true Athenian experience try a traditional taverna, retsina barrels and all.

Best old-school food joint Diporto (p72)

Must-try Greek wines Attica region (p58)

CONNECT & FIND YOUR WAY

Wi-fi There are hundreds of free wi-fi hotspots around the city, but in central locations the connection can be lousy during peak times. There is almost universal 5G coverage in the city and all three mobile operators (Cosmote, Vodafone and Wind) offer internet-only packages.

Navigation Once you sort internet access, any navigation app is good to get yourself acquainted with the city centre.

FREE-ADMISSION DAYS

All museums and archaeological sites are open to the public for free on the first Sunday of the month from November to March, the last weekend of September, 28 October, 18 April, 18 May and 6 March.

WHERE TO STAY

Every neighbourhood in Athens has a distinct character. The city centre is relatively compact, so wherever you stay you'll be within walking distance from the main attractions.

Neighbourhood	Pro/Con
Koukaki	The hottest neighbourhood these days is buzzing with tourists and options for going out.
Kolonaki	Posh, elegant, central and relatively quiet but pricey.
Plaka	Picturesque but touristy, with many dining options and close to the ancient sites.
Historic centre	The beating heart of the city, between Ermou, Stadiou and Athinas streets. Commercial flurry in the daytime, vibrant at night.
Exarhia	Youthful and alternative; probably the most affordable option.
Pangrati	Hip neighbourhood slightly away from the centre but with many dining and drinking options.

MONEY

Credit and debit cards are accepted everywhere; some taxi drivers may frown but the ones working with apps should be fine. Shops catering to tourists can be pricey – you can always ask for a better price but avoid hard haggling.

01 Breathtaking CITY VIEW

VIEWS | WALK | SUNSET

Lykavittos Hill looms above central Athens, dominating the city's glorious skyline along with the Acropolis. It's a cherished natural park, with meandering footpaths among shrubs, pines and other greenery, topped by the whitewashed Chapel of Agios Georgios. The 360-degree panorama of the city is stunning – this is arguably the best place in Athens to watch the sun setting.

FOTOKON/SHUTTERSTOCK ©

How To

Getting here You can either walk, catch a taxi or take the funicular to the 277m summit of Lykavittos.

When to go Late afternoon, when the heat subsides and the sun goes down, is the perfect time to go.

Funicular The 10-minute service operates half-hourly between 8.30am and 2.30am. Return/one-way tickets cost €10/7 (children €6).

ANDERS BLOMQVIST/LONELY PLANET ©

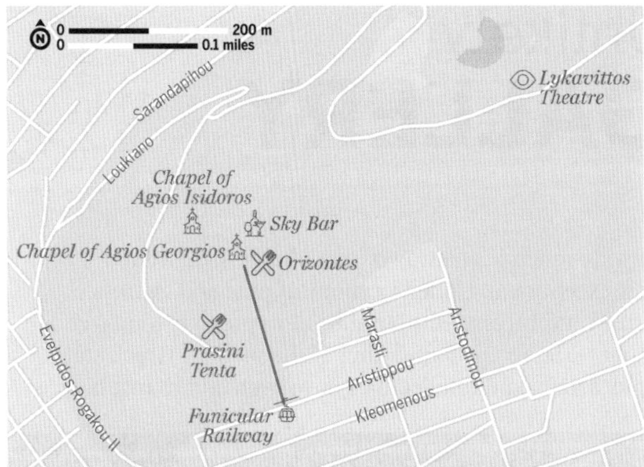

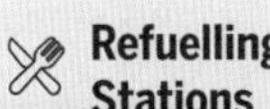

Top Lykavittos Hill seen from the Acropolis
Bottom Chapel of Agios Georgios

Take a break from the city's buzz with an invigorating urban hike up the so-called 'Hill of the Wolves', an Athenian landmark you can't miss no matter where you stand in the city centre.

If you're up for some serious hiking, start your ascent from Plateia Dexamenis in Kolonaki and follow the footpaths or go along the road that will take you to the hilltop car park. On the way you'll meet locals from the nearby neighbourhoods of Kolonaki and Exarhia jogging, walking their dogs or just enjoying a stroll on the leafy paths. The hilltop is also one of the favourite romantic spots for Athenian couples.

Located on the site of a former stone quarry, the open-air **Lykavittos Theatre** next to the car park is a time-honoured cultural facility that has seen outstanding performances throughout the years. (It is currently undergoing maintenance with a view to opening to the public again.)

From the car park, another footpath ascends to the **Chapel of Agios Georgios**, where weddings and baptisms often take place. The tiny **Chapel of Agios Isidoros** in a nearby cave is one of the oldest in Athens, built after the city became the capital of Greece.

From the open viewing area around the church, as the afternoon progresses, the spectacle is reminiscent of a low flight over the metropolis.

Refuelling Stations

If you want to complement your visual experience with a gastronomic one, there are several options for grabbing a cup of coffee, a quick bite to eat or a full-course meal on Lykavittos Hill.

The historic **Prasini Tenta**, located on the southern slope of the hill, was closed for many years but has recently been restored and is the perfect place to rest before continuing up the hill.

The **Sky Bar** serves appetizers and cocktails alongside the breathtaking views, while **Orizontes** is the more upscale alternative for fine dining with an extensive wine selection.

Finally, outside the theatre there's a canteen where you can get a quick snack or a drink to go.

02 Unlikely GALLERY

WALK | ART | HISTORY

Cemeteries rarely provide much in the way of remarkable sightseeing, but Athens' First Cemetery is exceptional. Under a canopy of pine and cypress, hundreds of wonderful marble sculptures and thousands of impressive tombs create an eerie but tranquil atmosphere. Since the foundation of the modern Greek state, the most famous statespeople, artists and intellectuals have been laid to rest here.

GEORGE PACHANTOURIS/GETTY IMAGES ©

How to

Getting here The cemetery is within walking distance of the Panathenaic Stadium in the district of Mets.

When to go It is open every day from 8am to 8pm; entrance is free of charge.

Be mindful This is a functioning cemetery where funerals take place daily, so try to be discreet and respectful. On a hot day, bring a bottle of water.

JANA_JANINA/GETTY IMAGES ©

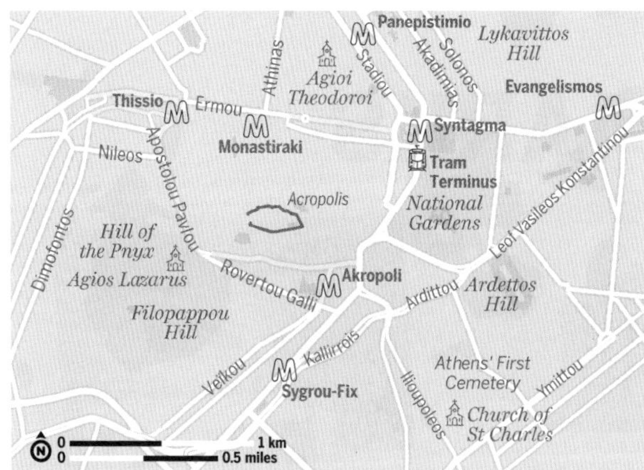

A peaceful stroll in an art garden The tombs, mausoleums and the grassy alleyways between them are lavishly decorated with marble tombstones, statues and every imaginable adornment. More than 800 magnificent works of art may be found here, while some of the tombs are so large that they resemble ancient temples. Don't miss the mausoleum of archaeologist Heinrich Schliemann (1822–90), decorated with scenes from the Trojan War. A visitor can even admire a reproduction of the **Choragic Monument of Lysicrates**, whose original is located near the Acropolis. The cemetery is also home to three churches: the Greek Orthodox **Agioi Theodoroi** and **Agios Lazarus**, and the Catholic **Church of St Charles**.

A lesson in modern Greek history Take notes or look up some random names you see in the inscriptions on the tombstones, and you could instantly be transported to different periods of modern Greek history through the stories of the deceased. Actor and politician Melina Merkouri, songwriter and musician Demis Roussos, poets Elytis and Seferis, film director Theo Angelopoulos, as well as former prime ministers, mayors, painters, actors, writers, state benefactors, church figures and fighters from the Greek Revolution, are buried here among ordinary Athenians. The caretakers are friendly and used to answering questions, and when they have the time, some lucky visitors even get short impromptu tours.

Sleeping Beauty

The *Sleeping Maiden* is the highlight of the cemetery's art and probably the most famous and recognised modern Greek sculpture.

It was created by the famous Greek sculptor Yannoulis Chalepas in 1877 on the commission of a wealthy, prominent Greek to adorn the tomb of his 18-year-old niece, Sofia Afentaki, who had died from tuberculosis in 1873.

The white-marble statue is a life-size depiction of the young girl, lying on her bed with her eyes closed and holding a cross to her chest. It's widely considered a neoclassical masterpiece and one of the greatest works ever created by the artist from Tinos island.

Athenian LANDMARKS

01 Parthenon

The eternal Athenian symbol and main sight at the sacred Acropolis, built in the 5th century BCE during the city's 'Golden Age'.

02 National Archaeological Museum

Housed in a magnificent neoclassical building, one of the most important Greek museums has a huge and splendid collection.

03 Panathenaic Stadium

Constructed as the exact replica of an ancient stadium that existed on the site to host the first modern Olympic Games in 1896.

04 National Gallery

A brand-new impressive building for the capital's largest collection of paintings by Greek masters.

05 Acropolis Museum

The state-of-the-art home to all artefacts discovered in and around the Acropolis rock.

06 Parliament

Originally the royal palace of the first king of modern Greece, Otto,

it now houses the Greek parliament.

07 Ancient Agora

The heart of public life in ancient Athens, where democracy was born and flourished.

08 Hadrian's Arch

The monument to the Roman Emperor Hadrian, built in 131 CE, combines Roman and Greek architectural elements.

09 Odeon of Herodes Atticus

A magnificent open-air Roman theatre that still hosts almost daily performances every summer.

10 Athenian Trilogy

The three-building architectural spectacle consists of the old National Library, the University of Athens ceremonial hall, and the Academy of Athens.

11 Roman Agora

Together with Hadrian's Library, this is the most important Roman-era site in Athens.

03 Picnic under an OLIVE TREE

OUTDOORS | ARCHITECTURE | CULTURE

In the labyrinthine paths snaking under cypress, olive and plane trees and through the array of blooming herbs and green shrubbery of the vast seaside Stavros Niarchos Park, you'll find the perfect cool shade to escape the city bustle. Bring a picnic, enjoy a book or just unwind in true Athenian style.

PIT STOCK/SHUTTERSTOCK ©

How to

Getting here
There's an hourly free shuttle bus from Plateia Syntagmatos; most bus lines to Piraeus also pass by. A taxi takes 10 to 15 minutes from the centre.

When to go The park is open year-round from 6am until midnight (2am during summer weekends). Of course, its full glory can be best enjoyed on a warm, sunny day.

Tours Entrance to the park is free; there are also daily free guided tours in English for groups of up to 20 people (booked online at snfcc.org).

ARCHITECT: RENZO PIANO BUILDING WORKSHOP
IMAGE: GIANNIS KATSAROS/ALAMY STOCK PHOTO ©

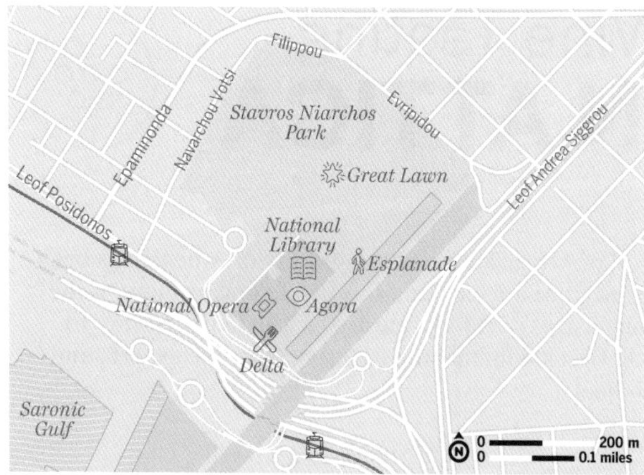

Fragrant blossoms and lush greenery Large trees native to Greece such as olives, pines, carobs and laurels abound, and a variety of typical Mediterranean herbal plants like lavender, oregano and thyme have been carefully arranged around the park's 21 hectares to provide a seasonal feast for the senses all year round. Even during the park's busiest days (summer weekends), there's always a quiet shady corner under the greenery where you can indulge in a spontaneous picnic or a carefree rest, complete with the archetypal cicada song.

World-class architecture The Stavros Niarchos Foundation Cultural Center is a magnificent Athenian landmark, designed by the renowned Italian architect Renzo Piano, and hosts the **National Opera** and the **National Library**. The lighthouse on top of the building offers splendid 360-degree views, while the **Agora**, an open space inspired by the ancient concept, is the focal point of the building complex. Along the 400m canal, the **Esplanade** allows for an idyllic stroll to and from the rest of the park.

Dancing fountains, free concerts and open-air movies The choreographed fountains are one of the most spectacular aspects of the park. They are daily water shows in the canal, put on by water jets and rotating fountains to the sounds of jazz, classical and pop music. The **Great Lawn** is the park's main open space, where visitors can enjoy free concerts and screenings of classic movies during the summer.

Top Stavros Niarchos Park
Bottom Stavros Niarchos Foundation Cultural Center

A Greek Feast

If you don't want to bring your own snacks and drinks, there are kiosks, canteens and a bistro scattered around the park and inside the buildings.

And if you are looking for an exceptional culinary experience, **Delta** – the only Greek restaurant with two Michelin stars – offers contemporary Greek cuisine accompanied by stunning views of the city. With an emphasis on high-quality ingredients and sustainability, the restaurant boasts an exceptional wine list featuring the best wineries from Greece as well as the rest of the world.

04 Wine Tasting IN ATTICA

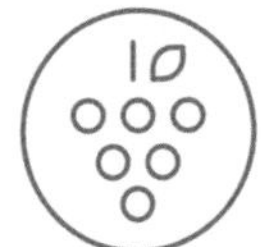

WINE | NATURE | FOOD

The sun-drenched soil of Attica, surrounding the city of Athens, has been producing fine grape varieties since ancient times. A trip to one or more of the many wineries in the Mesogeia area's vast vineyards is a great opportunity to learn all about the emerging Greek winemaking industry from the experts and try some delicious wines to boot.

LAOKOON/SHUTTERSTOCK ©

How to

Getting here Most wineries are a short drive outside Athens, and the best way to reach them is by car or taxi.

When to go The wineries are usually open to the public during working hours, but most of the larger ones accept visitors at weekends too.

Booking ahead You must call a few days in advance to schedule a visit.

THEASTOCK/SHUTTERSTOCK ©

Top Attica vineyard
Bottom Wine making in Attica

Let's Drink to That

Domaine Papagianakos This bioclimatic winery was built on the site of an old monastery.

Kokotos Estate A family winery that's been producing organic wines for more than 40 years.

Nikolou Winery For a century and a half, it's been producing wines in Koropi from selected vineyards in Attica and the rest of Greece.

Oenotria Land Established in Kapandriti in 2000, it's a branch of the famous Drama estate.

Strofilia Estate Located in Anavyssos as well as Nemea, the famous *agiorgitiko* region of the Peloponnese.

Zeginis Winery Located near the archaeological site of Ramnous in Marathon.

Heritage and tradition Wine has been produced in Greece for millennia, and there are vineyards with uninterrupted production since antiquity. However, during the last few decades, a new generation of winemakers has invested in all stages of production, and as a result, Greek wines are finally taking the place and credit they deserve on the world stage. There are about 200 distinct regional varieties, many with a 'Protected designation of origin' indication. Attica boasts the world-famous retsina, considered inferior in the past but making a quality comeback these days. The most frequent grapes in this region are *savatiano, roditis* and *malagouzia,* but in recent decades Attica has seen the cultivation of a plethora of other varieties – both indigenous and international – that harmoniously marry the grapes' core qualities with the Greek climate and terroir.

An experience to thrill your senses Visiting a winery on the outskirts of Athens is the perfect opportunity to learn about the history of Greek winemaking, walk around magnificent vineyards, have a peek into their cellars and, of course, savour their wines, usually accompanied by matching delicacies. Most places offer guided tours, tastings and the chance to buy your favourite bottles straight from the producers at very affordable prices. The larger estates even have their own wine museums and they often host events on the grounds, such as music concerts, masterclasses and family-friendly activities.

05 Party Like A GREEK

FUN | NIGHTLIFE | MUSIC

Plate-smashing is a thing of the distant past, but the Greeks have never ceased partying the night away in their own way. Going to one of Athens' many live clubs, big or small, to see Greek singers and musicians perform live among ecstatic crowds is an extraordinary cultural experience and a unique entertainment opportunity.

FRANCESCO DE MARCO/SHUTTERSTOCK ©

How to

Where to go Check out listings when in Athens, as shows are usually on for a limited time. The action moves from the city to the coast in summer.

When to go Clubs usually open after 10pm, but the fun doesn't start before midnight.

How much If you want to be seated at a table, you must share a bottle of spirits between four or wine between two (roughly €40 to €50 per person). If you just stand, a drink costs €10 to €20.

What about food Although food is sometimes offered, these are not places to dine.

BASILT/ALAMY STOCK PHOTO ©

TERRY HARRIS/ALAMY STOCK PHOTO ©

Top left and right Bouzouki players
Bottom left Athens nightclub

Huge clubs, big names, heaps of fun The largest clubs (*bouzoukia* or *pistes*) are impressively glamorous venues that regularly feature the hottest names on the Greek contemporary *laïka* and pop scene, both genres based on the sounds of timeless Greek bouzouki. The clubbers tend to overdress and show up well after midnight. The show kicks off with the supporting acts, and the atmosphere and fun build up until it's time for the real stars to appear. At this point the night lights up and there's singing and dancing all over the place until the morning hours. The audience quickly floods the stage, dancing around the performers and the band while whole trays of carnations are tossed at the stage.

Low-key, high emotion The Greek *entekhno* music scene is more subtle, with elements of Greek folk. It's known for being gloomier and more artistic, and its devotees consider it classier and more upscale than its 'rival' mainstream and mass-market *bouzoukia* world. The respective artists are equally popular and have a large fan base, yet they are very different and prefer playing in more intimate settings without the extravaganza of their pop counterparts. Despite the lack of dancing, the atmosphere and the intensity of the singing are on par with the *bouzoukia* experience, but the average cost is slightly lower.

Name-Dropping

Nikos Vertis, Konstantinos Argyros, Anna Vissi, Giorgos Mazonakis, Antonis Remos – these are only a few of the most popular performers currently active on the Greek pop scene. During the winter, you may catch them at clubs on **Iera Odos** and **Pireos** streets, while in the summer they play at open-air venues along the coast.

On the other hand, Socratis Malamas, Giannis Charoulis, Foivos Delivorias, Natassa Bofiliou and Miltos Paschalidis are all luminaries in the field of *entekhno*. They perform largely in outdoor summer concerts and only a handful of winter events in more modest venues like **Stavros tou Notou**, **Kyttaro** and **Sfiga**.

06 Among the MONUMENTS

HISTORY | ART | FOOD

A day spent hopping around Athens' ancient sites is an experience of a lifetime. It starts with the absolute highlight, the sacred rock of the Acropolis, followed by its glorious museum, including dinner on its terrace facing the floodlit Parthenon, and ideally culminates in a concert at the Odeon of Herodes Atticus.

VIACHESLAV LOPATIN/SHUTTERSTOCK ©

How to

Getting here The main entrance to the Acropolis is the Propylaia at the southwest side of the hill, but there's a less busy southeast entrance gate.

When to go Early in the morning is the best time to beat the tour groups, or go in the last two hours when crowds thin out. The Acropolis Museum restaurant stays open until midnight every Friday and Saturday year-round (book by phone or email).

Combo tickets The best option is a €30 five-day ticket valid for many archaeological sites.

ERICA RUTH NEUBAUER/SHUTTERSTOCK ©

Awe & Inspiration

Getting an early start will allow you to avoid both the crowds and the heat (if you're visiting in summer) at the **Acropolis**. Climb the rock and wander around the magnificent site to fully immerse yourself in the ambience and marvel at the classical beauty and harmony of the enduring monuments.

Try to imagine the place through the centuries and be captivated by the magic of classical Greece. Democracy, science, art, drama and philosophy flourished centuries ago in these very surroundings. The likes of Socrates, Plato, Aristotle, Pericles, Thucydides and Solon once trod these same grounds. It's impossible not to feel the Acropolis' magnetic pull as you roam among the living manifestations of ancient Athens' loftiest ideals.

PRETO PEROLA/SHUTTERSTOCK ©

The World's First Theatre

Built on the southern slope of the Acropolis rock and originally part of the sanctuary of Dionysus Eleuthereus, the **Theatre of Dionysos** is considered the world's oldest theatre, the place where ancient tragedy, comedy and satire were first formally performed to celebrate the cult of Dionysos.

Top left Propylaia
Top right Theatre of Dionysos
Bottom left Odeon of Herodes Atticus

Marble Wonders in the Home They Deserve

After a break for a light snack or a refreshment in the winding alleys of Plaka, the old town, head to the **Acropolis Museum**, one of the finest and most important in the world.

The museum building, an architectural masterpiece in itself, stands in direct correspondence with the rock and houses original marble sculptures taken to safety from the ancient site.

Take a guided tour or simply wander around the four flours to admire the stunning sculptures, friezes and other exquisite artefacts, and conclude in the glorious **Parthenon Gallery** reflecting on timelessness, beauty and human achievement.

The Most Uplifting Dinner of Your Life

The Acropolis Museum boasts a fine restaurant, with tables on its terrace facing

The Acropolis Monuments

The crowning glory of the Acropolis and the city, **Parthenon** is the apex of classical Athenian monuments and the city's eternal trademark. Dedicated to goddess Athena, the temple was constructed during the Golden Age of Athens (5th century BCE).

The **Erechtheion** features replicas of the glorious Caryatids, the larger-than-life maiden columns that held up the temple. The originals were moved to the Acropolis Museum – but one of the positions remains empty, awaiting the lone Caryatid kept in the British Museum.

On the rock you can also admire the imposing **Propylaia** entrance and the small but beautiful **Temple of Athena Nike**.

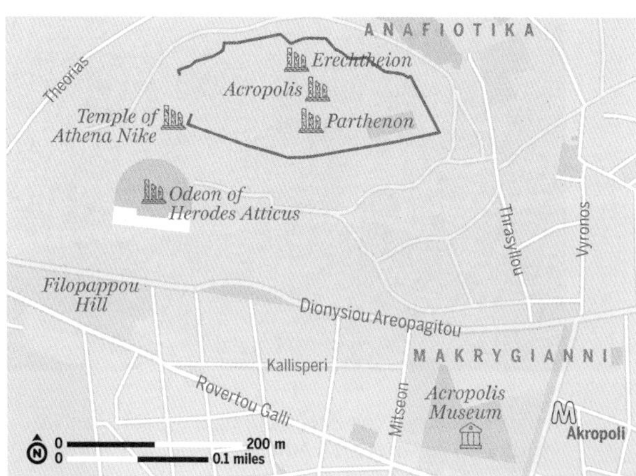

the Acropolis – an al fresco dinner here will perfectly complement a fulfilling day.

The fare is traditional Greek, carefully prepared with high-quality local seasonal ingredients, and the prices are surprisingly affordable for a location every restauranteur in the world would kill for.

Both the restaurant and the museum cafe also serve a rich traditional Greek breakfast until noon, in case you prefer to reverse the schedule and start your day at the museum.

A Worthy Close to a Unique Day

The **Odeon of Herodes Atticus**, built in 161 CE at the foot of the Acropolis, hosts almost daily performances of music, theatre, dance and opera during the summer's **Athens and Epidaurus Festival** (aefestival.gr). Many international and local stars have performed in this spectacular setting since the 1950s, when it was fully restored.

If you can get tickets for any performance, don't miss this opportunity for a grand finale of a day that will stay in your memory forever.

Left Propylaia
Below Aerial view of the Acropolis

Art During Economic Crisis

IN ATHENS, ART ENDURED AND FLOURISHED

One may have expected the opposite, but art in Athens not only endured but also flourished during the decade of economic crisis – and it continues to do so to this day. To understand why this is the case, one has to look at the big picture.

Left Onassis Stegi interior
Centre Odeon of Herodes Atticus
Right National Theatre

PIT STOCK/SHUTTERSTOCK ©

At the beginning of the 2010s, during the great financial crisis that peaked in 2012, Athens constantly featured in major world media. The near-daily protests and occasional riots were front and centre, along with images of indignant people and poverty. No one knew what to expect; Greece could have left the eurozone, a national disaster if things had gone south. Thus, a feeling of social solidarity developed at a time when institutions and the status quo were being openly questioned. Inevitably, radicalisation – to a greater or lesser extent – followed in certain parts of Greek society.

The Athens Biennale, the largest international exhibition of contemporary art held in the city, first raised the question 'And now what?' in 2013. The next one, in 2015, brought into focus activist cultural groups and self-organised art ventures.

Then came the idea of Athens co-hosting the Documenta – the largest European exhibition of contemporary art – in 2017. It was unprecedented for such a large event to focus on Athens, especially under the circumstances, and the fact changed the dynamics of the city's art scene. Immediately, the spotlight of the world's art community turned on the Greek capital. Many artists wanted to take part with special works themed after the crisis, and many were convinced that a huge injustice was taking place. So they arrived en masse to see and study the situation on the spot.

Suddenly, Athens began to take on another character. It looked like the new revolutionary centre, a laboratory where one of humanity's greatest experiments was being

BYVALET/SHUTTERSTOCK ©

LAZAROS PAPANDREOU/SHUTTERSTOCK ©

carried out: the search for a better and more just society. The Greek capital appeared like the (artistic) land of opportunity, and people from all over the world came to be part of the ongoing artistic climax.

One school of thought insists that it was precisely this radicalisation of society that brought about Documenta, which in turn was the starting point for the cultural explosion, mostly in the visual arts and to a lesser extent the performing arts – theatre and music.

> Greece could have left the eurozone, a national disaster if things had gone south.

A different interpretation is given by journalist Yannis Konstantinidis, an expert on the Greek art scene: 'I don't think it was so much the radicalisation of society. This had a greater impact on the economy, in the sense that there was a demand for solidarity markets without intermediaries, shared ownership etc. The Documenta came to Athens because there was a feeling that the situation was of wider concern, beyond the Greek crisis. Bearing in mind Germany of the 1930s and the rise of Nazism, the question was whether history was repeating itself.'

Since then, every day something new was happening. The Onassis Foundation's cultural hub, Onassis Stegi, embraced the alternative scene, and dozens of small independent galleries were established. Some were mainstream but many were underground, formed by groups of artists who didn't seem interested in communicating their work to the media.

Performing Arts

Athenians love going to the theatre, and the country has the highest number of theatres per capita in the world.

From glorious neoclassical buildings to tiny basement spaces, there are hundreds of venues across the city, staging a huge number of plays each season – at the height of the economic crisis in 2015, more than 1500 plays premiered in the city!

The most important venues are the **National Theatre**, the **National Opera** (in the Stavros Niarchos Foundation Cultural Center) and the **Athens Concert Hall** (aka Megaron).

During the summer months, the action – like with every other form of art – moves outdoors to a number of municipal venues and, of course, the magnificent **Odeon of Herodes Atticus**.

At the same time, ventures that started underground, such as the Victoria Square Project – an attempt to bring the visual arts into the neighbourhoods, making old residents, immigrants and artists their interlocutors – had evolved into an institutional presentation of art.

The new galleries in turn changed the landscape. The older ones addressed the Athenian middle and upper classes and the big collectors, while the new ones targeted 'the people'.

International street artists arrived in the city and joined their Athenian counterparts, creating murals and graffiti that still adorn large surfaces in the central neighbourhoods, often coexisting with pointless tagging and littering of every wall in the city – a trend that during those years expressed pure anger devoid of any artistic ambition.

International street artists arrived in the city and joined their Athenian counterparts.

Today, Athens is once again the centre of attention for totally different reasons. Stylish hotels are mushrooming, as the city is no longer just a stopover to the islands but a destination in its own right. In this environment, artistic expression continues to flourish.

Many Athenians spend their afternoons in reading clubs or on literary walks, while the artistic direction of the new, emblematic National Museum of Contemporary Art (EMST) has been taken over by the internationally renowned curator and art historian Katerina Gregou, returning to Greece after 15 years of international experience.

EMST hosts permanent and periodic exhibitions of great Greek and foreign artists, with a social footprint too, as it consistently advocates for the rights of communities such as LGBTIQ+ and showcases their work.

The brand-new complex of the National Gallery is impressive, with many important new exhibits.

The Basil & Elise Goulandris Foundation – a dream museum for every metropolis – houses one of the richest collections of modern, mainly European art, while the Stavros Niarchos Foundation Cultural Center hosts concerts and performances by mainstream and alternative artists.

Yannis Konstantinidis' view on the future is mixed: 'Athens is certainly not the new Berlin, as it has been claimed, but it has formed its own character. It is very important that the people who live, work and create here are

AEL/ALAMY STOCK PHOTO ©

ARCHITECT: RENZO PIANO BUILDING WORKSHOP IMAGE: PIT STOCK/SHUTTERSTOCK ©

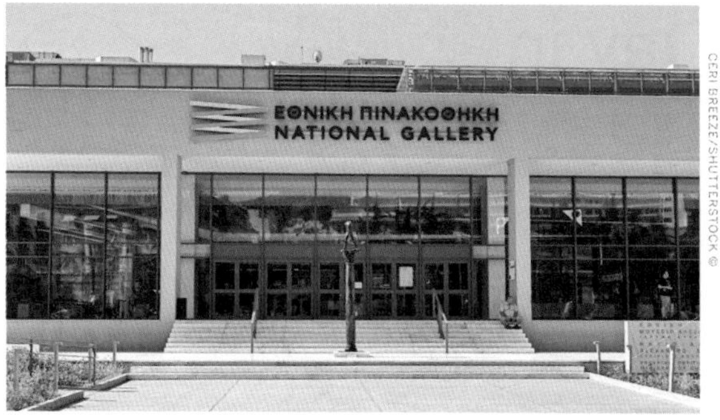

CERI BREEZE/SHUTTERSTOCK ©

LAZAROS PAPANDREOU/SHUTTERSTOCK ©

happy because they produce important work. But the next day largely depends on whether they stay in the city, and that in turn has to do with several things: whether life in the city continues to become more expensive and whether the city itself will continue to be interesting. You know, artists are not attracted to places where everything runs calm and smooth. I'm not saying that they necessarily look for social upheaval, but something has to be at stake. I do not know what is going to happen in Athens – the Biennale insists that the crisis is not over and that any remediation was not to the benefit of the people.'

Regardless of the Biennale's assessment, the reality is that these days Athens and Greece as a whole are a world apart from the crisis years. The International Monetary Fund left the country long ago, while the European institutions have become much more flexible with Greece, mainly because of its strong economic growth.

At the same time, the cultural seeds of the past decade appear to have set firm roots, putting Athens among the world's leading creative hubs for good.

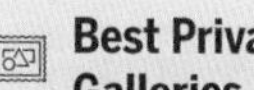

Best Private Galleries

There are more than 50 private art galleries in the city. Here's a selection of the most representative venues:

Backspace Athens An experimental space for visual arts in Exarhia.

Callirrhoë Athens An independent exhibition space for contemporary art in Koukaki.

Carwan Gallery An international contemporary design gallery in Piraeus.

ERGO Collective A creative platform founded on the premise of collaboration.

Hot Wheels Athens Individual and group exhibitions and collaboration with other art spaces internationally.

Rodeo An international gallery in Piraeus – a 'production house' with a London branch.

Opposite page left National Museum of Contemporary Art (EMST)
Opposite page right Stavros Niarchos Foundation Cultural Center
Above left National Gallery
Above right Basil & Elise Goulandris Foundation

07 A Day in PIRAEUS

WALK | SEASIDE | FOOD

The joys of Athens' hectic port have gone mostly unnoticed for years, as it was considered merely a transit point for getting from the capital to the islands. But Piraeus is an exceptional and diverse city in its own right, worth at least a day of every urban explorer's stay in Athens.

RICHARD CUMMINS/ALAMY STOCK PHOTO ©

How to

Getting here Metro line 1 terminates right in the heart of the busy harbour and line 3 at the Municipal Theatre. Bus 024 from Plateia Syntagmatos operates 24 hours. A taxi ride from the centre of Athens takes about 30 minutes.

When to go A weekday is best for getting the full flavour of this bustling city.

Local flavour If you arrive by metro line 1, take the time to wander the narrow streets behind the terminal, packed with small shops and workshops retaining the great harbour's old-fashioned charm.

Art & History

Piraeus boasts a number of small but interesting art and history hubs including the **Piraeus Archaeological Museum** and **Electric Railway Museum**.

The **Municipal Gallery** hosts works from top Greek painters and sculptors. Worthwhile private galleries include **Rodeo**, **The Intermission**, **Carwan** and **212 Arts**.

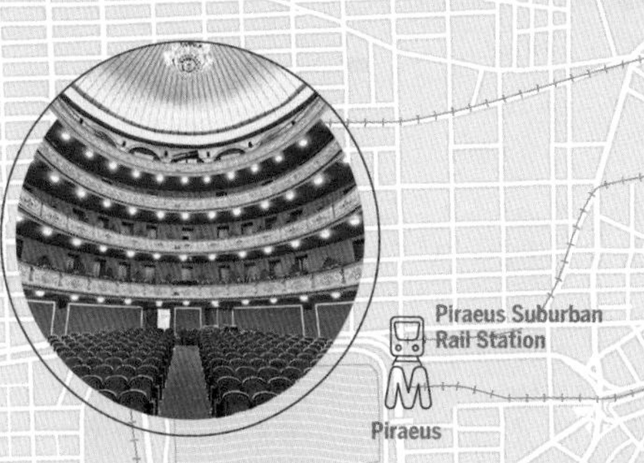

05 A magnificent neoclassical building inaugurated in 1895, the **Municipal Theatre** stands on Plateia Korai, the commercial heart of the city.

03 The smallest harbour in Piraeus, mainly used by fishing boats, **Mikrolimano** boasts a brand-new promenade and an array of fish restaurants with sea views.

01 The compact (yet the largest of its kind in the country) **Hellenic Maritime Museum** (pictured left) has a fine collection of rare books, maps, flags, naval weaponry, and the fin of the legendary submarine *Papanikolis*.

04 **Kastella** is a hill worth exploring if only for the views of the whole city and the Saronic Gulf. Working-class areas mix with luxurious villas and the open-air Veakio theatre at the top.

02 The second of the city's three harbours, **Zea Harbour** is lined with an array of mainstream bar-restaurants with views towards the hundreds of luxurious yachts moored in the marina all year long.

Piraeus Suburban Rail Station
Piraeus
Municipal Gallery
Dimotiko Theatro
Lambraki Grigoriou
Leof Vasileos Georgiou A
Leof Vasileos Georgiou B
Megas Limani (Great Harbour)
Plateia Terpsitheas
Plateia Kanari
Vasileos Pavlou
Piraeus Archaeological Museum
Zea Marina
Kaningos
Akti Koundouriotou
Mikrolimano
Akti Moutsoupoulou
Leof Freattydos
Plateia Alexandras
Plateia Freatidas
Saronic Gulf
0 500 m
0 0.25 miles

Listings

BEST OF THE REST

Museums & Art

National Archaeological Museum

Five superb permanent collections span the Neolithic and Bronze Age, Cycladic and Mycenaean civilisations, as well as the Roman era. Simply unmissable!

Basil & Elise Goulandris Foundation

Naming just a few of the artists whose works are housed in this stupendous new addition to the city's cultural scene would be like a 'who's who' of world-class art.

National Gallery

Housed in a brand-new, state-of-the-art building, the gallery has historically been home to the crème de la crème of Greek painters.

National Museum of Contemporary Art (EMST)

Athens' long-lasting lack of modern art establishment is now fixed with this interesting conceptual art museum housed in an old brewery in Koukaki.

Benaki Museum

A complex of five museums featuring works of art from Greek history. The concise and beautiful Museum of Islamic Art, near Keramikos, is a real gem.

Technopolis

An old gas factory has been transformed into a cultural hub hosting exhibitions, concerts and other events.

Traditional Tavernas

Diporto €

Simplicity and authenticity enjoyed at communal tables in a downtown basement. Athens' worst-kept secret is an apotheosis of no-frills, scrumptious Greek food.

Klimataria €

A family-run restaurant in the heart of Athens that dates back a century and is known for its beautiful garden and regular performances of live Greek music. Open all day.

Damigos €

The oldest taverna in Athens (since 1864) is located in a Plaka basement. Its speciality has always been fried codlings with garlic dip and other simple but tasty fish meals.

Kriti €€

Tucked away in an arcade on Plateia Kanigos, this is the place to enjoy authentic Cretan cuisine with fresh ingredients sourced from the island.

Gourmet Gems & Fine Dining

Nolan €€

Creative fusion cuisine with traditional Greek and Asian touches, all under the watchful eye of Sotiris Kontizas, a judge from the Greek version of *MasterChef* TV show.

Klimataria

Birdman €€

With carefully selected and superbly grilled meats, a burger many insist is the best in town, Japanese spirits and eclectic tunes, it's like dining in a Tokyo bar.

Seychelles €€

A gourmet tavern in trendy Metaxourgio. Greek food with unexpected twists and a pleasant setting on Plateia Avdi, ideal for a leisurely al fresco meal on a warm day.

Spondi €€€

The dining benchmark in the Greek capital for more than a quarter of a century – world-class cuisine and service.

Varoulko €€€

Michelin-star chef and owner Lefteris Lazarou offers the finest seafood experience in town coupled with a terrific location on the promenade of Mikrolimano in Piraeus.

Vintage Drinking

Galaxy Bar €

This narrow bar with a stylish '70s vibe has been serving regulars and international celebrities for 50 years. Come to drink and chat in a quaint ultra-civilised ambience.

Au Revoir €

The oldest bar in Athens, unchanged since 1957. The 'time capsule', as it's called by its second-generation owners, has served most Athenian night owls, intellectuals and artists.

Jazz in Jazz €

With a heritage going back to southern Crete in the '70s, this old-school jazz den could still operate as a genre museum if somehow all alcohol was removed from the premises.

Batman €

A small bar in Neos Kosmos that plays Greek retro music and gets packed every night, after midnight until the morning hours. A cult institution on the Athenian nightlife scene.

Varvakios Agora

Shop Till You Drop

Varvakios Agora

The biggest Athenian food market since 1886. Hundreds of merchants offer their fresh produce in the constantly buzzing surroundings of a splendid listed building.

Monastiraki Flea Market

In the flea market at Plateia Avyssinias, sift through the piles of junk for strange findings, antiques and retro objects, and you might unearth hidden gems.

Ermou

This is the main commercial street in the centre of Athens. Large department stores, international brands and local boutiques create a shopper's paradise.

Apivita

A Kolonaki-based 'experience store' that features a spa, a fresh juice bar and a 'green' hairstyling service, in addition to retailing a line of natural cosmetics.

Scan to find more things to do in Athens.

THESSALONIKI & NORTHERN GREECE

NATURE | GASTRONOMY | HISTORY

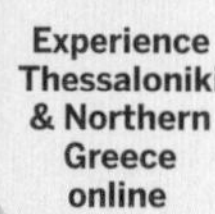

Experience Thessaloniki & Northern Greece online

NORTHERN GREECE
Trip Builder

Rugged mountains, magical waterfalls, crystalline beaches, perfectly preserved ruins that demonstrate a deep history, limestone villages seemingly lost in time, excellent cuisine – northern Greece is one of the least-visited regions in the country, which is all the more to the benefit of the adventurous traveller.

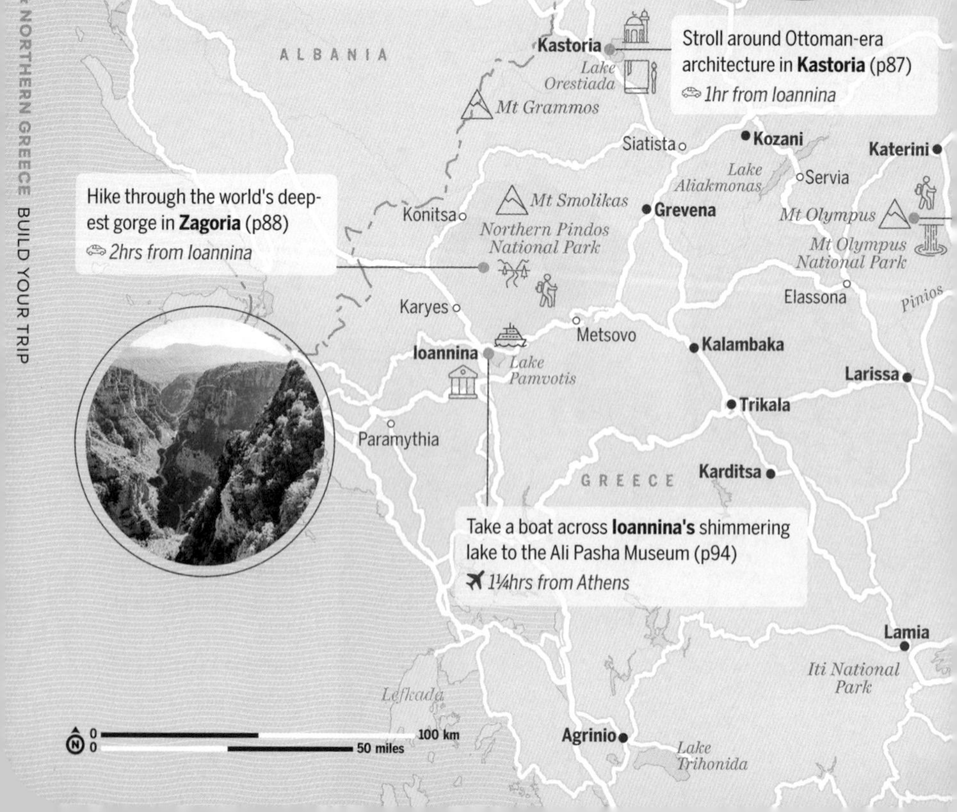

Stroll around Ottoman-era architecture in **Kastoria** (p87)
1hr from Ioannina

Hike through the world's deepest gorge in **Zagoria** (p88)
2hrs from Ioannina

Take a boat across **Ioannina's** shimmering lake to the Ali Pasha Museum (p94)
1¼hrs from Athens

ALBANIA
GREECE
Kastoria
Lake Orestiada
Mt Grammos
Siatista
Kozani
Katerini
Lake Aliakmonas
Servia
Mt Smolikas
Grevena
Mt Olympus
Konitsa
Northern Pindos National Park
Mt Olympus National Park
Elassona
Pinios
Karyes
Metsovo
Ioannina
Lake Pamvotis
Kalambaka
Larissa
Trikala
Paramythia
Karditsa
Lamia
Iti National Park
Lefkada
Agrinio
Lake Trihonida
0 100 km
0 50 miles

BULGARIA

Soak up Greek-Islamic culture in **Xanthi** (p86)
2hrs from Thessaloniki

Indulge in Greece's most delectable cuisine in **Thessaloniki** (p96)
5hrs from Athens

Mt Falakro
Drama
Xanthi
Komotini
Serres
Alistrati
Lake Vistonida
Kilkis
GREECE
Strymonas
Hrysoupoli
Nestos
Fanari
Kavala
Nigrita
Keramoti
Alexandroupoli
Gulf of Kavala
Thasos (Limenas)
Lake Korónia
Lake Vólvi
Stavros
Thasos
Thracian Sea
Evros Delta
Thessaloniki
Strymonic Gulf
Panorama

Observe **Mt Athos**, the most important site for the Greek Orthodox Church (p93)
2hrs from Thessaloniki

Stratonion
Halkidiki Peninsula
Epanomi
Ierissos
Samothraki
Nea Moudania
Ouranoupoli
TURKEY
Gulf of Thessaloniki
Gulf of Agion Oros
Gökçeada (Imvros)
Vourvourou
Sarti
Mt Athos

Hike through **Mt Olympus** and cool off in waterfalls (p84)
1½hrs from Thessaloniki

Find your perfect beach on **Halkidiki's** second 'finger' (p92)
2hrs from Thessaloniki

Aegean Sea
Sporades
Skyros
Gulf of Evia
Evia

Practicalities

FRANTICOO/SHUTTERSTOCK ©

ARRIVING

Makedonia International Airport The region's main transport hub for international and domestic flights; there are smaller regional airports servicing domestic flights in Ioannina, Kavala and Alexandroupoli. Taxis to the centre of Thessaloniki cost between €20 and €30 depending on the time of day or night, and take about 30 minutes. Bus X01 comes every 40 minutes, and takes between 50 and 70 minutes to reach the centre, depending on traffic; tickets cost €2.

HOW MUCH FOR A

Gyros
€2.70

Tsipouro
€7

Freddo espresso
€1.90

GETTING AROUND

Walking Thessaloniki's centre is compact, and most of the sites are within close distance, so exploring by foot is your best bet. For cities like Ioannina, Xanthi and Kavala, you can also rely on your feet to get around.

Bus The metro is still under construction so for public transport, hop onto the city's bus system. You'll need exact change (€1) to purchase a ticket from the *periptera* (kiosks) or the onboard blue machines.

Car You'll definitely want to rent a car to travel across the region. Driving in Thessaloniki is not for the faint of heart, though – double parking, running red lights and kamikaze pedestrians are seemingly the norm.

WHEN TO GO

JUN–AUG
Hot and humid days, perfect for the beach.

SEP–NOV
The tail end of summer, when you can beat the crowds.

DEC–FEB
Wet, cold, occasionally snowy weather.

MAR–MAY
Warmer days, perfect for city jaunts and hikes.

EATING & DRINKING

Northern Greece has some of the best food in the country, and Thessaloniki is the gastronomic capital (don't tell the Athenians). In the city, you'll find world-class restaurants and plenty of casual places dishing out souvlaki and *gyros* (eaten with pitta bread). Along the coast, expect fresh fish and seafood, while in the mountains, grilled meat, boiled greens and fragrant cheeses are the norm. Northern Greece also makes the country's best pies and baked goods. There's a distinct Ottoman influence on the cuisine thanks to the many Anatolian refugees who settled here in the 20th century.

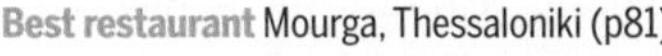

Best restaurant Mourga, Thessaloniki (p81)

Must-try bougatsa Select, Ioannina (p95)

CONNECT & FIND YOUR WAY

Wi-fi Buy a SIM card from Vodafone or Wind in stores and at the airport; special tourist packages cost €10 and provide ample data. Most cafes and restaurants have wi-fi, but service can be spotty in the more rugged areas.

Navigation Google Maps works well in most of the region. In some areas, like eastern Zagoria, you won't have good mobile service; pre-load maps to avoid getting lost.

WHERE TO STAY

From atmospheric guesthouses to design hostels, you'll be spoiled for choice. In Thessaloniki, note that hotels in the centre can be a bit noisy even at night.

Place	Pro/Con
Thessaloniki	A cosmopolitan hub with a diverse range of places to stay. Ano Poli is quiet, but an uphill hike. The waterfront has the best views, but can be noisy with nightlife.
Zagoria	Atmospheric stone guesthouses nestled in the mountains.
Halkidiki	Beachfront hotels and apartment rentals to suit any budget.
Ioannina	Ottoman-era boutique hotels with views of the lake.

ARCHAEOLOGICAL SITES

A handy app to download is Topos Text, which geolocates ruins and provides a historical overview.

MONEY

Most places in northern Greece now accept contactless payment through card or phone, but it's always a good idea to have small notes on you to pay for taxis and more off-the-beaten-path restaurants.

08 Taking a BITE

FOOD | DRINKS | HISTORY

As the gastronomic capital of Greece, Thessaloniki is a place where you can literally taste your way through the city's history. With countless bakeries, *tsipouradhika,* souvlaki spots, tavernas and wine bars, each bite and sip will delight your senses and bring new understanding of its layered past.

How to

Getting here/around Fly direct from across Europe, or take a five-hour train from Athens. Most of the listed restaurants and bakeries are within walking distance; for locations slightly further away, a taxi is your best bet.

When to go Summer in Thessaloniki can be brutally hot and humid. The best time for a culinary tour is in May or September, when it's warm enough to dine outside.

Dress code Thessalonikians are known for their style and grooming – you'll look out of place if you're dressed shabbily!

Tyropita After the 1923 Greek-Turkish population exchange, Thessaloniki experienced a culinary boom, as Christians brought over Turkish cooking techniques and traditions – including the best way to make filo pastry. In the district of Neapoli, try the city's best cheese pie at **Milano Bakery**. Started by Anatolian refugees, it hasn't changed the recipe in nearly a century.

Gyros A hallmark of Thessaloniki cuisine, *gyros* is slow-roasted pork or chicken shaved off with a blade and stuffed into pitta bread with a smear of tzatziki, onions, tomatoes and plenty of French fries. The perfect hangover lunch, the best *gyros* is found in Toumba district known for its football stadium and a drink called Tuba Libre (mix of Coca-Cola and retsina). The best of several rival *gyros* spots is **Giotis**.

Neo-taverna As a port city, Thessaloniki is better known for fish than meat, with countless tavernas to feast on octopus, sardines and fish fillets. The most interesting seafood dishes can be found at neo-taverna **Mourga**. The menu changes daily – expect dishes like amberjack ceviche, giant grilled prawns and white *taramasalata* (fish-roe purée). The produce is regional and fresh; the wine list features Greek natural wines.

Sephardic cuisine During WWII, the city lost most of its once-prominent Jewish population, and only whispers of Sephardic culture remain. One such place is **Akadimia** in the historically Jewish neighbourhood behind Tsimiski. Sample (by pre-arrangement) a menu of typical Sephardic dishes, like meatballs with walnuts and parsley, and *huevos haminados* (braised hard-boiled eggs).

A Day at the Market

You could easily lose track of time at the **Kapani Market**, an atmospheric jumble of stalls selling everything from hunks of lamb to mastic from the island of Chios to mountain tea from nearby Mt Olympus.

It is the oldest continuously operating market in the city – since the time of the Ottomans – and the perfect place to stock up on picnic supplies or gifts to take back home.

■ **By Amber Charmei**
Amber's favourite aspect of life in Greece is the graceful way locals embrace the beauty of the moment.

Urban Pedigree

CONTEMPORARY CULTURE WITH PLENTY OF CONTEXT

With its sun-kissed Mediterranean glamour, Roman gravitas, lots of Byzantine glory and sounds and flavours of Asia Minor, Thessaloniki offers a compelling urban experience. This shimmering port city has reinvented itself many times since its founding in 315 BCE. Its latest manifestation is an engaging destination for contemporary art and culture.

Left Archaeological Museum
Centre Museum of Byzantine Culture
Right Stream in Pozar

In a world where secrets are ever scarcer, Thessaloniki offers that rare quality of being a discovery. With over two millennia of continuous urban life, it has an easy confidence – a city with nothing to prove. Yet it can't help but make a dazzling first impression, with a row of elegant facades so close to the sea you'll taste the salt on a stormy day. Poised between east and west, Thessaloniki has been a magnet for empires – Roman, Byzantine, Ottoman – and a nexus of cultures and faiths. With the arrival of Sephardic Jews expelled from the Iberian Peninsula in the 15th century, it became the main Jewish city of Europe. The lilting cadence of Ladino (Judeo-Spanish), along with Ottoman Turkish, Greek and French, filled the streets of sophisticated Salonica, as it then was called. This petite multicultural metropolis finally joined modern Greece only on the eve of WWI. A decade later, the great influx of Greek refugees from Asia Minor reinforced the city's Greek identity, while underscoring its eastern cultural orientation.

Thessaloniki has absorbed a lot and abandoned little, forging a deeply cosmopolitan culture and complex urban landscape. Worldly yet disarmingly quaint, this is a city of juxtapositions. Roman ruins and Ottoman mosques and bathhouses punctuate ungentrified stretches of grand prewar apartment buildings, belle époque beauty and juicy bites of '60s pop. More than a picturesque backdrop, history is integrated into the city's contemporary life. Bells peal at Byzantine churches, some over a millennium old (13 of them Unesco-recognised monuments), and locals still shop at the Ottoman-era Kapani Market; join them as they break for a *tsipouro* and mezedhes amid swirling crowds and fresh fish.

SAIKO3P/SHUTTERSTOCK ©

MUART/SHUTTERSTOCK ©

With such wealth to draw on, Thessaloniki's Archaeological Museum and Museum of Byzantine Culture are superb. Engagement with modern and contemporary culture is equally inspiring. At the MOMus Museum of Contemporary Art, A-list collections and special exhibitions explore currents in 20th- and 21st-century art. The Costakis Collection, one of the most complete collections of Russian avant-garde art outside Russia, is at the MOMus Museum of Modern Art. Museums at the pier feature experimental art, photography and cinema. The city adores film – cinephiles and luminaries converge for the Thessaloniki International Film Festival, as well as the Short Film Festival and notable Documentary Festival. The highlight of the visual arts calendar is the Thessaloniki Biennale of Contemporary Art, encompassing a performance art festival when the city shines as a surreal stage.

> With a row of elegant facades so close to the sea you'll taste the salt on a stormy day.

Nightlife here is an art itself, with many expressions both Greek and international. As a city with a large student population, Thessaloniki has always had a famously active music scene. Thanks to its excellent crowds and a couple of choice venues, it's also a favourite stop for touring bands of all genres. Over a dozen music festivals supplement a full concert programme. And with an after-hours food scene to match, no one goes home hungry; there's *patsas* (tripe and trotter soup) for the bold, and many other choices for the rest of us.

Bathhouse Culture

Bathing in one of the city's grand public baths was part of Thessaloniki's culture for centuries; the last closed only in the 1960s. But you can still enjoy the experience at **Loutra Lagada**, half an hour from town.

Natural warm waters fill the Byzantine pools (dating from 900 CE and 1400 CE), separated by gender in the daytime and reserved for private use in the evenings.

At the gorgeous **Loutra Pozar**, about two hours from Thessaloniki, you can bathe in warm natural pools and waterfalls as steam rises into the trees above. It also has private indoor baths, and stays open until late.

09 Up in the CLOUDS

HIKING | WATERFALLS | RUINS

As the loftiest peak in Greece, Mt Olympus has a history as impressive as its height (2918m): here, after all, is the mythical home of the ancient Greek gods, and the palpable energy of the 12 Olympians remains. Today it's better known as a hiker's paradise, with wild nature full of endless waterfalls and natural pools, and the unmissable ruins of Ancient Dion.

How to

Getting here/around Mt Olympus is an hour's drive from Thessaloniki. You'll need a car to get around the area (aside from hiking in the mountains).

When to go Hiking is best in spring, summer (when the water is most refreshing) and autumn. The temperature can drop quickly at night, so bring layers. Avoid hiking in winter, as the top of the mountain becomes very unsafe.

Where to sleep Litohoro makes a practical base, though you can also stay in the refuges that dot the landscape. Wild camping is not permitted.

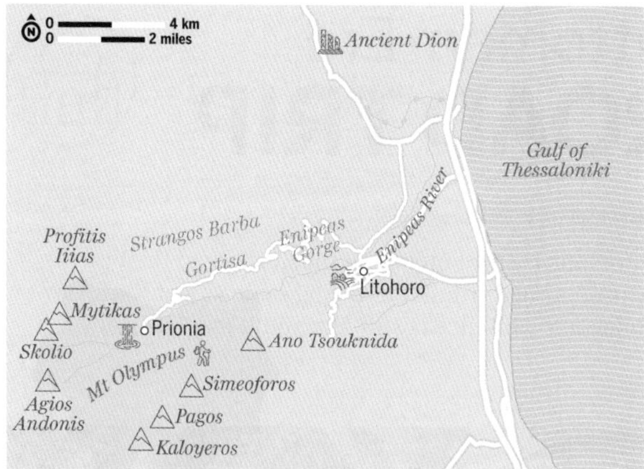

Pay your respects In the shadow of Mt Olympus lies **Ancient Dion**, one of the most important sites in classical Greece – this is where Alexander the Great made sacrifices to Zeus before going to war. Take your time walking through the grounds, sitting by the river and eating figs that generously grow off the trees. Don't miss the **Sanctuary of Isis**, goddess of fertility; in the heat of summer, watch out for the snakes that slither through the tall grass (in ancient times, they were believed to protect the temples). Entry includes access to the park and the **Archaelogical Museum of Dion**.

Wild swimming There's a number of hiking trails around **Mt Olympus**, among them the E4 European path that begins in the village of **Litohoro** and ends in Prionia at an altitude of 1100m (the hike takes about five hours). The springs of Prionia feed the mountain with gushing waterfalls and deep natural swimming pools, beckoning you to jump in. Most are accessible just off the main hiking trail, and the further up the mountain you go, the icier the water gets.

A bacchanalian evening What would the gods want you to do after a day in nature? Get drunk, of course. In the village of Litohoro, make a beeline for **Disko Romeiko,** an all-day cafe-bar that sits by the Enipeas River. Run by a former DJ and her husband, it always has excellent music, generously poured drinks and delectable mezedhes. Most evenings, the party goes on until late and the bar turns into an impromptu dance floor.

A Small Feast

Fasoladha (bean soup) is, surprisingly, the national dish of Greece – and one of the best places to eat it is at the entrance of **Prionia**.

There, a tavern by the same name welcomes weary hikers with fiery shots of raki and steaming bowls of bean soup, flecked with red pepper and served with warm, homemade bread.

10 Ottoman-Era ROAD TRIP

HISTORY | RELIGION | ARCHITECTURE

The legacy of the Ottomans is still tangible in the north, and the best way to soak up the history is on a road trip. From the lakeside city of Kastoria to Xanthi, where a distinct Islamic presence is still felt, you'll feel like you've stepped back in time.

PANOS KARAS/SHUTTERSTOCK ©

Ottoman-Era Thessaloniki

Don't miss the **Bey Hammam** (the old public baths, pictured), **Alaca İmaret Mosque** and **Eptapyrgion** (or Yedi Kule, a defensive fort turned into a prison).

History buffs should also stop at the birthplace and residential home (now museum) of **Mustafa Kemal Atatürk**, the founder of modern Turkey.

How to

Getting here/around Thanks to the Egnatia Odos highway, completed in 2017, it's never been easier (or safer) to drive through the mountainous terrain connecting these once distant cities.

When to go Spring or autumn is the best time to visit. Avoid winter, when the roads can become icy and dangerous.

Road-trip snacks The most portable snack is *koulouria* – a yeasted bread ring coated in sesame seeds. It's crunchier and thinner than its Turkish counterpart, *simit*, but the culinary parallels are obvious.

03 A former Islamic seminary built by Pasha Mohamed Ali in **Kavala**, Imaret features vaulted stone ceilings and a jaw-dropping hammam. The impressive grounds and delightful restaurant are open to the public, or splurge and spend the night.

02 It's a two-hour drive to **Thessaloniki**, one of the Ottoman Empire's most important cities. A walking tour around the centre will reveal many architectural gems, though most buildings are today used as markets, cafes and churches.

Kalambaka
Larissa
Trikala
GREECE
Lamia
Gulf of Evia
Skyros
Evia
Aegean Sea

01 The atmospheric lakeside city of **Kastoria** has some of the most interesting Ottoman-era buildings around. The single-domed Koursoum Mosque in the historic centre is the only one surviving in the area.

04 Some 600 Ottoman-style mansions built in **Xanthi** include the impressive Kouyioumtzoglou Mansion. Xanthi has Greece's largest Muslim population, with working mosques and shops selling Islamic books and prayer rugs.

0 100 km
0 50 miles

11 Zigzagging ZAGORIA

HIKING | VILLAGES | GASTRONOMY

Nestled between the Pindos Mountains and the Ionian Sea, Zagoria, located in the region of Epiros, is one of the last relatively unknown parts of Greece – largely thanks to its isolation. With nearly 50 villages dotting the landscape, stone forests, gorges, waterfalls and musical festivals, it's a truly entrancing part of the country.

VALERY BOCMAN/SHUTTERSTOCK ©

How to

Getting there/around Ioannina serves as the gateway to Zagoria, but you'll need a car to get around the mountain.

When to go Winter: ice climbing and snowshoeing. Summer: foraging for blackberries and cooling off in mountain springs.

Pop some tunes A special kind of Greek blues comes from Epiros; Grigoris Kapsalis is the most prolific *klarino* (clarinet) player – load up a playlist for melodic beats.

Pack a map The eastern side of Zagoria has no mobile service; make sure you pack a paper map.

MNSTUDIO/SHUTTERSTOCK ©

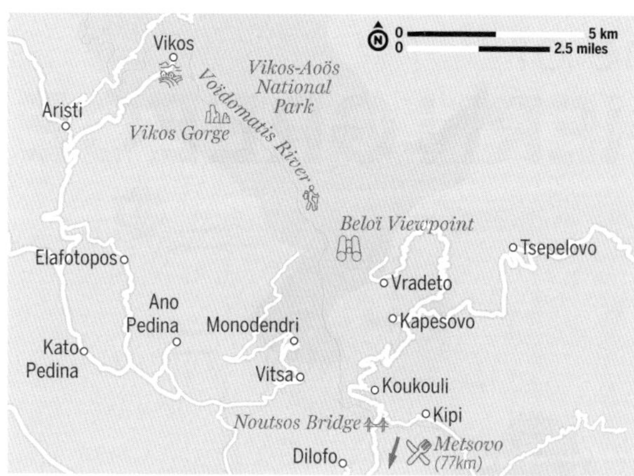

Top Vikos Gorge
Bottom Monodendri

Bridges There are more than 100 soaring stone bridges across Zagoria, built in the 18th and 19th centuries by craftspeople trying to connect isolated villages to each other. These impressive feats of engineering are artworks, seamlessly built into the environment. Some can be easily spotted from a car, like the **Noutsos Bridge** on the road from Dilofo to Koukouli. To reach others, such as the **Plakida Bridge**, with its triple arch on the edge of the village of Kipoi, you'll need to hike.

Hike the gorge The 12km-long, 900m-deep **Vikos Gorge** is the world's deepest gorge relative to its width. Those who have no fear of heights can head to the **Beloï Viewpoint** for jaw-dropping views of the canyon (the acoustics up here are pretty great, too). You can also trek through the gorge along the **Voïdomatis River**; it's best to do this in summer. The classic route starts in **Monodendri** and ends in Vikos or vice versa; in either case, follow the O3 signs and budget up to seven hours for the hike.

Villages Collectively, the 44 villages of Zagoria are known as **Zagorohoria**, and each one is seemingly more beautiful than the next. All are built out of limestone, with quiet squares shaded by plane trees and framed by bougainvillea – you'll feel like you've stepped into a fairy tale. For a truly magical experience, don't miss the three-day mid-August *panigyri* (religious festival) in the village of **Vikos**, where you'll experience traditional Epirot music and dance.

Metsovo Magic

You'll smell **Metsovo** before you see it – a heady mix of chimney smoke, pine trees and, most importantly, grilled meat.

The most delectable can be found at **5 Fs**, an outdoor taverna that has been doling out perfect portions of grilled meat, unceremoniously served on butcher paper, for decades.

This is the best place to try *provatina* (female sheep), and more adventurous eaters should go for *kokoretsi* (lamb sweetbreads and liver wrapped in intestines).

Round out the meal with smoked cheese and fried potatoes.

The Cuisine of NORTHERN GREECE

01 Florina pepper

A sweet red pepper that is pickled, grilled or preserved in olive oil. Around Greece, it is revered for its delicate taste and structure.

02 Tsoureki

Greece's answer to challah, this yeasted, braided bread has a complex flavour thanks to the addition of mastic and mahlepi (wild cherry bark).

03 Bean soup *(faso-ladha)*

Some of the country's best beans come from the north, around the Prespes region. Boiled until creamy and tender, it's the perfect post-hike or winter meal.

04 Kokoretsi

No part of the animal goes to waste in Greece. *Kokoretsi*, or offal wrapped in intestines and grilled to perfection, are a favourite in the north.

05 Tsipouro

Triple-distilled grape alcohol reminiscent of grappa, served in tiny glasses – you can easily have 20 before realising what's happened.

06 Bougatsa

This breakfast pastry is made with filo dough

and stuffed with either sweet custard cream or salty cheese.

07 Soutzoukakia

These oblong kebabs spiced with cumin are usually grilled over an open fire and served with a little pile of crushed *boukovo* (red-pepper flakes).

08 Galotyri

A combination of sheep's cheese and yogurt, this delicious spread originated in Epiros. It's often eaten with meat to aid digestion.

09 Metsovone

This semi-hard, smoked cheese is a mountain speciality from the village of Metsovo. It's eaten plain or served grilled and sprinkled with paprika.

10 Spoon sweets

Ultra-sugary preserved fruits suspended in unctuous syrup. It can be made with any fruit and is usually served with Greek coffee or yoghurt.

11 Mushrooms

There are more than 2000 varieties of mushrooms in central northern Greece, and during the autumn you can go mushroom-hunting yourself.

12 No Place Like HALKIDIKI

BEACHES | BOAT TRIPS | DIVING

Forget the islands – some of Greece's best beaches are actually on the three-fingered, potbellied peninsula just an hour's drive from Thessaloniki. 'There's no place like Halkidiki', the local saying goes, and it's true. From crystalline beaches to the most important site for the Greek Orthodox Church, Halkidiki has something for everyone.

ICARUS AERIAL FILMING/SHUTTERSTOCK ©

How to

Getting around For travelling around the peninsula, opt for a car rental.

When to go Try and avoid August, when crowds are at their peak.

Choose a peninsula Kassandra Peninsula is the most developed for package tourism. Sithonia has the best beaches and a more relaxed vibe. Athos is the holy prefecture and only part is accessible.

Religious permits Men wishing to visit Mt Athos will need to apply for a special permit (called a *diamonitirion*) from the Pilgrims' Bureau in Thessaloniki or Ouranoupoli.

ALEKSANDAR TODOROVIC/SHUTTERSTOCK ©

Boating Ever dreamed of being a captain? You don't need a special licence to rent a small boat and navigate the turquoise waters between the Sithonian Peninsula and Mt Athos. In **Vourvourou**, you'll find dozens of retailers renting out boats for the day; bring your own food or snacks and set sail for **Diaporos Island**. You'll be able to drop anchor wherever your heart pleases.

Holy mountain One place you can't visit unaccompanied is **Mt Athos**, the most holy place for the Greek Orthodox Church and a World Heritage Site with a 1700-year-old history. Women aren't permitted to visit the area, so for a more inclusive experience, book a three-hour cruise from Ouranoupoli with **Athos Sea Cruises**, which will give you a glimpse of the 20 monasteries from a distance.

Diving As impressive as Halkidiki's shores are, what's going on underneath is even more jaw-dropping. At the village of **Nikiti** in Sithonia, **Atlantis Diving Center** offers one-day diving excursions. There's no need to be a professional – they have options for first-time divers and children, and you're guaranteed to spot silvery schools of fish.

Beaches There's no shortage of beaches in Halkidiki. Organised beaches (with lounge chairs, bars and pulsing music) can be found in Kassandra, while undeveloped beaches are the norm in Sithonia. Alternatively, head to the hidden naturist beach of **Kalamitsi**. Here, people pitch tents and drop their clothes for weeks at a time. Nudism and free camping is a big part of the Greek summer experience, and this is the perfect place for it.

Top Mt Athos
Bottom Beach in Sithonia

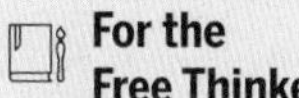

For the Free Thinker

Philosophy buffs should make a pilgrimage to the seaside village of **Stagira**, the birthplace of Aristotle, one of the greatest names in European philosophy and Plato's most famous student.

Nearby, a 'theme park' has been erected in his honour, and while you won't find rollercoasters or Ferris wheels, you will see replicas of many scientific inventions mentioned in Aristotle's textbooks, including optical discs and a playable pentaphone (sounding bars).

13 Ioannina's MAGIC

HISTORY | CRAFTS | GASTRONOMY

Set on Lake Pamvotis, Ioannina has an atmospheric city centre, perfectly preserved ruins and a strong arts and crafts scene. The air smells like figs or firewood, depending on the season, the morning fog rolls in over the silvery lake, while the chants of the Orthodox priests float above the abandoned Ottoman-era minarets.

KOSTASGR/SHUTTERSTOCK ©

How to

Getting around Unless you're planning on travelling outside the city, Ioannina is compact enough that you don't need a car or public transport.

When to go Ioannina is stunning year-round but particularly magical around Christmas, when the city is awash in twinkling lights and snow caps the mountains.

Where to stay Book a room in the Its Kale district, which is pleasantly quiet but still close enough to the centre that you'll be in on the action.

GEORGIOS TSICHLIS/SHUTTERSTOCK ©

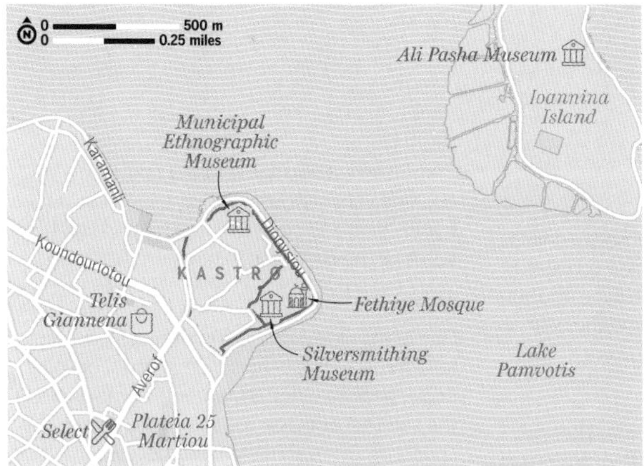

Catch a ferry to the tiny island on Ioannina's **Lake Pamvotis**, famous for being the summer residence of Ali Pasha – and the place where his life came to a gruesome end. The enchanting island has been inhabited for centuries and today, aside from some local residents, it hosts the small **Ali Pasha Museum**, located in his former home. The islet is also famous for fried frog legs, which you can munch on at **Prasini Akti**.

Spend some time wandering around the **Kastro**, where you can soak up centuries of Ioannina's history in a few hours. Start at the **Municipal Ethnographic Museum**, housed in the former Aslan Pasha Mosque (keep an eye out for the ketubahs, or Jewish wedding contracts), before heading onto the ruins of the fortress, the 1430 **Fethiye Mosque** and the ornamented tomb of Ali Pasha. Here you can also check out the **Kahila Kedosha Yashan Synagogue**, which is the oldest Romaniote synagogue in the Balkans (visit by appointment only). The whole fortified area is now wheelchair-accessible; you can purchase one ticket that will give you access to all the sites.

As the former silversmithing capital of Greece, Ioannina is known for all things shiny (and for being the hometown of Bulgari). Head to the **Silversmithing Museum** to learn about the city's historic contributions to this ancient craft. While you'll find plenty of jewellery stores along the town's main drag, a much more unique gift is a hand-forged knife – and the best ones can be found at **Telis Giannena.**

Top Autumn in Ioannina
Bottom Fethiye Mosque

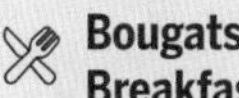

Bougatsa Breakfast

Make a beeline to **Select**, a family-owned *bougatsa* (a type of pastry) spot in downtown Ioannina serving two things: custard-filled *bougatsa* and cheese-filled *bougatsa*.

Served piping hot and haphazardly cut with a double-handled knife, this is the most traditional – and delicious – way to start the day.

Select is one of the oldest bakeries in town, and it's been doling out *bougatsa* for decades.

Listings

BEST OF THE REST

Local Flavours

Souvlaki Kostas €

Little cubes of pork, chicken or lamb are grilled to perfection on a wooden stick, basted with olive oil and garnished with lemon juice. You can eat them plain or in a sandwich, and the best ones in Thessaloniki can be found here.

Bantis €

Since 1969 this little corner shop in Thessaloniki has been doling out *bougatsa,* crispy filo pastries filled with cheese or vanilla cream. Served piping-hot out of the oven and sold by the weight on an old-fashioned scale, they make the perfect breakfast.

Ktima Bellou €€€

On the eastern side of Mt Olympus, where few tourists venture, lies this hotel-restaurant where all the (organic) ingredients are grown on their own land.

Thomas €€

Opened in 1970, this family business in Sklithro is one of the best in Greece. Come here to try wild-mushroom orzo, local *saganaki* cheese with red-pepper jam, and any of their meat dishes. All regional ingredients and only Greek wines.

To Psaradika €

A very cute cafe next to the Prespa Lakes that's the perfect place to try the famous Prespes beans and smoked trout.

Kanella & Garyfallo €€

Northern Greece is abundant in mushrooms, and this mountain restaurant in the Zagori village of Vitsa is the best place to try them in a million different ways – stuffed, fried, sautéed, or pureed into soup are just a few examples.

Genteki €€

This little restaurant in Florina takes slow cooking very seriously – all the ingredients are hyper-local and cooked over an open fire. It's some of the best food in northern Greece.

Akanthos €

One of the oldest *kafeneia* in Greece, Akanthos in Tzoumerka has been serving honest country cooking for decades. Sit under the grapevines in the summer or inside the cafe in the winter. The speciality is *provatina* (female sheep).

Coffee & Wine

Kofi Microroastery €

A cute third-wave coffee shop for takeaway; perfect for strolling Ioannina's town centre.

Its Kale Cafe €

In the castle ruins of Ioannina, with a breathtaking view of the lake and mountains, this is the most atmospheric place to have a cuppa.

Domaine Ligas €€

The winery that put natural Greek wine on the map, now in its second generation in

BOAZ ROTTEM/ALAMY STOCK PHOTO ©

Bantis

Giannitsa. Come here to sample some of the most interesting wines in Greece. Visits by appointment.

SHED €

One of the best in Thessaloniki: a third-wave coffee shop with outdoor seating located next to a sunken Byzantine church.

Domaine Karanika €

The only winery in Greece producing sparkling wine is run by a gregarious Greek-Dutch winemaker near Florina. By appointment.

Chatzivaritis Estate €€

One of Greece's only female winemakers runs this family business in Goumenissa, making low-intervention natural wines from local grapes. Visits by appointment.

Outdoor Thrills

Arcturos Bear Sanctuary

The brown bear, Europe's largest land mammal, exists only in small numbers – and several of them have been placed in the Arcturos Bear Sanctuary near Kastoria. It's a delightful outing.

Tzoumerka National Park

The Arachatos River in Tzoumerka, south of Ioannina, has some of the country's best white-water rafting – you'll float through gorges and under stone bridges. Whether you're an experienced rafter or a newbie, there are cascades for any skill level.

Prespa Lakes

Near the border with Albania and North Macedonia lie the twin Prespa Lakes, Greece's most impressive. Swimming, strolling and bird-watching are all fun activities around the lakes.

Papingo Rock Pools

In Zagorohoria, millennia of erosion have created a karst terrain with natural rock pools and

JEKATARINKA/SHUTTERSTOCK ©

Archaeological Museum, Pella

waterfalls. Come in spring or early summer, when the water is still high enough to bathe.

Historical Vibes

Art of Silk Museum, Soufli

Just across the border from Turkey, Soufli is the former epicentre of silk production in the Ottoman Empire. This informative museum is a great place to learn about the trade and purchase a few silk items.

Vergina Royal Tombs Museum

The ancient royal tombs of the Macedon Kingdom make for an arresting experience – the *tumulus* (burial mound) has been turned into an underground museum. The undisputed star is the marble tomb of Philip II, Alexander the Great's father.

Archaeological Site of Pella

Pella rose to fame in late 5th century BCE when King Archelaos made it Macedon's capital. Also visit the adjoining Archaeological Museum, where burial treasures including remarkable gold jewellery are on display.

Scan to find more things to do in Thessaloniki & Northern Greece.

DELPHI & CENTRAL GREECE

ANCIENT MARVELS | MOUNTAINS | ADVENTURE

Experience Delphi & Central Greece online

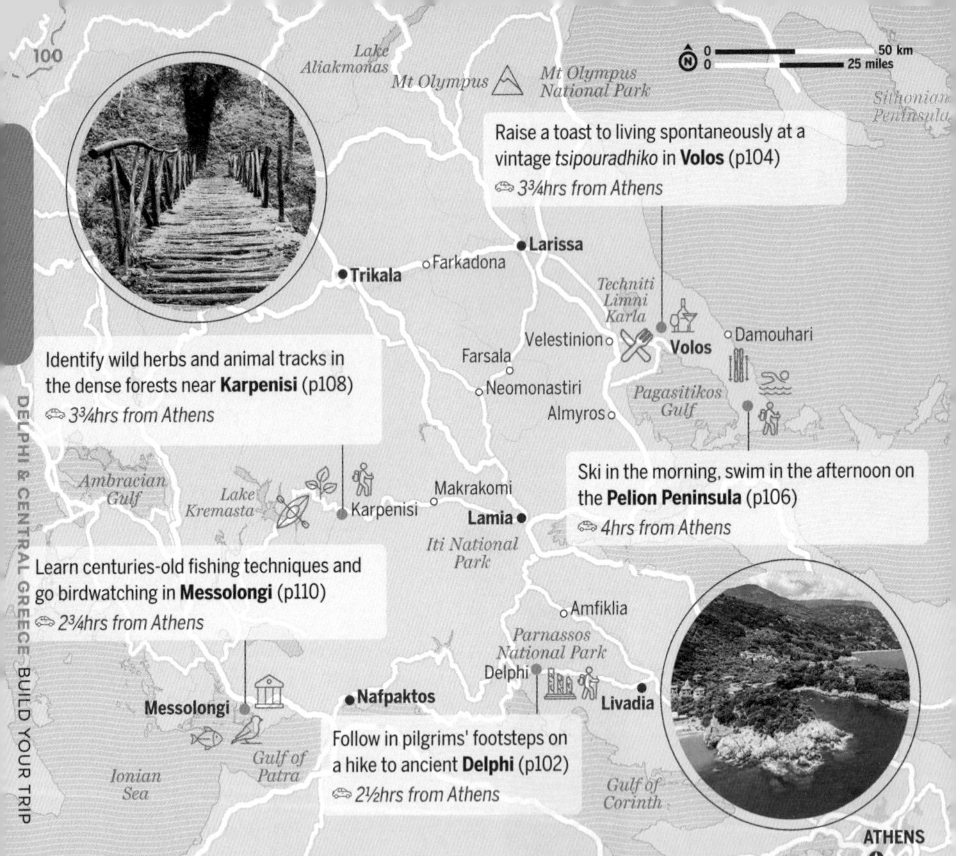

Raise a toast to living spontaneously at a vintage *tsipouradhiko* in **Volos** (p104)
3¾hrs from Athens

Identify wild herbs and animal tracks in the dense forests near **Karpenisi** (p108)
3¾hrs from Athens

Ski in the morning, swim in the afternoon on the **Pelion Peninsula** (p106)
4hrs from Athens

Learn centuries-old fishing techniques and go birdwatching in **Messolongi** (p110)
2¾hrs from Athens

Follow in pilgrims' footsteps on a hike to ancient **Delphi** (p102)
2½hrs from Athens

CENTRAL GREECE
Trip Builder

Sure, central Greece's Unesco World Heritage Sites of Meteora and Delphi are must-sees. Dare to venture beyond these ancient marvels to discover bird-filled wetland habitats, spirit-fuelled sociocultural rituals, river trekking, winding mountain trails, skiing with sea views and more.

Explore bookable experiences in Delphi & Central Greece

Practicalities

ARRIVING

Athens International Airport Express buses from central terminals connect with the extensive KTEL intercity bus network, reaching Pelion and Messolongi.

Volos Airport KTEL intercity buses run from airport to Volos. Regular routes operate between Volos and Pelion's villages.

MONEY

You can pay by card pretty much anywhere, but bring some cash just in case. ATMs are harder to come by in villages.

FIND YOUR WAY

GPS works fairly well in most towns and villages. Google Maps and Waze can be unreliable in more remote areas.

WHERE TO STAY

Place	Pro/Con
Delphi	Mountain views and easy access to ancient site. Town and accommodation on the plain side.
Pelion Peninsula	B&Bs in traditional mansions. Inconvenient without a car.
Karpenisi	Snug guesthouses in pretty villages. The capital has lost character.
Messolongi	Renovated city-centre apartments and lakeside studios. Lagoon views are a rarity.

GETTING AROUND

Car The best way to explore the region. Be prepared for road tolls, particularly between Athens and Volos.

Bus The KTEL intercity network is reliable. Buy tickets at bus terminals or online.

Train Services are limited and less convenient. Buy tickets at stations or online (hellenictrain.gr).

EATING & DRINKING

The region's fare is meat-focused – this is where spit-roasting originated. Chargrilled lamb chops are found everywhere, though locals favour chewier mutton. In Pelion, try *spetsofaï* (stewed pork sausages and peppers); in Karpenisi, wild-boar *stifadho* is often on the menu. In Thessaly, veggie-based dishes are plentiful. Also sample feta and other cheeses like Arahova's *formaela*.

Best fish Dimitroukas, Messolongi (p115)

Must-try chargrilled meats Gousios, Kalambaka (p115)

JAN–MAR
Ski and snowboard season in Pelion, Karpenisi and Arahova.

APR–JUN
Warm, sunny days and mountains filled with wildflowers.

JUL–SEP
Peak season for ancient sites, swimming and festivals.

OCT–DEC
Ideal for hiking and intimate fireside escapes.

14 Delphi Done DIFFERENTLY

ANTIQUITY | TREKKING | OLIVES

There's more than one way to get to know Delphi. Trek the archaic footpath that pilgrims once followed to reach the sacred religious sanctuary in order to consult high priestess Pythia. Below the ancient site, a silvery sea of more than 1.5 million olive trees – some dating back 3000 years – spreads towards the sea, still producing fine olive oil.

LEFTERIS PAPAULAKIS/SHUTTERSTOCK ©

How To

Getting here Delphi is a 2½-hour drive from Athens. Alternatively, take the train from Athens to Amfiklia followed by a 60-minute taxi ride to Delphi. KTEL intercity buses run regularly from Athens' Liossion bus terminal to Delphi.

When to go In spring, when wildflowers are abloom, or September through early November, when there are fewer visitors.

Local flavour Stock up on speciality goods like *hilopites* (fettucine-style pasta) at the nearby town of Arahova.

HERACLES KRITIKOS/SHUTTERSTOCKT ©

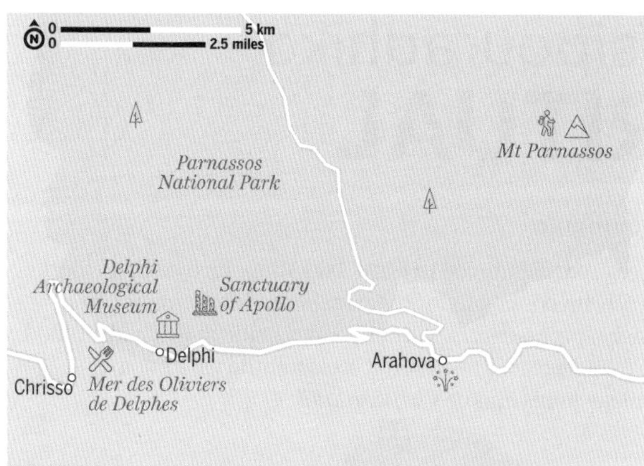

Hike to the ruins Follow in the footsteps of pilgrims, kings and commoners alike, who made their way to Delphi to seek counsel from mystical Pythia on everything from warfare strategy to fertility. **Trekking Hellas** leads guided tours along the European E4 trail down **Mt Parnassos**' slopes, through a riverbed and down ancient rocky steps to the ancient site. Expect knockout views of Mt Kirfi, over 1.5 million olive trees and the Gulf of Corinth.

A sea of olive trees At **Mer des Oliviers de Delphes**, sample intense, fruity, cold-pressed extra virgin olive oil (EVOO) produced with handpicked local Amfissa olives. Cousin co-founders Vasilis and Vassilis Kanatas represent new blood in a family olive-oil-producing tradition harking back five generations. Their gold-medal-winning 1000 Ans has a delicate aroma reminiscent of the wild herbs, almond and fig trees with which these perennial trees share the soil. This premium monovarietal partly originates from 3000-year-old trees that elicited oil which ancient Pythian Games athletes slathered on their bodies and priests used for clay lamps to illuminate Delphi's **Sanctuary of Apollo**.

Seeking Percy Jackson If your kids are Percy Jackson and the Olympians fans, they'll be excited to dig below the surface of ancient Delphi and its **museum** via a fun-filled guided tour with **Greek Mythology Tours** inspired by Rick Riordan's best-selling fantasy novels.

Top Ancient site at Delphi
Bottom Mt Parnassos

Festival of Agios Georgios

In the nearby ski town of **Arahova**, a 12-minute drive east of Delphi, Greeks gather at cosy tavernas and chi-chi bars during snow season.

But few know of the annual **Panigiraki** feast that takes place at or after Orthodox Easter. With Homeric-era roots, this exuberant four-day celebration honours the village's patron St George.

Local men don fustanellas (knee-length pleated skirts) and women wear traditional *sigounia* (a sleeveless overcoat) and dance around the **Church of Agios Georgios** and in the streets, to the sound of the archaic *pipiza* (pipe) and *daouli* (tabor).

Hill races, discus throwing and wrestling count among its many sporting events.

15 Tsipouradhiko RITUAL

CULTURE | GASTRONOMY | DRINKING

In the early 1920s, Greek refugees forced to leave Asia Minor arrived in the port town of Volos. Proving that crisis breeds creativity, they established the *tsipouradhika* (small restaurants), serving fiery spirit *tsipouro* with mezedhes made of fish and seafood from the Pagasitikos Gulf and the Aegean. This revered sociocultural gastronomic tradition lives on at Volos' vintage joints and neo-*tsipouradhika*.

VERVERIDIS VASILIS/SHUTTERSTOCK ©

How To

Getting here/around Drive to Volos or take a KTEL intercity bus from Athens or Pelion Peninsula. Volos is easy to navigate on foot or by bicycle.

When to go Unless you don't mind the cold, short-sleeve season runs from April to October. July and August are busy, which may mean long wait times.

Decipher an unwritten code Volos artist Alexandros Psychoulis reveals some of the mystery surrounding the *tsipouradhiko* in his book *Drinking Tsipouro in Volos.*

RUBEN M RAMOS/SHUTTERSTOCK ©

Gold school Venture to Volos' working-class Nea Ionia district, where the refugees brought their taste for unusual seafood to port workers. Pick from classics like **Demiris**, which has endured for more than four decades. Anise-infused *tsipouro* accompanies rarely found sea fig, native delicacy fried sea anemone and octopus ink sacs.

Vintage finds Another hive of authentic *tsipouradhika* can be found in the Palaia neighbourhood. Regulars, many of them local university professors, gather under mulberry trees at **Nikos-Gianna** for chargrilled octopus with *tsitsiravla* (pickled wild pistachio shoots) and fried skate with garlic dip. Down a backstreet, no-nonsense **Kavouras** has drawn a devout fanbase from politicians to plumbers for over 70 years. Smooth, well-rounded draft *tsipouro* is served with specialities such as monkfish liver and sun-dried horse mackerel.

The new generation Chef Grigoris Helmis has been blazing a path since opening new-wave *tsipouradhiko* **Mezen** in 2013. Painstakingly selected *tsipouro* is paired with mezedhes in what only can be described as an ambrosial art form. Back in Nea Ionia, Pelion-born Timoleon Diamantis returned from Michelin-starred restaurants to revive much-loved **Ouzerie Karakatsanis** in 1969. The *MasterChef* winner takes inspiration from Mt Athos' humble monastic fare and prepares signature slow-food dishes like lemony cod with plums exclusively on a wood-fired hearth.

Top Making *tsipouro*
Bottom Volos

Tsipouradhiko's 10 Commandments

Thou shalt not peruse the menu. Let your server decide.

Thou shalt not covet meat. Fish and seafood are king.

Honour the holy spirit *tsipouro* (or *tsikoudia* or ouzo).

Thou shalt only decide on *tsipouro* with or without anise.

Thou shalt not take a sip without a bite of food.

Thou shalt not snub dishes, no matter how peculiar.

Thou shalt not eat, drink and run. Take it slow.

Thou shalt not monopolise mezedhes. It's meant to be shared.

Thou shalt only drink beer if it's your final round.

Thou shalt not refuse a complimentary *tsipouromeze*.

Recommended by Andreas Diakodimitris, *co-owner of Mezen @an_diakodimitris*

16 Action-Packed PENINSULA

SWIMMING | HIKING | SKIING

Swimming, skiing and hiking – it all awaits you on one incredibly varied peninsula. Hard to believe, but it's true when it comes to Pelion, which is home to some 24 traditional villages. Immerse yourself in the Aegean's invigorating waters on beaches fringing its eastern coast, trek forested mountain trails where mythical Centaurs galloped, and dash down snow-clad slopes with sea views.

GEORGIOS TSICHLIS/SHUTTERSTOCK ©

How To

Getting here/around Fly into Volos or Athens. Driving is the best way to move around, but factor in sufficient travel time along winding roads.

When to go Year-round, or April to October for warm-weather activities and December to March for skiing and romantic getaways.

Wine down Book a wine tasting at Patistis (patistis-wines.gr) to sample terroir-forward organic vino, including unconventional labels like mandarin- and peach-scented Rodito Active, produced with the *roditis* grape varietal.

THEASTOCK/SHUTTERSTOCK ©

Skiing with sea views Situated at an altitude of 1471m, the family-friendly **Pelion Ski Centre** may be pint-size but it's one of few European resorts so close to the sea. On a clear day you'll ski or snowboard with far-reaching Aegean and Pagasitikos Gulf views. Warm March days mean you can hit the slopes in the morning and swim at nearby **Agii Saranda** beach in the afternoon. Open from around mid-December, the centre has five ski lifts and six runs, including a 5km-long cross-country piste that whooshes through poplar and beech forest.

Swim the Aegean side The peninsula's finest beaches are found on the Aegean-washed eastern coast. Cool off in **Mylopotamos'** sapphire waters and dig your toes in tiny, multicoloured pebbles. Pelion's best-known swim spot sports a photogenic stone arch. Minuscule **Fakistra** may involve a steep trek but its turquoise waters are worth the effort. Get to this lovers' cove early to snag a spot beneath shrub-draped cliffs. Crowd-dodging locals prefer untamed **Kalamaki**, where flat pale-grey stones lead to crystalline waters.

Trek between villages Throughout Pelion, a network of *kalderimia* (ancient cobblestoned paths) links villages, beaches, churches and plentiful springs. **True Adventure** offers a challenging but doable nine-day 168km-long hike on the **Long Pelion Trail**, through olive groves and maple, oak and beech forest to villages including **Makrinitsa** but also lesser-known **Lafkos**, plus **Damouhari** beach of *Mamma Mia!* fame.

Top Mylopotamos
Bottom Mountain village, Pelion

Festival Fun

Music Village unites a diverse array of global artists and music lovers in **Agios Lavrentios** village, where everyone is invited to be part of the creative process.

Held from August through early September, the festival features scheduled and spontaneous performances and workshops hosted in traditional homes, squares and forest clearings.

Agricultural producers, chefs and agritourism cooperatives count among members of the peninsula's flourishing gastronomic community who gather at the annual **Pelion Gastronomy Festival** held at **Karaiskos Farm**, usually in late September.

Watch cooking demonstrations, chat with farmers about their produce and sample traditional delicacies like spoon sweets but also local craft beer.

17 Cavorting in KARPENISI

NATURE | ACTION | LAKE

Karpenisi may be a cosy winter escape for Greek city dwellers, but look beyond its serene stone-built villages at the foot of Mt Kaliakouda and Mt Velouchi and you'll find plenty of opportunities to chase adventure. Among the pulse-quickening pursuits on offer are canyoning, river trekking and rafting, while artificial Lake Kremasta remains virtually undiscovered and undeveloped, for now.

22IMAGES STUDIO/SHUTTERSTOCK ©

How To

Getting here/around Fly to Athens and drive to Karpenisi, as the area is best explored by car. Otherwise, KTEL intercity buses operate between Athens and Karpenisi.

When to go Throughout summer for the ongoing Forest Festival; October for the chestnut festival; November for the *tsipouro* festival; December to March for skiing on Mt Velouchi.

Karpenissi Trail Choose between four mountain trail races, including the tough 26km Kaliakouda Trail (karpenissitrail.gr).

PAUL SHARK/SHUTTERSTOCK ©

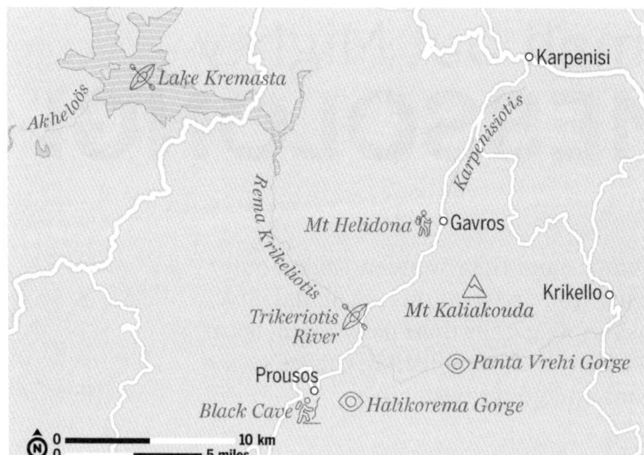

Top Lake Kremasta
Bottom Krikeliotis River

Adventures on land Jump in a 4WD with a knowledgeable guide who will expertly navigate the lofty heights of **Mt Helidona**, passing through minute, single-digit-population villages and following gravel roads down to riverside beaches framed by sheer cliffs. Ramp up the adrenaline with a fir-forest hike across wooden bridges and past waterfalls to the **Black Cave**. From there, you'll traverse across a craggy vertical rock-face following a via ferrata route consisting of steel fixtures that allow even inexperienced climbers to safely complete the course.

Water action If you're in Karpenisi between mid-May and September, don't miss seeing its biggest natural drawcard, **Panta Vrehi** gorge. Join a river trek through the **Krikeliotis River** to witness this marvel of nature. Springwater flowing from **Mt Kaliakouda** creates a curtain that resembles rain. Between December and May, the **Trikeriotis River** offers thrilling rafting experiences featuring technical turns yet suitable for families. More water fun can be had in red-limestone-lined **Halikorema Gorge**, which is ideal for easygoing canyoning. Rappel your way through four waterfalls reaching up to 10m high, then take a dip in natural pools.

Take to the lake Canoe the aquamarine waters and islets of artificial **Lake Kremasta**, which was formed from four rivers and by sinking 20 villages underwater in the mid 1960s as part of a hydroelectric project.

Book activities with **F-Zein Active** and **Trekking Hellas**.

Forest Wandering

Mountain escort **Yannis Liaskonis** (@Yannis Liaskonis) knows Karpenisi's highly biodiverse forests like the back of his hand.

Follow his lead through a dense plane-tree forest along an unmarked fairy-tale-like trail between the villages of **Koryshades** and **Gorianades**.

He'll point out wild herbs like lemon balm, mint and snow-resistant thyme and, in early autumn, cyclamens.

Walking among Greek fir, horse chestnut, kermes oak, willow and hornbeam trees, you'll breathe in some of Europe's cleanest air.

At dusk, as you cross streams fit for drinking, keep your eyes peeled for shy roe deer but don't expect to spot their well-camouflaged predator, the Eurasian wolf.

18 Small but Mighty MESSOLONGI

HISTORY | BIRDS | FISHING

Messolongi's twin lagoons and their wooden fishing huts are what you first notice when you arrive in this small, flat city. Beyond discovering how fisherfolk gather their daily catch, learn about Messolongi's remarkable role in establishing Greece's independence, visit museums and go birdwatching.

ALIKA OBRAZ/SHUTTERSTOCK ©

Following Nature's Flow

Messolongi's fisherfolk utilise traditional aquaculture techniques inextricably linked with the seasons, fish breeding cycles and the unique lagoon habitat.

In spring, fish from the Gulf of Patras enter the shallow lagoons, where the sun fattens them. Find out more about these sustainable fishing methods on a fisher-led boat tour (messolonghibylocals.com).

Trip Notes

Getting here/around Fly into Athens and drive to Messolongi. Alternatively, take the KTEL intercity bus from Athens.

When to go April for the Exodus of Messolongi commemoration; May to June for Ai Simiou *panigyri* (festival); September for the fish festival; October to March for birdwatching.

Avian nation Around 290 endemic and migratory bird species, including flamingoes, avocets and curlews, pass through or reside in Messolongi, home to one of the Mediterranean's most significant wetland habitats.

05 **Aitoliko** islet hosts a museum dedicated to Greek painter and engraver Vasso Katraki. Politically and socially charged expressions of the human form constitute the majority of her riveting catalogue.

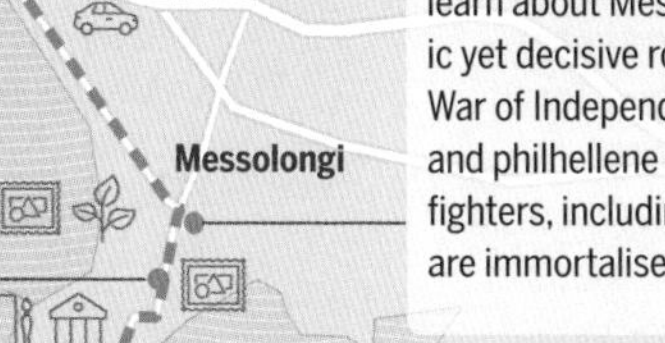

Aitoliko

Messolongi

Klisova Lagoon

Tourlida

01 Visit the **Garden of Heroes** with a guide to learn about Messolongi's tragic yet decisive role in Greece's War of Independence. Greek and philhellene freedom fighters, including Lord Byron, are immortalised.

02 At the **History and Art Museum**, moving artworks like François-Émile de Lansac's *Episode of the Siege of Missolonghi* (1828) convey the immeasurable courage of the city's 'free besieged'.

03 Drive around **Klisova Lagoon** at sunset to see traditional fisher's huts and boats in their best light but also Dalmatian pelicans and other species from the observatory. Soothing mudbaths also await.

04 Cycle to **Tourlida** islet (pictured left) and cool off at a Gulf of Patras beach. At the Salt Museum, find out how Messolongi's precious 'white gold' is produced and see salt pans.

N 0 5 km
0 2.5 miles

Gulf of Patra

FROM TOP: GIANNIS PAPANIKOS/SHUTTERSTOCK ©, RINI KOOLS/SHUTTERSTOCK ©

Escape to the Country

YOUNG GREEKS SHUN THE BIG SMOKE

Throughout central Greece, a palpable energy emanates from its vast fertile ground. New generations with innovative ideas are taking over family businesses while safeguarding centuries-old traditions. Above all, they're making a conscious decision to return to or stay rooted in their ancestral lands.

Left Aitoliko
Centre Mt Parnassos
Right Fishing near Aitoliko

GEORGIOS TSICHLIS/SHUTTERSTOCK ©

Standing beside a traditional fisher's hut above glimmering Klisova Lagoon, Alexandras Panagiotopoulos speaks passionately about his native Messolongi's potential to draw sustainability-minded travellers. 'We're not interested in mass tourism, though. We want to keep it small-scale so as to protect the environment. When we talk about responsible tourism, we want those who visit to become a part of our day-to-day lives,' he says.

Following university studies in Athens, Alexandras returned to Messolongi. In 2018, he and his partner, ex-Thessaloniki architect Kyra Papanikolaou, founded non-profit Messolonghi by Locals, whose welcoming hub doubles as a tourism information centre. Their goals are multifold, including the development of historical, cultural and environmental tourism in this intriguing corner of the country. They consider community participation and mobilisation to be equally crucial. Among other initiatives, the organisation runs programmes for local schoolkids, educating them about fishing traditions, wetland habitats and wildlife.

Alexandros and Kyra count among growing numbers of young Greeks finding positive reasons to stay in, return to or relocate to the region, following a severe brain drain during Greece's decade-long economic crisis. Their chief motive: achieving a better quality of life.

Some, like the 20-something Nikos Kontopanos, want to build on a successful family business. Together with his brother Panagiotis, Nikos is gradually taking over the reins at Saloon Park, a horse-riding ranch and fun park founded by his father below Karpenisi's Mt Velouchi. 'There are opportunities for work here as long as you have drive and

SEH KIN WAI/SHUTTERSTOCK ©

HERACLES KRITIKOS/SHUTTERSTOCK ©

enjoy being in nature. I love this environment and the animals. I don't need anything else,' he says.

Others have no connection to the location where they've resettled. In the cosmopolitan ski town of Arahova, near Delphi, French-Greek industrial designer Eleni Prablanc crossed skis with future husband, Giorgos Korodimos, on the slopes of Mt Parnassos. In 2015, they founded a Delphi branch of pioneering Greek operator Trekking Hellas. 'I love the fact that I can be snowshoeing on Mt Parnassos one day and trekking an ancient footpath pilgrims took to Delphi the next,' says Eleni.

> 'We're not interested in mass tourism. We want to keep it small-scale.'

Giorgos, who grew up roving the mountains around Arahova with his shepherd grandparents, has never considered leaving his birthplace. An experienced mountaineer, he is happiest when rock climbing, downhill skiing and guiding visitors on hikes through stone-built villages and up alpine summits.

The young parents and their two children embrace local folk customs such as the annual Panigiraki feast celebrating St George and commemorating the 1826 Battle of Arahova. Reflecting a burgeoning interest among Arahova's youth to preserve traditions on the brink of oblivion, Giorgos hand-sews his *fustanella* (traditional skirt) for the event. 'During the crisis, Arahova received much fewer visitors from Athens and Thessaloniki, our two main markets,' he says. 'Many of us had to find a way to keep busy. This proved an opportunity to revive traditions like loom weaving. While cultivating a newfound respect for these near-forgotten arts, we realised it's something we really enjoy.'

Local Know-How

Farm-to-fork Gather vegetables at **Karaiskos Farm** and learn how to prepare village-style spinach and feta pie from scratch with chef Dimitris Varalis, who gave up Mykonos' fat tips to head cooking lessons at the Pelion agritourism venture.

Ancient superfood At age 12, Paris Andreou Leontios planted the seed for what has evolved into a successful family-run business. Based in Arahova, **5 Raches** organically cultivates archaic *lathouri* (grass pea), high in protein and fibre, at an altitude of 1200m.

Oracle insider Certified guide **Penny Kolomvotsou** (@penny.kolomvotsou.9) has a way of making ancient Delphi entertaining even for its youngest visitors.

Listings

BEST OF THE REST

Historical High Points

Moni Megalou Meteorou

In 1340, St Athanasios scaled Meteora's highest rock and described a feeling of *meteoron* (levitation). View precious 9th-century manuscripts, rare Byzantine icons and a mid-16th-century kitchen at one of Greece's most revered monasteries.

Delphi Archaeological Museum

Among museum highlights are two stone-carved *kouroi* statues dating to the early 6th century BCE. The idealised muscular forms are thought to depict brothers Kleobis and Biton and feature characteristic braided hair.

Outdoor Adventuring

Visit Meteora

Follow the guides along forested trails in the foothills of the monoliths up to viewpoints where you'll see an abandoned monastery, the endless Thessaly plain and the imposing Pindos Mountains. Based in Kalambaka.

Pelion Scout

This Horefto-based operator runs family-friendly sea-kayaking and boat tours to the isolated sea caves of Thetis and six-day experiences combining coastal hiking, canyoning in waterfalls and beach-hopping.

Velouchi Ski Centre

Choose between 16 slopes, including free-ride pistes and black-run Hercules, and a snowboard park. Weekend night skiing is a highlight, when two runs are illuminated and Ice Bar hosts parties.

Lake Plastira

Two-wheeled experts Tavropos lead guided MTB and e-bike rides around the lake and further afield. Alternatively, hire a canoe, waterbike or stand-up paddleboard and cool off with a swim afterwards.

Panigyria Revelry

Domnista

This village near Karpenisi hosts a rousing three-day autumnal toast to *tsipouro,* central Greece's favourite firewater, with plenty of traditional song and dance that lasts until late.

Ai Simiou

In Messolongi, local men don folk clothing and celebrate this deeply symbolic, tradition-rich *panigyri* with fervour and devoutness over four days in May or June.

Meat & Fish Specialities

Kaplanis €€

Famished skiers gather by the fireplace at this family-run spot in Arahova for *sarmadhes* (dolmadhes made with cabbage), fried cour-

Moni Megalou Meteorou

gette flowers and soul-warming cockerel casserole with *hilopites* (fettucine-style pasta).

Gousios €€

Known throughout Thessaly, Gousios is worth the drive from Kalambaka or Kastraki. Try wood-fire-grilled lamb chops derived from the rare Kalaritiko sheep, village sausages and hand-cut fried potatoes.

Agios Athanasios €€

Swaying willow tree views and soft jazz accompanies huge, juicy pork chops and garlicky eggplant dip, setting this otherwise traditional taverna in Megalo Horio apart from others in the Karpenisi area.

Dimitroukas €€

Situated in downtown Messolongi, this fish taverna serves lagoon-fresh delicacies like salt-cured mexinari (grey mullet), ligda (gilthead sea bream) and butterflied flathead mullet with aromatic, locally produced Trikene ouzo.

Spiti tou Psara  €€

Butter-fried rainbow trout, sourced from a nearby fish farm, is the plat du jour at this family-run riverside joint in Gavros village near Karpenisi. Keep an eye out for the century-old thick woollen cape adorning one wall.

 Refined Restaurants

Meteoron Panorama €€€

Reservations are necessary at this popular Kalambaka restaurant. Experience incomparable Meteora views (illuminated at night), coupled with indigenous black pork and steaks from steppe cattle with ancient lineage.

Bebelis  €€

Local speciality *kelemnia* (onions stuffed with mince, rice, tomato and herbs) and slow-braised pork shank are classics at this longtime Galaxidi favourite. Don't miss the mini folklore 'museum' upstairs.

Lake Plastira

Maritsa's €€

Also in Galaxidi, this breezy portside restaurant beloved of weekending Athenians serves handmade black-and-white orzo with mussels, scallops and prawns, among other well-executed seafood dishes.

 Up-and-Coming Wineries

Tsililis

Book a wine tasting at this family-run winery near prehistoric Theopetra Cave, close to Meteora. You'll want to try its award-winning red made from native *limniona* grape and fine *tsipouro*, a potent clear spirit.

Meteoro

The Tsinas family might be new to winemaking but their Cabernet Sauvignon–Syrah is phenomenally good. Pick up a bottle or two from the winery, located in Megarchi near Meteora, to take home.

Liakou

Near Kalambaka, sample fruity Asproparis, named after a protected vulture local to Meteora and produced from indigenous *malagousia*.

Scan to find more things to do in Delphi & Central Greece.

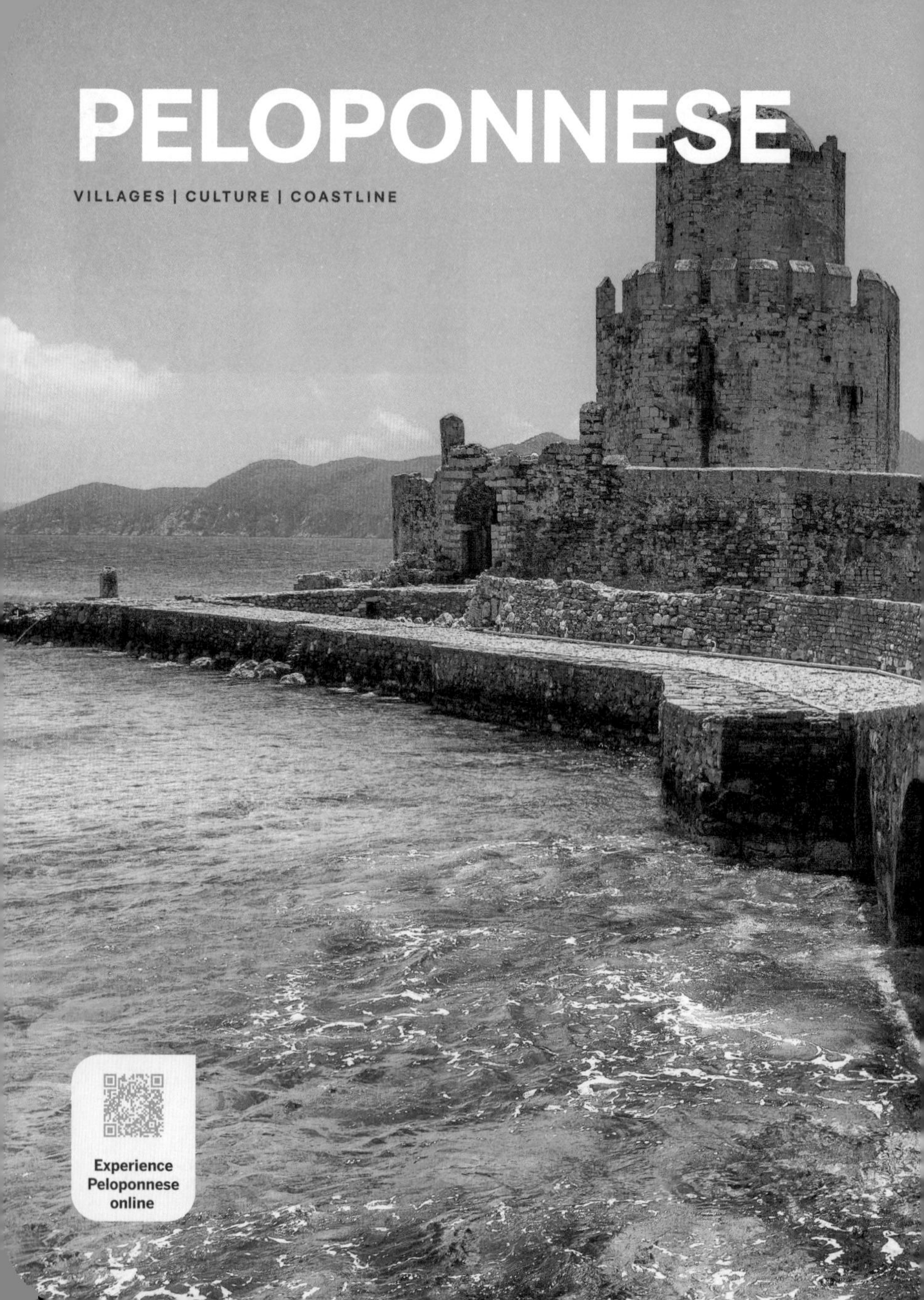
PELOPONNESE
VILLAGES | CULTURE | COASTLINE
Experience
Peloponnese
online

PELOPONNESE

Trip Builder

Greece's southernmost peninsula, lapped by both Ionian and Aegean waters, has ancient fortresses and monasteries, hiking trails, Byzantine villages and long stretches of pristine coastline – not to mention it's the birthplace of the Olympic Games at Ancient Olympia. Many visitors are drawn back year after year.

Cut through the **Vouraïkos Gorge** on a unique rack-and-cog train journey (p133)
55mins from Corinth

Visit the uninhabited **Alkyonides Islands** and get the chance to spot dolphins (p121)
30mins from Corinth

Reconnect with nature while hiking in the Arkadian surroundings of **Abeliona** retreat (p123)
1½hrs from Kalamata

Set out from a Byzantine mansion to explore the walled town of **Monemvasia** (p128)
3hrs from Athens

Discover the secrets of olive oil at **Eumelia** farm in the Lakonia region (p125)
2½hrs from Kalamata

Explore bookable experiences in the Peloponnese

Practicalities

ARRIVING

The small city of Kalamata has a regional airport accepting domestic flights and European charters in the summer. It's best to fly into Athens, then hire a car.

MONEY

Most places accept credit cards and Apple Pay. Take some euros for those mountain villages that may not.

CONNECT

Wi-fi can be found in most places to stay, restaurants and cafes. Connectivity is a little sketchy in the mountain villages.

WHERE TO STAY

Town/ Village	Pro/Con
Nafplio	Romantic weekend getaway by the coast, near Athens; it gets busy in summer.
Olympia	Gateway village for experiencing the ancient history of the Olympics.
Patra	Busy port town at the foot of Mt Panachaikon; more of a transport hub.

GETTING AROUND

Car By far the best way to reach the region's historic villages, secluded beaches, ancient sites and vineyards is with your own wheels. Driving gives you the flexibility and freedom to explore at your own pace.

Bus A good bus network services the region; however, buses require a change at a main transport hub.

TOP: DINOSMICHAIL/SHUTTERSTOCK © BOTTOM: NATALIYA NAZAROVA/SHUTTERSTOCK ©

EATING & DRINKING

It's not an exaggeration to say you can eat like a god when visiting this region. Home to the world-famous Kalamata olives, it also has an abundance of fresh produce such as watermelons and citrus fruits. An annual eggplant festival takes place in July in the port town of Leonidio – expect delicious mince-stuffed eggplant with béchamel sauce.

Best drinks with a view Emvasis, Monemvasia (p135)

Must-try olive oil Eumelia farm (p125)

JAN–MAR
Mild temperatures, perfect for hiking the many trails.

APR–JUN
Weather gets warm, though it's still a bit chilly to swim.

JUL–SEP
August is perfect for swimming; water temperatures up to 26°C.

OCT–DEC
December is the wettest month; possible to ski in the mountains.

19 Mythical ISLANDS

BOAT TRIP | MYTHOLOGY | DOLPHINS

In Greece, the Halcyon myth is very popular – but what's not so well known is that lying in the eastern part of the Corinthian Gulf is a cluster of four small islands of the same name, demanding to be explored by boat. Here you'll find a monastery, a chapel and a few houses, all abandoned after their collapse in the tragic 1986 Kalamata earthquake.

ELENKALO/SHUTTERSTOCK ©

How to

Getting here Boat trips leave from the small Peloponnese marina of Kiato, a 1¼-hour drive on the National Toll Road from Athens; or catch a train, then a short taxi ride.

When to go Late summer and early autumn, when the crowds start to dissipate, are best.

Boat tours Lido Blue (lidoblue.gr) offers private and group boat tours to the islands, with the possibility to spot dolphins in the summer months.

CHRISTOFOROS WESTRA/SHUTTERSTOCK ©

MAZAREKIC/SHUTTERSTOCK ©

Far left Zoodochos Pigi
Bottom left Daskalio
Above left Dolphins

Alkyonides Islands With so many popular islands in Greece, the so-called 'Halcyon Islands' – encompassing **Daskalio**, **Glaronisi**, **Prasonisi** and the largest, **Zoodochos Pigi** – are probably the least known of all. There are no facilities here, only an abandoned monastery on Zoodochos Pigi with a chapel that is surprisingly well maintained by the local visitors, so expect to see icons inside (you can also light a candle if you wish).

Untouched nature Half an hour by boat from the port town of Kiato and you're in a different world. It's possible to camp here at night, but be aware that some cats run wild on the islands (at least they keep the vermin population down). Spend time swimming and relaxing, and bring a picnic. There's good hiking on each island, with unique wildlife; the islands are also the place where the Halcyon birds (a type of kingfisher) breed during the winter months.

Dolphin-spotting It's not a very well-known fact that dolphins can be seen in Greece. Yet come to the Gulf of Corinth – an area protected by the Natura 2000 network for its rich biodiversity – in the summer months, and that's exactly what you'll hopefully get to see. Your boat trip to the Halcyon Islands can be the perfect chance to spot the common dolphins and striped dolphins, known as the most sociable inhabitants of the Greek seas.

The Alkyonides Myth

In Greek mythology, the goddess Alkyone (Halcyon) was married to King Ceyx, a mortal.

One day, the king was caught in a storm at sea and drowned. Halcyon found her husband's body on the shore and, completely distraught, she threw herself into the waves.

The gods were so impressed by their devotion that they brought them back as sea birds, or Halcyons, and stipulated that the females only lay eggs in the winter near the islands where they drowned.

For this reason, for 14 days during winter you'll find Greece uncharacteristically mild – a period known as the Halcyon Days, when birds migrate here.

20 Reconnect with NATURE

RETREAT | SPIRITUALITY | OUTDOORS

If you're looking to rediscover yourself in a non-clichéd way and reconnect with a natural environment, you can't go wrong with this escape in the mountains of Arkadia. Restore your balance in what's considered a place of unique spirituality – the region of Arkadia was home to Pan, the flute-playing god of the wild, fields, groves and wooded valleys.

VALES1989/SHUTTERSTOCK ©

How to

Getting here A car is essential; the drive takes 2½ hours from Athens or two hours from Corinth.

When to go The retreat is open year-round but while its mountain location will be cosy in winter, it might be harder to reach. Spring and autumn are excellent times to appreciate the nature.

Village escape The small mountainous village of Abeliona has cobbled streets, traditional stone houses and fountains, surrounded by a chestnut forest and springs.

PIT STOCK/SHUTTERSTOCK ©

YIANNISSCHEIDT/SHUTTERSTOCK ©

Far left Mountain lake near Arkadia
Bottom left Dimitsana
Above left Menalon Trail

Not all retreats are the same, and **Abeliona** (abeliona-retreat.com) certainly proves this. It's built on a mountainside overlooking the picturesque Arkadian landscape, and you get to relax in a suite located in traditional stone houses scattered across the hillside. The yurt at the top of the retreat offers yoga sessions, or you can choose to simply relax next to a roaring log fire. Either way, a retreat in the mountainous Greek countryside is sure to revitalise, if not transform, you.

In keeping with the principle of treating oneself with respect, the food at Abeliona retreat is an important part of the experience. Expect dishes prepared using locally grown fruits, vegetables and herbs (more often than not from their own land), plus free-range eggs from their own chickens. Both meat and vegetarian dishes are offered, and meals are served in the traditional communal dining room in front of the signature log fireplace during the cooler months.

The more active visitors can take part in a range of outdoor activities such as river or mountain trekking, mountain biking and rafting. The **Apollo Trails** cover nine routes over 26km that take you through local villages, over stone bridges and to nearby ancient sites like the World Heritage–listed **Temple of Apollo Epicurius** within the sanctuary of Bassae, which was built in the 5th century BCE.

Hike to Medieval Villages

For more hiking in the heart of Arkadia region, tackle a section of the **Menalon Trail**.

The well-signposted, 75km trail stretches from Stemnitsa to Lagkadia, passing the dramatic scenery of the Lousios Gorge and the Mylaon River valley.

It's divided into eight sections of varying difficulty; the 12.5km section between the villages of **Stemnitsa** and **Dimitsana** is the most popular for a day hike.

A picturesque descent into the Lousios Gorge past Prodromos Monastery is followed by an ascent to the Filosofou Monasteries.

The trail then follows the course of the river before ending at Dimitsana. Both villages have places to stay and eat.

21 Secrets of the OLIVE

GASTRONOMY | NATURE | REJUVENATION

Nestled in the heart of the Lakonia region lies a unique farmhouse estate offering lodgings in traditional stone eco-houses scattered amongst the ancient olive groves, with views across to the surrounding mountains. Immerse yourself in all things olive oil, learn about its many uses, and take part in farm activities, from harvesting the centuries-old trees to cooking and olive-oil tasting.

ANDRONOS HARIS/SHUTTERSTOCK ©

How to

Getting here
The nearest airport is Kalamata. A car journey from Athens to the village of Gouves, where the farmhouse is located, takes just over three hours. A bus goes via the Isthmos of Corinth where you change to Skala, then catch a short taxi ride.

When to go The olive season is in the autumn months (particularly October), so if you'd like to take part in a workshop, this is the time to do so.

Into wine? You can also take part in their grape harvest in September and October, complete with stomping and using a traditional press.

THEASTOCK/SHUTTERSTOCK ©

FRANTISEK CEKAL/SHUTTERSTOCK ©

Far left Vineyard, Nemea
Bottom left Local olives
Above left Olive orchard near Sparta

An olive-oil immersion workshop at **Eumelia** (eumelia.com) is perfect for those wanting to understand more about the number-one Mediterranean ingredient while taking home tips to introduce it into their everyday lifestyle. Olive oil greatly boosts the immune system – combined with regular exercise, it can significantly improve your life.

Join in the harvest of the three unique varieties of olives grown on the farm: Myrtolia, Koroneiki and Agrelia. Learn how to prepare the harvest nets, pick olives and prepare them for the olive mill. Throughout a five-day stay, you'll be treated to meals prepared with organic products straight from the farm, free-range poultry and herbs grown in their garden; the dinners feature dishes paired with organic wines.

You can also visit the **Museum of the Olive & Greek Olive Oil** in nearby Sparta, one of only nine in the world, to learn how the ancient Greeks made olive oil and how it's evolved over the last 5000 years, plus get a tour of the olive mill to witness the process of making oil in the press.

To complete the experience, you'll get to taste the difference between the three varieties of olives once they've been processed, make your own olive-oil soap using the herbs from the farm, and even have a High Phenolic EVOO massage – a massage using olive oil, naturally.

Nemea Wine Route

Apart from olives, the Peloponnese has also been known for its fine wines since ancient times.

In the rolling hills southwest of Corinth, the **Nemea** region is one of Greece's premier wine-producing areas. It's famous for its smooth, full-bodied reds, many produced from the local *agiorgitiko* grape.

There are 40-odd wineries in the region, signposted as part of a wine route. Many are open to the public, though some must be prebooked. Visits usually include a winery tour and a tasting with local cheese and bread.

During the *anoichtes portes* (open doors) weekend in May, most wineries are open and tastings are often free.

22 Stay in a MANSION

RELAXATION | HISTORY | NATURE

At the southernmost tip of the Peloponnese sits a Byzantine mansion and farm, restored to reflect its eclectic past and offering visitors the opportunity to take part in its working traditions. It's a great base for exploring the region, including the imposing fortified town of Monemvasia.

How to

Getting here/around Monemvasia is about a three-hour drive from Athens. It's best to hire a car so you have the freedom to explore the area.

When to go The mansion is usually open from Greek Easter until mid-autumn. Spring and autumn are the best times; the end of the summer is still warm enough to use the infinity pool.

Monemvasia from a boat Kinsterna Hotel can organise a boat trip around this magnificent rock.

A Historic Mansion

A perfect example of an original Byzantine mansion in the Peloponnese, **Kinsterna Hotel** (kinsternahotel.gr) has been meticulously restored with great respect for its long history.

It's set on a 25-acre estate of citrus and olive groves, farmland and a herb garden, with magnificent views across to the Monemvasia rock and the sea beyond.

Owned by the Kapitsini family since 1870, the mansion was gradually abandoned by the 1980s. Its current owners decided to renovate it using craftspeople from the region whose skills had been passed

Top Kastania Cave
Bottom Kinsterna Hotel

HERACLES KRITIKOS/SHUTTERSTOCK ©

REUTERS/ALAMY STOCK PHOTO ©

Cave Wonderland

The extraordinary **Kastania Cave**, 13km northeast of Neapoli, has some of the best examples of rare stalactites and stalagmites in Europe, estimated to be around three million years old. As you walk around a lit 3km circuit, guides point out unique 'Disney' characters, octopuses and otherworldly creatures cast in stone.

down for generations. The result is a unique getaway.

Take a tour around the estate to understand its history and join in the activities – all open to nonguests, too, to encourage an appreciation of a typical mansion of its era.

The Grape Harvest

The many activities on offer at Kinsterna include taking part in the harvesting and pressing of grapes to make wine from mid-August to mid-September.

The grapes are collected from the 5-acre vineyard across from the mansion, then brought back to the estate and crushed in the traditional way in a *patitiri* (ancient stone tub). Some 40 days later, the production of the typical Greek *tsipouro* (distilled spirit of grape must) starts. The whole process is good fun for guests and nonguests alike.

A Scandinavian-Style Fjord

At mainland Greece's southernmost tip lies a unique destination. **Gerakas,** a mere 30 minutes from Kinsterna, is Greece's only fjord – it was created from a sea lagoon, making it a perfect shallow wetland with plenty of food for rare species of migrating birds such as great egrets, grey herons and the occasional swan and mallard duck. Legend has it that it was an unknown shelter for many years, accidentally discovered by a fisherperson and his son. Swim off the rocks at the end of the small port, or relax in one of the waterfront tavernas or cafes with sea views backed by mountains.

The Castle Town of Monemvasia

You don't need to be a history enthusiast to automatically fall in love with this Byzantine jewel. The ancient fortified town of **Monemvasia**, only a 15-minute drive from Kinsterna, was built in the 6th century on a rock jutting out to sea, hence the nickname 'the Gibraltar of the East'. The fortified medieval village is

Monemvasia & Gerakas Tips

Having lived in Monemvasia for a long time, my favourite activity is to hike up to the ancient city at the top of the rock during sunset, followed by a tasty feast at **Matoula** tavern in the castle for some comfort food. I'd highly recommend the stuffed vine leaves *(ntolmadakia)* and the rooster with Greek pasta. Another great spot to relax is **Gerakas port**, a charming marina that feels like a Scandinavian country. My personal choice for lunch is **Remetzo** tavern, and the traditional *tsaiti* (local pie) and grilled octopus with *tsipouro*.

By Ismini Papadaki, *marketing manager at Kinsterna Hotel @kinsterna_hotel*

PIT STOCK/SHUTTERSTOCK ©

Far left Monemvasia's lower town
Above Gerakas
Below Monemvasia laneway

divided into the lower town, featuring a cobbled main street lined with souvenir shops, hotels and tavernas, and the upper town, with its ruins and fortress.

History envelopes you as you wander past buildings – some derelict but many preserved – that date back to Byzantine, Venetian or Ottoman periods, all vestiges of Greece's eclectic past occupiers. Once you've paid a visit to the medieval **Kastro** (be warned, it's quite a hike but worth it both for the fortifications and the sea views), challenge yourself to see if you can find all 40 churches, some of which are ruined. The 12th-century Byzantine **Church of Agia Sofia** is one of the oldest in Greece; it sits at the highest point of the rock, surrounded by spectacular scenery.

Fortresses & Ancient Sites of the PELOPONNESE

01 Acrocorinth

In Ancient Corinth, this fortress is linked to the myth of Sisyphus, the king who built it and witnessed Zeus fooling around with Aegina.

02 Palamidi, Nafplio

One of the biggest and best-preserved Venetian fortresses, with views across Nafplio and the Argolic Gulf. Beware the 999 steps to climb.

03 Ancient Olympia

The birthplace of the Olympic Games, where the Olympic flame is still lit. Supposedly Zeus celebrated beating his father Kronos at wrestling here.

04 Mystras

A former Byzantine capital, this fortified city is a compelling set of medieval ruins spread over a steep mountainside and surrounded by verdant olive trees.

05 Bourtzi Fortress, Nafplio

Located on a tiny island just offshore from Nafplio, this was the residence of the executioner of convicts held in Palamidi Fortress and more recently a hotel.

06 Ancient Nemea

Located in one of Greece's premier wine regions, this was once the venue for the biennial Nemean Games, held in honour of Zeus.

07 Ancient Mycenae

The most powerful kingdom in Greece for four centuries was home to Agamemnon, the king who commanded the Greeks during the Trojan War.

08 Kastro, Methoni

One of the largest in the Mediterranean and surrounded on three sides by the sea, lending stunning vistas. The entrance is via a 14-arched stone bridge.

09 Theatre of Epidavros

The best-preserved of all ancient Greek theatres, with phenomenal acoustics. It's where the worship of Asclepius, god of medicine, originated.

10 Kastro, Koroni

At the Cape of Akritas in the south of the Peloponnese, this 13th-century Venetian gem still has well-preserved houses and temples within its walls.

23 Kalavryta Rail JOURNEY

RAILWAY | GORGES | OLD TOWNS

Experience stunning mountainous landscapes and gorges of the northern Peloponnesian Achaïa region on a vintage rack-and-cog railway journey – a steep-grade railway with a toothed-rack rail – between the towns of Diakofto and Kalavryta, chugging through seven curving tunnels along the way.

Rack or Cog?

Built between 1889 and 1895, the railway was a remarkable feat of engineering for its time, with only a handful of equivalents in the world. Between 2007 and 2009 the entire rails and cog sections were replaced, as well as the former carriages. The original steam engines can still be seen outside Diakofto and Kalavryta stations.

How to

Getting here/around The railway journey starts from Diakofto and runs for 22km through the mountainous landscape with several small stops along the way, before ending in Kalavryta.

When to go It's recommended year-round. Combine it with a trip to Kalavryta ski resort (one of the biggest in Greece) in the winter.

Top tip Aside from the unique journey, it's possible to combine a mountain and coastal retreat as the beach at Diakofto is only 20km from Kalavryta ski resort.

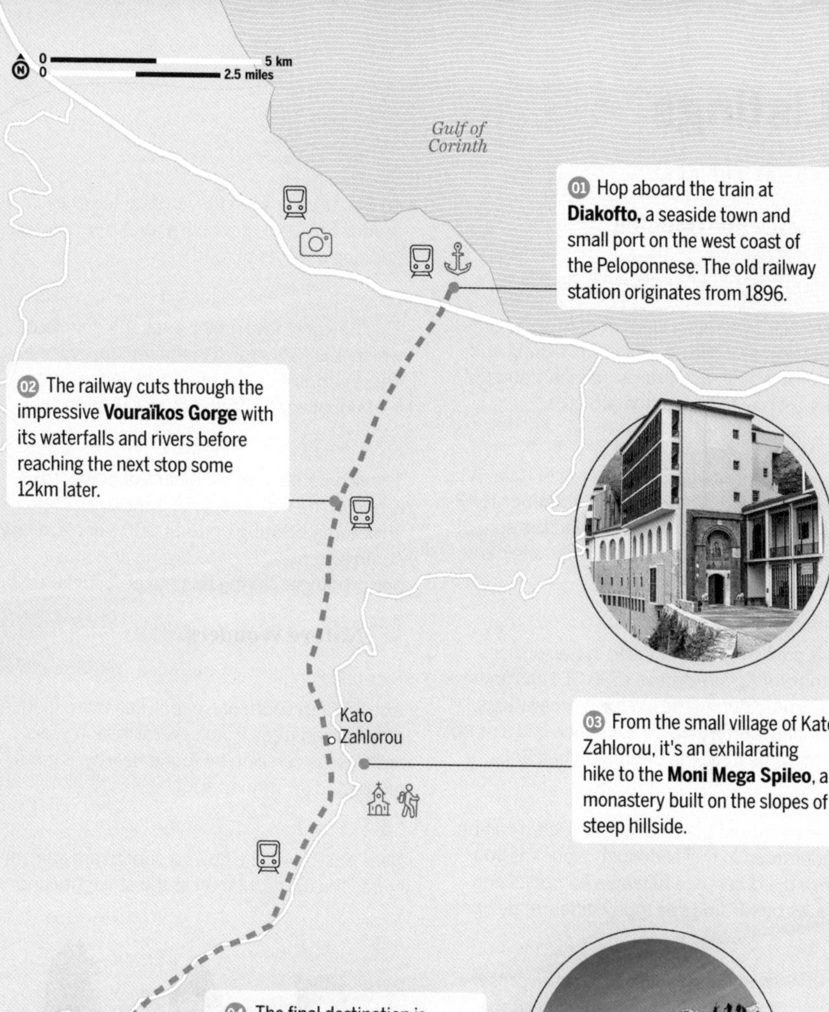

01 Hop aboard the train at **Diakofto,** a seaside town and small port on the west coast of the Peloponnese. The old railway station originates from 1896.

02 The railway cuts through the impressive **Vouraïkos Gorge** with its waterfalls and rivers before reaching the next stop some 12km later.

03 From the small village of Kato Zahlorou, it's an exhilarating hike to the **Moni Mega Spileo**, a monastery built on the slopes of a steep hillside.

04 The final destination is **Kalavryta** whose name means 'Good Waters'. There are cave systems and lakes in the area, plus a ski centre to the east of town.

Listings

BEST OF THE REST

Museum-Hopping

Museum of the History of the Olympic Games in Antiquity

In Ancient Olympia, learn about the original events of foot racing, wrestling, boxing and chariot racing. Sculptures, mosaics and pottery art pay tribute to the athletes.

Museum of the Kalavryta Holocaust

Poignant tribute to the residents of Kalavryta who were slaughtered on 13 December 1943 by the German army who burned the schoolhouse with women, children and the elderly inside.

Monemvasia Archaeological Collection

This small museum housed in the former temple of Agios Andreas (596 CE) has findings unearthed during the old town excavations, including pottery from Asia Minor, and a marble door frame from the Church of Agia Sofia.

Komboloi Museum

Greece's most popular souvenir item can be understood in this Nafplio museum as you learn the difference between *komboloï* and prayer beads and see many different designs.

Museum of Traditional Greek Costumes

Victoria Karelia, an advocate for the preservation of Greek folk tradition and heritage, has donated a large collection of Greek male and female folk dresses from the 18th to 20th centuries to this small museum in Kalamata.

Spectacular Festivals

Patras Carnival

The largest carnival event in Greece, Patras Carnival usually starts mid-January and ends on Clean Monday in the lead-up to Greek Orthodox Easter. Expect parades, street parties, dancing and lots of food.

Leonidio Eggplant Festival

This tiny port town celebrates the eggplant, which is widely grown in the region, every July. There's music, dancing and, of course, many traditional eggplant dishes to sample.

Athens & Epidavros Festival

The 4th-century BCE Theatre of Epidavros is one of the best-preserved ancient Greek structures. Seating up to 14,000 people, every summer it plays host to drama and music performances during this major festival.

Nature Wonders

Petrified Forest, Lakonia

About 16km south of Neapoli lies this expanse of fossilised trees from several million years ago; fossils can also be found nearby. A great picnic and swimming spot.

Cave of the Lakes, Kalavryta

Near Kastria village flows a subterranean river, hence the name. Marvel at the stalactite and

Traditional Greek costumes

PELOPONNESE REVIEWS

stalagmite formations and cascading lakes on three levels inside this vast cave.

Diros Caves, Pyrgos

Flooded Neolithic Age caves near the beach of the same name, 14km in length and explored by boat and on foot. The stalactites and stalagmites form odd shapes.

Didyma Caves, Argolis

Near the village of Didyma are two huge sinkholes, collapsed thousands of years ago. One holds the tiny Agios Georgios chapel and the other is a haven for nesting birds.

Cape Tenaro, the Mani

One of Europe's most southerly points, on the Mani peninsula, is mentioned in Homer's *Iliad*. Walk 2km to the restored lighthouse from the car park and hear about the nearby underwater cave, thought in ancient Greece to be the entrance to Hades.

Monastic Life

Prodromos Monastery

On the Menalon Trail between Dimitsana and Stemnitsa villages, this monastery is literally clinging to the rock face. There are many frescoes inside and sweeping gorge views. It's inhabited by monks; dress appropriately to enter.

Filosofou Monasteries

Two monasteries near Prodromos, Lousios Gorge. The older one was built in the 10th century on a precarious cliff-face ledge; it's said to have been a school during Ottoman rule. The newer, 17th-century one has magnificent floor-to-ceiling frescoes.

Moni Mega Spileo

Near Zahlorou village, 10km north of Kalavryta, this imposing monastery built into the slopes of a hillside has had a turbulent past; it was burned down and taken over by German troops in WWII. There are many icons to admire as well as the views.

Prodromos Monastery

Church of Agios Spyridon

This small 18th-century church is a place of significant historical importance in Nafplio. Ioannis Kapodistrias, the first president of newly independent Greece, was assassinated here in 1831.

Unique Bars & Cafes

Fougaro, Nafplio €

Originally a canning factory, this large venue with a pleasant courtyard now hosts cultural events as well as an all-day cafe-bar popular with tourists and locals.

Emvasis, Monemvasia €

A three-storey cafe at the entrance to the Kastro. The romantic rooftop offers panoramic sea views over a cocktail; it's open all day so come for breakfast or relax with a coffee.

Beer Bar Q, Patra €

One for the beer lovers – a popular bar with live Greek music that serves a range of 17 different kinds of draft beers accompanied by tasty platters and desserts.

Scan to find more things to do in the Peloponnese.

24 Saronic Gulf ESCAPE

SOCIAL | HISTORY | SWIMMING

The Saronic Gulf Islands dot the waters nearest Athens and offer a fast track to Greek island life. As with all Greek islands, each has a unique feel and culture, so you can hop between classical heritage, celebrity-studded harbours, exquisite architecture and remote escapism.

AERIAL-MOTION/SHUTTERSTOCK ©

How to

Getting here/around Frequent conventional and fast ferries from Piraeus serve these islands. Allow 30 minutes (Aegina) to two hours (Spetses). Skip the car – all the towns are best on foot, and some prohibit vehicles. Exception: to explore Aegina widely, it's best to hire wheels.

When to go Late spring and early autumn, to avoid busy summer but still have great weather.

Ice-cream stop Get homemade goat's-milk ice cream at Flora's in Hydra.

LEOKS/SHUTTERSTOCK ©

From Ancient History to Azure Seas

Beyond its bustling port, **Aegina** has the seductive, easygoing character of a typical Greek island. The added bonus are prestigious ancient sites such as the splendid 500 BCE **Temple of Aphaia**, celebrating a local goddess of pre-Hellenic times, and the magical Byzantine **Paleohora** ruins. Weekending Athenians spice up the mix of laid-back locals, creating lively waterfront life.

Tiny **Angistri** lies a few kilometres off the west coast of Aegina and, out of high season, its mellow pine-clad lanes and azure coves make a brilliant day trip or, even better, a longer escape. Dirt paths through the pine trees lead to beaches like the broad, pebbly and clothing-optional **Halikadha Beach** with crystalline waters.

ROMAN SIGAEV/SHUTTERSTOCK ©

Seafaring Champions

Hydra's and Spetses' history as maritime powerhouses and their important roles in the War of Independence are significant even today, celebrated annually in Hydra's **Miaoulia Festival** (June) and Spetses' **Armata** (September). It's a blast to come for days of celebrations culminating in fireworks and explosive staged battles in the harbour.

Top left and right Aegina
Bottom left Temple of Aphaia

Car-Free Island Showstopper

Whether you sail or ferry into **Hydra**, the sparkling boat-filled **harbour** and the bright light striking the tiers of carefully preserved stone houses make for a scene you'll never forget. Breathtaking Hydra is one of the only Greek islands that is free of wheeled vehicles. No cars or scooters – just tiny marble-cobbled lanes, donkeys, rocks and sea. Artists (Brice Marden, Nikos Chatzikyriakos-Ghikas, Panayiotis Tetsis), musicians (Leonard Cohen, David Gilmour), actors and celebrities (Melina Mercouri, Sophia Loren) have all been drawn to Hydra over the years. In addition to the island's exquisitely preserved stone architecture, divine rural paths and clear, deep waters, you can find a good cappuccino along the harbour which is great for people-watching.

If you're an outdoors type, don't forget the island's idyllic coastal paths and hidden swimming bays. Another unbeatable experience is the long haul up to **Moni Profiti Ilia**. The

Where to See Hydra Arts & History

Faneromeni Harbourside monastery complex with 17th-century Kimisis Tis Theotokou Cathedral.

Lazaros Koundouriotis Historical Mansion Handsome ochre-coloured *arhontiko* (stone mansion) of Greek war hero. Exquisite 18th-century architecture, furnishings, outfits and annual art exhibition.

Studio of Panayiotis Tetsis Home and atelier of one of Greece's best painters, with paints and paintings intact, plus perfectly preserved shop.

Historical Archives Museum of Hydra Portraits and naval artefacts, plus well-curated art and cultural exhibitions and summer concerts.

Deste Foundation Small former slaughterhouse with a high-season exhibit of top-name international art.

■ **Recommended by Dimitris Fousekis,** *local artist and illustrator @dimitris.fousekis*

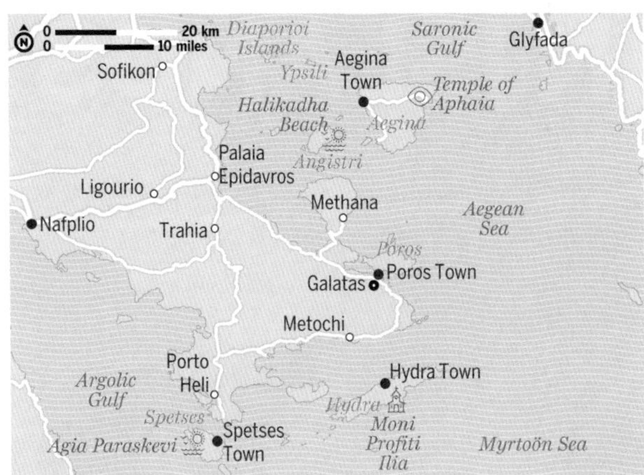

wonderful monastery complex contains beautiful icons and boasts endless, dramatic views.

Historic Haven with a Ring of Beaches

Spetses stands proudly a few kilometres from mainland Peloponnese, but there is a stronger sense of carefree island Greece here than in other Saronic Gulf destinations. The lively, historical old town is the only village on the island. The rest, ringed by a simple road, is rolling hills, pine forests and aquamarine-clear pebble coves. With a rich naval history, it is still incredibly popular with yachties, and its vibrant culture attracts artists, intellectuals and lovers of a good island party. The mansion of Spetses' famous daughter, the 19th-century seagoing commander Laskarina Bouboulina, has been converted into **Bouboulina's Museum**.

From the main **Dapia Harbour**, lined with shops and cafes, and passing the church of **Moni Agios Nikolaos**, you'll arrive at the attractive **Palio Limani** (Old Harbour) yacht anchorage and more bars and restaurants.

Hire a bike or scooter, or hop on the bus or summertime caïque to get to tiny, pretty **Xylokeriza Beach** or popular, long and pebbly **Agia Paraskevi** and the sandier **Agii Anargyri**. At the north end of Anargyri, you can follow a small path to submerged, swimmable **Bekiris Cave**.

Far left Historical Archives Museum of Hydra
Below Xylokeriza Beach, Spetses

IONIAN ISLANDS

NATURE | HISTORY | GASTRONOMY

Experience the Ionian Islands online

Explore bookable experiences in the Ionian Islands

Stroll the honey-hued twisting alleys of Corfu's Venetian-influenced **Old Town** (p148)

1¼hrs from Igoumenitsa

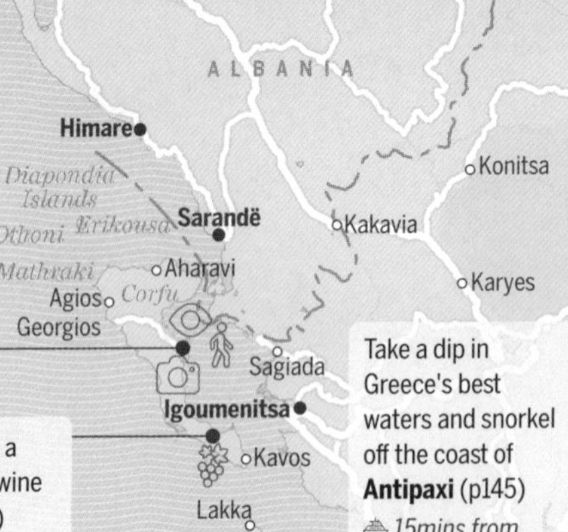

Visit hidden vineyards for a taste of the Ionians' best wine in **southern Corfu** (p146)

1¼hrs from Corfu Town

Take a dip in Greece's best waters and snorkel off the coast of **Antipaxi** (p145)

15mins from Paxi

Dine with locals at their favourite harbourside taverna on **Lefkada** (p144)

1¾hrs from Kefallonia

Hike deep into the olive groves and to pristine beaches of **Kefallonia** (p159)

1¾hrs from Lefkada

IONIAN ISLANDS
Trip Builder

It's no secret that the Ionians, greener and more lush than the rest of the Greek islands, are a haven for nature lovers. From elegant Venetian old towns and aquamarine waters frequented by dolphins, to hidden vineyards, charming farmstays and immersive culinary retreats, you'll find it all in the 'emerald' isles.

Practicalities

ARRIVING

Ioannis Kapodistrias Airport Taxis connect to Corfu Town (€20) and Gouvia Marina (€30).

Ferries From Albania, connect with Corfu Town via Saranda. From Italy, connect in Igoumenitsa which offers lines to Corfu, Paxi and Kefallonia.

FIND YOUR WAY

Most towns are easily navigated on foot, but GPS might find backstreets tricky. Sailors, use Windy and Navionics apps.

MONEY

ATMs more likely in main towns and larger villages. Most places accept cards and Apple Pay.

WHERE TO STAY

Place	Pro/Con
Corfu Old Town	Lively place to stay, with centuries-old Venetian apartments.
Gaios, Paxi	Pretty self-catering apartments on the waterfront.
Kefallonia	Beautiful stone villas and reasonably priced apartments near beaches.
Lefkada	Boutique hotels, all-inclusives and self-catering apartments at reasonable prices.

GETTING AROUND

Sailing Boats can be chartered with a captain or without (if you have a licence) from Corfu's Gouvia Marina (€500 to €800 per day).

Ferry Between Corfu, Kefallonia and Paxi (ferryhopper.com); smaller boats service the smaller islands.

Car The best way to get around. Car hire companies are at airports and ports.

EATING & DRINKING

The Ionians' regional dishes show influence from Italy. *Pastitsadha* (slow-cooked meat in a tomato sauce) along with *bourdeto* (spicy fish casserole) and *tsigareli* (wild greens in a spicy sauce) are just a few of the must-try dishes inspired by the Venetian rulers six centuries ago.

Must-try seafood Nautilus, Bay of Garitsa (p153)

Best wine Pontiglio Winery, southern Corfu (p155)

MAR–MAY
The islands are in full bloom. Great hiking weather.

JUN–SEP
Summer season in full swing. Beaches and tavernas fill up.

OCT–NOV
Cooler weather and olive harvest. Bargain rates.

DEC–FEB
Drizzly and wet. Corfu Town still buzzes with activity.

25 An Ionian Sailing ADVENTURE

BEACH | SWIMMING | SEAFOOD

Diehard sailors will tell you that you haven't truly seen the Ionians unless you've explored them by boat. Thanks to their unique topography and plenty of mountainous, green zones, these gorgeous islands have stretches of coastline that aren't easily reached by land. Prepare your sea legs – the dolphins, turtles and secret beaches await.

A Stop in Lefkada

If you're coming into Lefkada Town harbour on a boat, you have to drop by **Frini Sto Molo** taverna for lunch or dinner. It's a favourite with the locals and has excellent seafood dishes. Then, if you have time, sunset from **Exanthia** village with a drink at **Rachi** is a must.

Recommended by photographer Sandra Semburg @ *sandrasemburg*

Trip Notes

Getting around The best way to island-hop is on a chartered sailboat. Use sailogy.com to find the right boat for you, or head straight to the Sunsail or PlainSailing offices in Corfu's Gouvia Marina (pictured above).

When to go The Ionian Sea is plain sailing from late April until late September.

Top tip Stop off at tiny islands Ereikousa and Othoni for empty white-sand beaches, great hiking and caves that demand exploration with a snorkel or paddleboard.

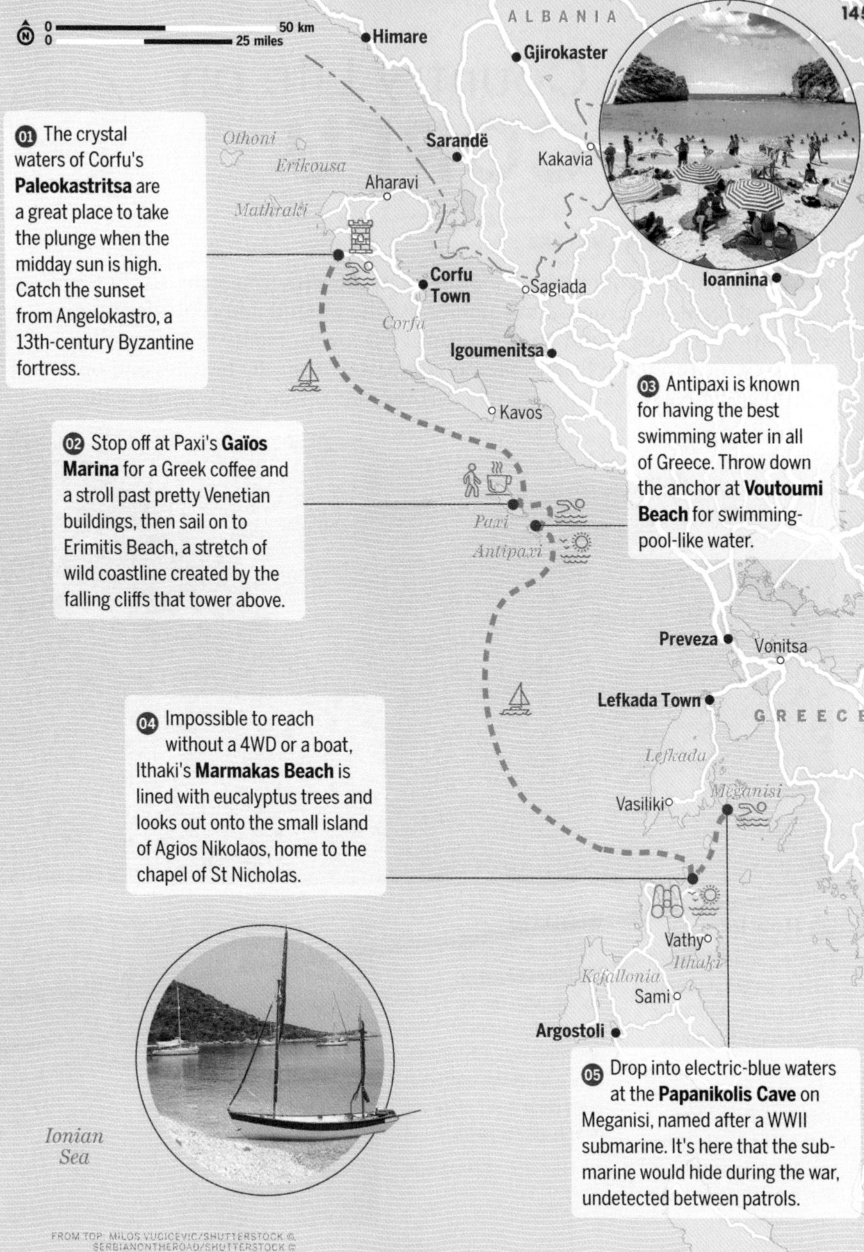

01 The crystal waters of Corfu's **Paleokastritsa** are a great place to take the plunge when the midday sun is high. Catch the sunset from Angelokastro, a 13th-century Byzantine fortress.

02 Stop off at Paxi's **Gaïos Marina** for a Greek coffee and a stroll past pretty Venetian buildings, then sail on to Erimitis Beach, a stretch of wild coastline created by the falling cliffs that tower above.

03 Antipaxi is known for having the best swimming water in all of Greece. Throw down the anchor at **Voutoumi Beach** for swimming-pool-like water.

04 Impossible to reach without a 4WD or a boat, Ithaki's **Marmakas Beach** is lined with eucalyptus trees and looks out onto the small island of Agios Nikolaos, home to the chapel of St Nicholas.

05 Drop into electric-blue waters at the **Papanikolis Cave** on Meganisi, named after a WWII submarine. It's here that the submarine would hide during the war, undetected between patrols.

26 Country Life on CORFU

HIKING | FARMSTAYS | NATURE

Benefitting from high precipitation in the winter months, Corfu is so lush that it can feel tropical in summer. Fertile ground and centuries of olive cultivation give the island an agricultural edge, with plenty of honey, olive oil and wine produced locally. Step inland, away from the beaches and onto winding dirt paths leading into olive groves, for a taste of the country life.

VLASOVS/SHUTTERSTOCK ©

How to

Getting around Local buses can get you around Corfu, but renting a car allows more freedom and gives you a better command over your own schedule. Public transport works on island time and arrival times often don't match up with bus timetables.

When to go
Wildflower-flecked meadows bloom in spring, with the best months for outdoor activities being April and May, just as the winter rains clear and before the heat really kicks in.

NICK N A/SHUTTERSTOCK ©

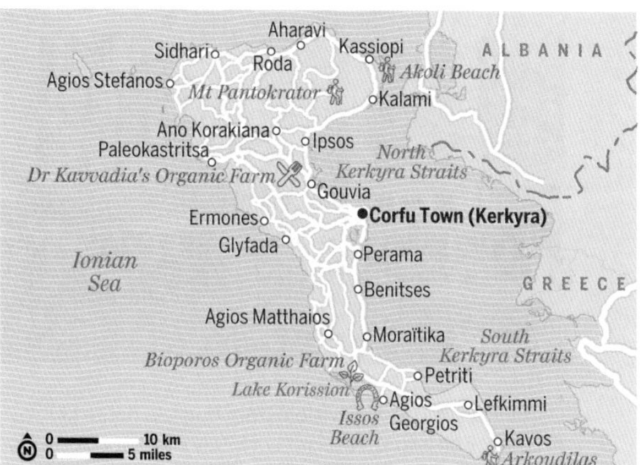

Hike it Lace up for the **Corfu Trail**, a 220km hiking route that runs from the south of the island at the monastery of **Arkoudilas** through dense forest, olive groves and onto wild, cliff-lined beaches, up to the mountain village of **Liapades** and the dramatic summit of **Mt Pantokrator** (906m), the island's highest peak. Visit thecorfutrail.com to tackle it solo; small, family-run **Aperghi Travel** handles tours and accommodation for walkers.

Live like a farmer Tucked into an olive grove only a short distance from Corfu Town, **Dr Kavvadia's Organic Farm** offers stays in its bright, modernist apartments and a chance to get immersed in agricultural lifestyle. Depending on the season, you can help out with the olive harvest in October, sow and pick organic vegetables in the garden or collect your own eggs from the hens each morning.

Lakeside activities Take a drive in the south of the island towards **Lake Korission** for horse riding around the cinematic dunes of **Issos Beach** with the Corfu Horse Riding Centre, or turn off the main road down a gravel path for **Bioporos Organic Farm**, where you can stay and keep the family donkey company. Completely enveloped by nature, Bioporos offers beekeeping experiences and organic cosmetics workshops. Through the olive groves and down a winding path on the farm is Bioporos' very own corner of Lake Korission, complete with rowing boat.

Top left Corfu Trail
Bottom left Corfu beaches

A Coastal Hike

Hike to the secret beach of **Akoli**, on the northeastern coast of Corfu. It's beautiful – the wild olive trees give ample shade to shelter from the sun. It's been a safe haven for activists to meet, organise and start action against tourist development in the region because it's a symbol of pristine beauty on the island.

It's rarely frequented by others in the spring months, and dolphins can often be spotted from the beach here off season.

Recommended by Xenia Tombrou, local environmentalist *@xenia313*

A Window onto Italy

CORFU'S VENETIAN LEGACY LIVES ON

Corfu's proximity to its neighbours is not the only reason the island feels more akin to Italy in places than to Greece. From singular Easter traditions and its characteristic rose- and gold-toned Old Town colour palette to the food that makes this island one of Greece's best for gastronomy, Corfu has the Venetians to thank for it all.

Left Corfu Town
Centre Mt Pantokrator
Right Old Perithia

CALIN STAN/SHUTTERSTOCK ©

On a clear day, Corfu is visible from Puglia's Santa Maria di Leuca. The island's proximity to Italy made it a strategic entry point to the east, first Byzantium and then the Ottoman Empire. Not actually falling under Greek rule until the 19th century, Greece's most western isle first came under Venetian influence in the 1200s. Even before then, Corfu was captured by the Sicilians twice over the course of a 200-year period and was jostled between Sicily and Venice until the late 1300s when the Corfiots themselves asked that Venice take over. The island was in the Venetians' hands from then until the late 18th century.

Under Venetian rule, Corfu's economy flourished. The island's oldest settlement, Old Perithia on the foothills of Mt Pantokrator, still holds onto the vestiges of its Venetian past – the crumbling mansion homes built in the 14th century by Venetian merchants stand testament to the wealth that was poured into the island from across the Ionians. By the mid 1700s, Kythira, Antikythira, Kefallonia and Lekfada also became colonies of Venice, with the main industry in the Ionians focused on the export of produce grown on the islands.

Corfu's dense olive groves can be accredited to the Venetians, who brought olive cultivation to the island, making its distinct and bitter Lianolia variety of olive oil Vatican-worthy produce. By the 16th century, it was Corfu that supplied olive oil to the Vatican.

To defend Corfu, their colonies and the blossoming industry there, the Venetians completed Palaio Frourio (Old Fort) in the 1540s and Neo Frourio (New Fort) a couple of decades later. Between these two examples of Venetian engineering,

PAWEL KUSEK/SHUTTERSTOCK ©

SZYMON MUCHA/SHUTTERSTOCK ©

Corfu Town began to take shape. In the same style as Ragusa in Sicily (also conquered by the Venetians), multistorey buildings began to crop up tightly around central gathering points, the *plateia* (squares), which developed organically around cisterns and wells. Off the *plateia* ran narrow cobblestone alleyways, which the Corfiots still call *kantounia*. This all exists today – one example is the charming Plateia Dimaercheiou, with the *kantounia* leading off towards the very heart of town and the Church of Agios Spyridon, the patron saint of Corfu.

> Greece's most western isle first came under Venetian influence in the 1200s

Apart from architecture and industry, the Venetians brought a culture of learning and music to the island. Corfu's first newspaper was printed in Italian and the Academy of Modern Greece opened under Venetian rule. Opera also found its way into the consciousness of the Corfiots, laying the foundations for the island's affinity to music that is still flourishing today, with its philharmonic orchestra being the most highly esteemed in Greece.

In villages across the island, signs of the Venetian reign remain – some locals are completely oblivious that the dishes they're accustomed to (*stifadho, pastitsadha, bianco* and *bourdeto*) were originally brought to Corfu by their Italian neighbours. Language, too, still hints at the Corfiots' Italian heritage. In Corfu, to wake up early is to get up *'A buon ora'*, while grandmothers are referred to as *Nonna* in some parts of the island. Italian is so woven through the Corfiots' daily life that some are not even aware of it.

After the Venetians

Following the demise of the Republic of Venice in the late 1700s, conquering Napoleon ensured the French were next to step in as the rulers of the Ionians.

Vestiges of the brief French era on Corfu can be found in the grand, photogenic esplanade in the heart of Corfu Town. Built between 1807 and 1814, the **Liston** – with its distinct arcades that nod to the elegant Parisian architecture of the period at Rue de Rivoli – was built by French architect Ferdinand de Lesseps.

At the time, the aristocratic families of Corfu were the only people permitted access to the Liston, now Corfu's best people-watching spot.

Corfu Town SECRETS

LOCAL LIFE | SHOPPING | CUISINE

Historic and elegant, Unesco-listed Corfu Town hides many secrets down its winding narrow lanes. Seek out the less touristy side of the Venetian-influenced Old Town, from shaded gardens to family-run tavernas, local designers and traditional workshops, and rub shoulders with Corfiots rather than the day-cruise crowds.

LORNET/SHUTTERSTOCK ©

How to

Getting around Corfu's main airport is walking distance to the Old Town. Take a taxi, local bus 15, or stroll into town; once you're there, the narrow streets demand to be explored on foot.

When to go Locals avoid the town in July and August because of the heat and influx of visitors. Go in April, May, September and October to get the best of the weather and avoid the crowds.

What's on Corfu Town has a lively cultural life; check corfuland.gr for current listings.

BALATE DORIN/SHUTTERSTOCK ©

The Old Fort or the New Fort?

Corfu's Venetian-built 14th-century **Palaio Frourio** sits on the water and can be spotted as you fly into the island. What visitors often overlook is the **Neo Frourio** (New Fort, built in the 1570s – so not as new as you might think), tucked behind the *laiki* (central market). It's completely free to stroll around and has the best views over the pastel-hued Old Town.

SUCHART BOONYAVECH/SHUTTERSTOCK ©

Wander the Kantounia

Corfiot for 'narrow alleyway', the *kantounia* of the Old Town were extolled by Greek singer Rena Vlahopoulou in her 1972 song 'Kerkyra, Kerkyra', dedicated to the island and its highlights. Taking a turn down one of these alleys – the washing strung high above your head, swallows flitting between the buildings – leads to Corfu's own world, one in which old men

Dream of Saponification

Visit Greece's oldest soap factory, **Patounis**, for traditional olive soap. Offering an age-old, tried and tested method for crafting soaps completely free of chemicals since the 1850s, the Patounis family still make soaps by hand in their workshop down Ioannou Theotoki street. Book your tour online (patounis.gr).

Top left Souvenir shops, Corfu
Bottom left and top right Palaio Frourio

play backgammon in a shaded square and students fill the air with the chords of their late-night bouzouki session. The *kantounia* are many and demand an exploration. Even locals can get lost here.

Escape for a Lunchtime Dip

Come summer, Corfu Town can be a swelteringly hot experience. If you're missing your own yacht, take a stroll to the swimming spots that locals go to and avoid the crowds in the heart of town.

At the end of the Bay of Garitsa, the **Anemomilos Windmill** is where Corfu Town's old-timers go to take the plunge as the mercury rises. A 15-minute stroll on from there is the **Mon Repos Estate**, where the late Prince Philip of Greece was born.

The estate's open gardens are shaded by cypress trees leading to **Kardaki Beach** with its long stone jetty that juts into blue-green waters surrounded by dense foliage.

Coffee like a Corfiot

What separates Corfu Town from an Italian old town (for there are many similarities) is the locals' ability to sit and while away the hours nursing a coffee. Whether it's a short, silty Greek number or an ice-cold 'freddo cappuccino', it's enjoyed in the shade and can take upwards of an hour to drink. The best place for people-watching with a coffee is **Josephine** cafe under the Liston arcade; also try **Coconella** or **Saltino**. Take some Greek coffee home from the family-run **Markosian Leon & Co**, a 100-year-old *kafekopteio* that feels like stepping back in time on entry.

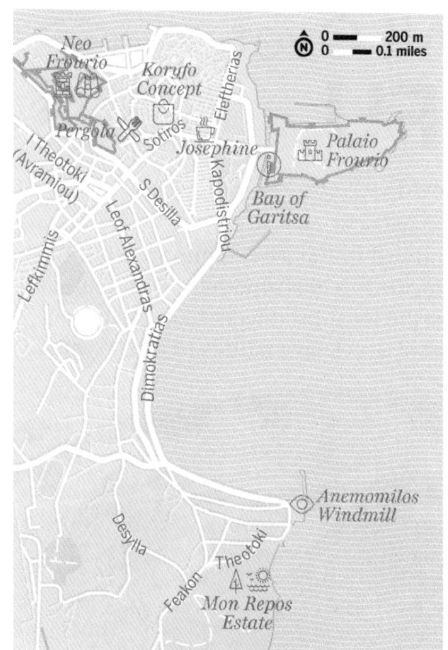

Where the Locals Eat

At the height of summer, escape the crowds and enjoy a fresh sea breeze with your ouzo and meze at **Nautilus** in the Bay of Garitsa, or dip into possibly the island's best *taramosalata* (a thick purée of fish roe and potato) at **Poseidonio** in the dappled shade of eucalyptus trees. In the heart of town, **Pergola** is the taverna of choice for locals, with plenty of hearty, home-cooked dishes like the island's famous *stifado* (stew). For gelato, the century-old, family-run **Papagiorgis** is really the only place Corfiots will go; the chocolate kumquat or wild strawberry sorbet are best sellers.

Shop Greek Designers

One thing Corfu Town is not lacking in is shopping – but how to sift through all the souvenir stores and actually get to the good stuff? Visit Corfiot designer Marianna Kastrinos' **Koryfo Concept**, tucked away behind a main thoroughfare, for Corfu-inspired jewellery, prints and loose linens. Other boutiques with distinct items by Greek designers you'll actually want to take home are **Muses** and **La Poupee**.

Far left Mon Repos Estate
Left Anemomilos Windmill

28 Eating All Over CORFU

CUISINE | WINE | CULTURE

Thanks to the distinctive blend of cultural influences stemming from the periods of Venetian, French and British rule, Corfu's gastronomy is standout and differs from that of the rest of Greece. Meet the local producers to experience the best of the food on the island, from classic Greek specialities to fresh seafood and Italian flavours.

SERGII KOVAL/SHUTTERSTOCK ©

How to

Getting around Hire a car and take your time visiting the island's best cooks and producers. Give yourself the time to road-trip and meet the people who will take your tastebuds on a trip.

When to go Producers offer tours year-round, but it's best to aim for May, June and September. They'll have more time for you outside the harvest seasons, and cooking classes outdoors are much more enjoyable when the heat of the summer isn't in full force.

WIRESTOCK CREATORS/SHUTTERSTOCK ©

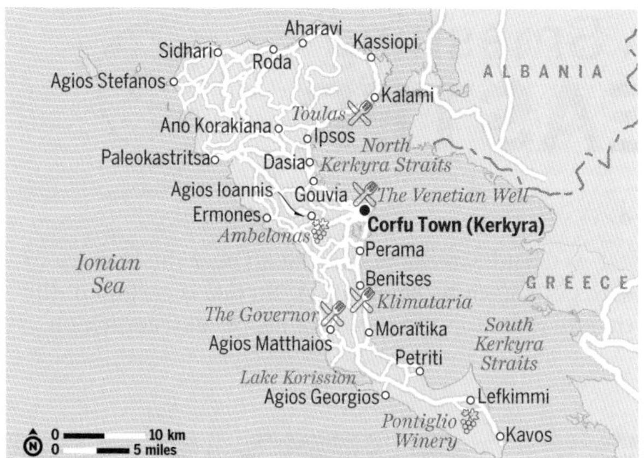

Cook with the experts Visit a Greek grandmother in her village home and make a traditional Greek coffee together, then spend a week foraging wild mountain herbs and cooking local dishes with Corfiot food writer Anastasia Miari on her **Flavours of Corfu** (matriarcheats.com) retreat. Or head to the centuries-old vineyard **Ambelonas** where Vasiliki Karounou, author of *Corfiot Cuisine,* does step-by-step cooking demonstrations followed by a feast.

Meet the producers The island's fertile land is one reason Corfu is known for its gastronomy. In the south of the island, **Pontiglio Winery** offers tours and tastings at the small, family-run vineyard that was set up in the years following the economic crisis and now provides wine for the island's best restaurants. Visit the **Governor** olive mill for a hike deep into its olive groves and a special tasting featuring unusual flavour combinations of its unique olive oil that boasts cancer-fighting properties.

Best bites For fresh seafood on the water, head to **Toulas** in Agni Bay and plump for a *bianco* (fish stew in a zingy lemon salsa). Further down the island, in the heart of Corfu's Old Town, the **Venetian Well** takes traditional recipes and serves them with an elegant twist in a pretty courtyard around a 500-year-old Venetian well. Visit Nikos Bellos' **Klimataria** in the fishing village of Benitses for the best octopus *pastitsadha* (traditional meat and pasta dish) and juicy tomatoes you'll find on Corfu.

Thank the Neighbours

The Corfiots have the Venetians to thank for their rich, spice-filled cuisine. The *stifadho* – from the Italian *stufato* – is a slow-cooked tomato stew featuring rabbit, beef or octopus and an injection of spices that can be accredited to Corfu's location on the spice trail. Cinnamon, spicy paprika, nutmeg and cloves have been known to feature in a *stifadho,* but each local will prepare it differently, some swearing by just a spicy paprika and others throwing it all in there.

29 A Smashing EASTER

FESTIVAL | CULTURE | HISTORY

Come Orthodox Easter weekend, Greeks flock from all over the country to Corfu's Old Town for a bizarre pot-smashing celebration. No one is certain of the real reason behind it, but that doesn't stop thousands of people descending on the town to take it all in.

VERVERIDIS VASILIS/SHUTTERSTOCK ©

How to

Getting around Arrive in advance of scheduled events, and if you're driving, make sure to park clear of the Old Town and walk from there. This is the busiest weekend of the year and you don't want to be stuck trying to find parking while the action is taking place.

When to go Greek Orthodox Easter is usually observed on different dates from the Easter celebrated in Western countries, so check ahead. The main events take place from Friday to Monday of the Easter weekend across the island.

VERVERIDIS VASILIS/SHUTTERSTOCK ©

Far left Philharmonic orchestra
Bottom left Throwing clay pots
Above left Carrying the Epitaph

Follow the band On the evening of Good Friday, follow Corfu's famous philharmonic orchestra through the town as Epitaphs (representing the funeral bier of Jesus Christ) decorated with wildflowers and paraded by Greek Orthodox priests begin to make their rounds down the grand esplanades. Locals light candles and burn frankincense along the procession, which ends with the Epitaph of the Mitropolis at the Liston arcade at 10pm.

Pot smashing Watch your head on Easter Saturday – this is the moment everyone's been waiting for. Thousands gather at the Liston arcade, looking up at Venetian balconies bedecked in red sashes, enormous *canates* (clay amphoras) painted crimson and filled with water teetering precariously on the edge. When the clock strikes 11am, the *canates* – some taller and wider than the grown men pushing them off – are thrown from the balconies, smashing into tiny pieces only metres from the crowds gathered below. When it's over, pick up a piece for good luck and grab a coffee as the Corfu philharmonic orchestra does its thing.

Fireworks and feasting In the evening of Holy Saturday, make your way to the bandstand in the park opposite the old fortress for a final Resurrection Mass in which the thousands gathered carry candles, creating a magnificent light display. Come midnight, fireworks fill the skies – a celebration of the resurrection of Christ and a final mark that 40 days of fasting are finally over. At this point, locals return home for a midnight feast with the family or head to the town's clubs and bars to celebrate the end of Lent until the early hours of the morning.

What's Behind It?

The story goes that the ancient Greeks would toss out their old clay pots once spring came to make way for new seeds planted in brand-new pots.

Later, around the 16th century, the colonising Venetians would mark the New Year in Corfu by tossing out all of their old belongings in a dramatic (if not wasteful) spring clean.

The Corfiots are then said to have adopted the tradition for their biggest religious holiday, Orthodox Easter.

Local priests say the crashing of the pots symbolises the earthquake-like tremors that were felt as Christ was resurrected.

Listings

BEST OF THE REST

Best Bites

Carnayo, Paxi €

A favourite with locals right on the waters of Gaïos. The mixed plate of starters alone is worth a visit.

Rachi, Lefkada €€€

Refined dishes with incredible views over Exanthia village and the island from high above.

Fish Eye, Corfu €€

Smart seafood flavours redefined on wild, sandy coastline; located on Marathias Beach in the southwest of the island.

Flya Restaurant, Corfu €€€

Elevated Mediterranean dining in an elegant setting on the picturesque east coast of the island.

Taverna Kouloura, Corfu €€

Enjoy the best catch of the day in a tiny fishing bay which looks out onto Albania.

Bars with Character

Josephine, Corfu Town €€

The best spot to people-watch over a cocktail from within the Liston's Parisian-style arcades in Corfu Town.

Home, Corfu €€

A transformed village home serving the best cocktails on the island. Located in Kavos in the island's south.

La Grotta, Corfu €€

Set on the atmospheric cliffside above turquoise waters, this bar serves up a party complete with diving board.

Erimitis, Paxi €€

The best Greek wines paired with panoramic views over rugged cliffs from an expansive deck.

Picturesque Villages

Kioni, Ithaki

An idyllic haven of mustard-and-cream Venetian houses that line a pretty harbour you can sail straight into.

Hora, Kythira

Narrow winding alleys of whitewashed houses set around an impressive medieval fortress.

Old Perithia, Corfu

Corfu's oldest settlement has ramshackle stone houses tucked into the foothills of majestic Mt Pantokrator.

Liapades, Corfu

Bougainvillaea winds around bright, whitewashed houses close to one of the island's best beaches.

Argyrades, Corfu

Walk to Agios Ioannis church at the heart of the village for panoramic southern views.

Kioni, Ithaki

Beaches to Seek Out

Arkoudilas, Corfu

Rugged, cliff-lined sandy beach that feels more akin to the tropics, with views to neighbouring Paxi.

Chouchoulio, Corfu

Pebble-strewn and tucked into a quiet bay with a charming seafood taverna just a stroll away.

Megali Petra, Lefkada

Pristine beach with electric-blue waters that are dotted with impressive rock formations.

Emplisi, Kefallonia

Completely surrounded by nature, with trees that reach right to the water's edge for extra shade once the heat kicks in.

Feeling Cultured

Achilleion Palace, Corfu Town

Used as the set for the James Bond film *For Your Eyes Only,* the Achilleion's sweeping views over the island's east coast are as impressive as its interiors.

White House, Corfu

More a living museum with a restaurant dropped into a pretty bay, this was once home to the famous British author Lawrence Durrell, who regularly hosted his equally famous brother Gerald.

Kapodistrias Museum, Corfu

The centuries-old home of the first governor of Greece, Ioannis Kapodistrias, tucked into a leafy estate at the heart of the island.

Mon Repos Estate, Corfu Town

Birthplace of the late Prince Philip of Greece, hidden amid a forest of cypress trees and moments away from a favourite swimming spot of Corfu Town locals.

Black moray eel

Outdoor Thrills

Kefallonia

Take the path from Antisamos to Koutsoupia with Outdoor Kefallonia for a paradisiacal beach reached after a verdant coastal road. The long-established operator offers all manner of trips throughout the island.

Ithaki

A superb half-day walk begins and ends in the village of Stavros, the centre of hiking activity on Ithaki. Along the way, it takes in a museum, historic sites, pretty woodlands, airy viewpoints and high goat pastures.

Lefkada

Specialising in learn-to-windsurf packages, Club Vassiliki also offers board hire, private lessons and a wide range of other activities from diving to mountain biking.

Paxi

With clear visibility and diverse habitats, Paxi offers some great diving. Paxos Oasi Sub offers try dives, snorkelling safaris and PADI open-water courses.

Scan to find more things to do in the Ionian Islands.

CRETE

SCENERY | HISTORY | CUISINE

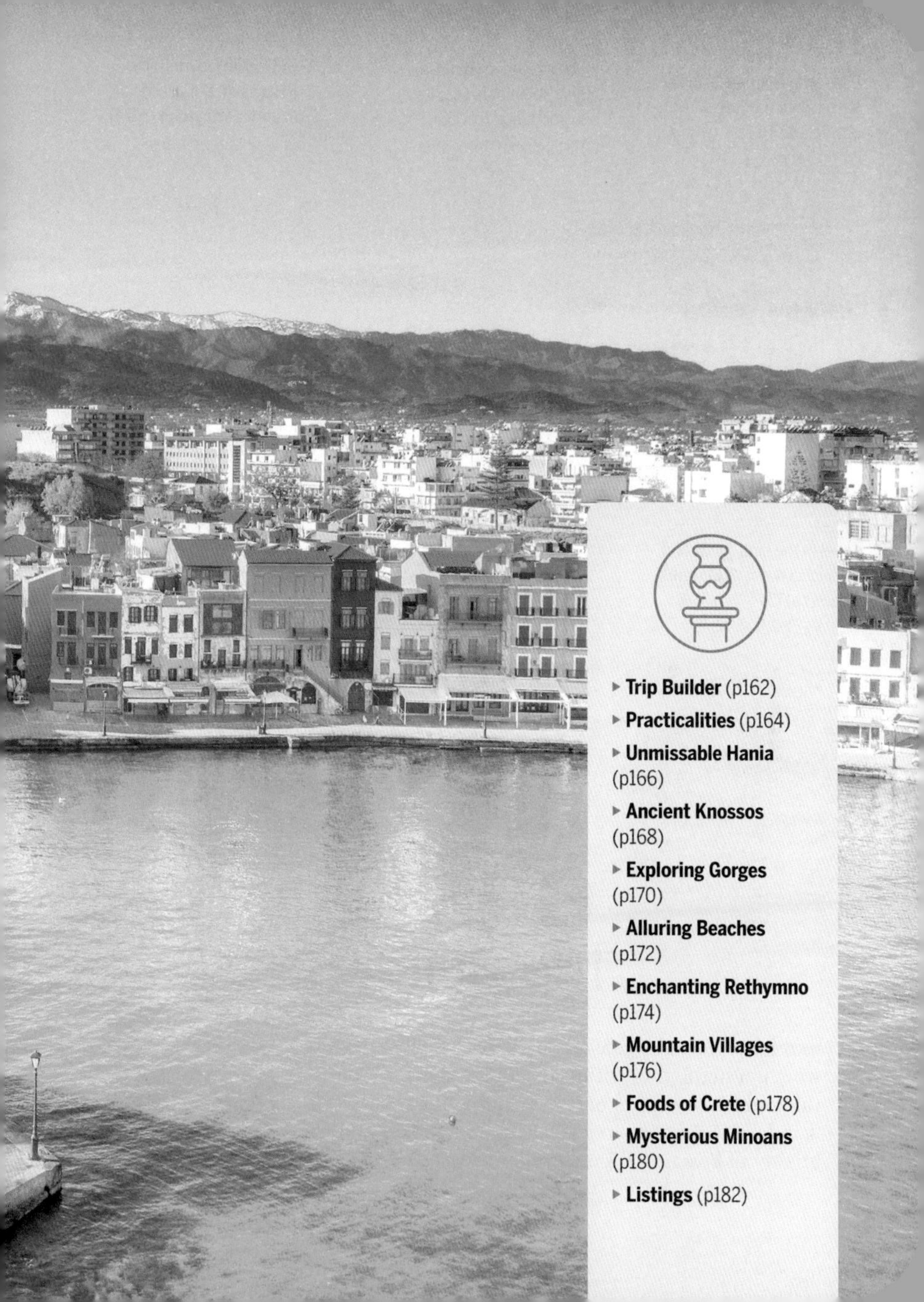

CRETE
Trip Builder

Crete is a large island that packs a country's worth of highlights within its craggy shores. From the immersive charm of its Venetian cities to the wonders of Knossos to its soaring mountains and bounty of beaches, it's a traveller's feast.

Laze away your days on **Falasarna Beach** where sunsets dazzle (p173)
1hr from Hania

Enjoy evocative **Hania**, a city of sensational sights and good food (p166)
1¼hrs from Rethymno

Get lost in labyrinthine, Renaissance-era lanes of historic **Rethymno** (p174)
1¼hrs from Hania

Revel in the pink sands and turquoise water of **Elafonisi Beach** (p173)
1½hrs from Hania

Start in the mountains and trek to the sea through **Samaria Gorge** (p170)
1½hrs from Hania

Wander **Argyroupoli**, an ancient mountain village built atop Roman ruins (p177)
30mins from Rethymno

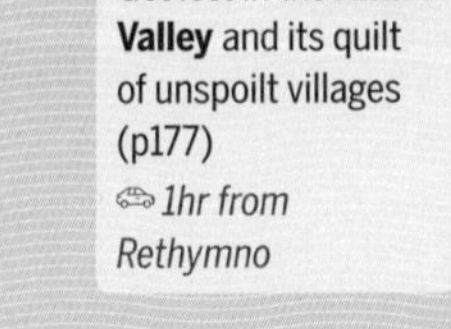

Get lost in the **Amari Valley** and its quilt of unspoilt villages (p177)
1hr from Rethymno

Rodopos Peninsula
Gulf of Hania
Stavros
Kalyviani
Spilia
Kissamos
Fournes
Theriso
Milia
HANIA
Samaria Gorge National Park
Omalos
Agia Irini
Vryses
Almyros Bay
Panormo
Bali
Perama
Episkopi
Sougia
Paleohora
Agia Roumeli
Aradena
Imbros
Loutro
Hora Sfakion
Plakias
Lefkogia
Spili
Amari
Agia Galini
Mesara Gulf
Mata
Gavdos

Explore Crete's top collection of Minoan artefacts at the **Heraklion Archaeological Museum** (p168)
1½hrs from Rethymno

Watch out for falling dates at the palm-shaded **Vaï Beach** (p173)
2½hrs from Iraklio

Rub shoulders with the Minoans at the **Palace of Knossos** (p168)
15mins from Iraklio

Mediterranean Sea

Practicalities

MARKUS MAINKA/SHUTTERSTOCK ©

ARRIVING

Airports Crete's two airports are in Iraklio and Hania. The former is convenient for travel in the east and the latter for the west. Both have plenty of car rental agencies (keep in mind that local Crete-based firms can be cheaper than international brands) and local bus services to their respective city centres. If using a taxi to reach the city centre, check the posted fixed price and get the driver to agree first.

HOW MUCH FOR A

Coffee
€2

Souvlaki
€3

Fresh fish
€15 or more

GETTING AROUND

Car The best way for exploring Crete's large and varied countryside. It gives you the flexibility to try any mountain-pass road that attracts you. Note that some very remote beaches will require a 4WD.

Bus Crete has an efficient network of buses that connect all the main cities and towns. On more remote routes they may only run two or three times per day, so opportunities for complex outings are limited.

Ferry The great joy of the south coast, frequent ferries in summer (less often at other times) provide a scenic and enjoyable way to travel between beach towns and are essential for car-free towns.

WHEN TO GO

JAN–MAR
Cold and blustery; much is closed.

APR–JUN
Warming weather, wildflowers; widespread openings after Orthodox Easter.

JUL–SEP
High temperatures, prices and crowds. September is beautiful and less crowded.

OCT–DEC
After October, Crete turns inward for winter.

EATING & DRINKING

Cretan cuisine evolved from the abundance of local produce, coupled with enormous ingenuity. You'll find a wonderful array of Cretan specialities, such as the dozens of wonderful cheeses, produced primarily from goat's or sheep's milk or a combination of the two. Another part of the magic of Cretan cuisine is the ingredients gathered from hillsides and around villages. The fresh bounty includes all types of fruit and vegetables. And don't miss the range of grilled meats served in village tavernas across the mountains and the fresh seafood in coastal towns.

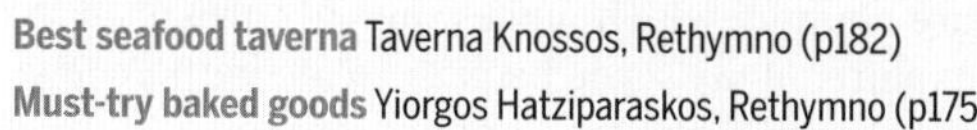

Best seafood taverna Taverna Knossos, Rethymno (p182)

Must-try baked goods Yiorgos Hatziparaskos, Rethymno (p175)

CONNECT & FIND YOUR WAY

Wi-fi Places to stay, cafes and some port areas have free wi-fi that's usually acceptably fast.

Navigation Map apps sometimes don't offer accurate or smart choices for smaller roads, especially in rural areas. A large paper map is very useful. Download Crete mapping data to your app for places with no mobile service.

WATCH THE SEASONS

Check what's fresh when, as the best Cretan cuisine uses seasonal ingredients. Summertime farmers markets are a joy to wander.

WHERE TO STAY

Crete is an affordable place to stay. Book as far ahead as possible to score good deals in peak season, and note that selection is limited from November to March.

Town	Pro/Con
Hania	Crete's most appealing city. It can fill up in summer.
Rethymno	Plenty of Venetian magic. Best for only two or three nights.
Iraklio	Close to the busiest airport. Less interesting for sightseeing.
Matala	Major beach town near ruins. Crowded in summer.
Agios Nikolaos	Beaches and good nightlife. Isolated in the island's east.
Paleohora	Close to many beaches, and on a ferry route, but somewhat remote.

MONEY

Nearly all places to eat and shops take cards (some even eschew cash). Even in high season, Crete's costs are moderate compared to western Europe. Book accommodation and rental cars well ahead to save money.

30 Unmissable HANIA

HISTORY | WATERFRONT | FOOD

Hania is Crete's most evocative city, with its pretty Venetian quarter criss-crossed by narrow lanes and culminating at a magnificent harbour. Examples of Venetian and Turkish architecture abound, which makes the old town a superb place to walk around and explore. Many settle back in a cafe with a view; restaurants that showcase the full range of Cretan food are aplenty.

How to

Getting around Everywhere worth getting to in Hania is easily reachable on foot.

When to go In summer Hania is thronged and steamy. In April, May, September and October everything is open and crowds are manageable.

Buying local food Hania is known for having some of the best food in Crete; the Saturday market boasts top produce and dozens of food vendors. Drandaki Bakery still uses a wood-fired oven.

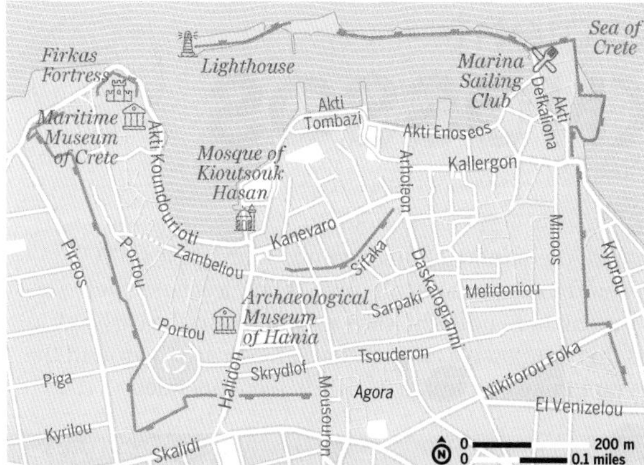

There are few places where Hania's historic charm and grandeur are more palpable than in the centuries-old **Venetian harbour**. It's lined with pastel-coloured buildings that punctuate a maze of narrow lanes filled with shops and tavernas. The eastern side of the harbour is dominated by the domed **Mosque of Kioutsouk Hasan**, now an exhibition hall. The waterfront curves onto the 14th-century breakwater, which is over 500m long. Clamber over the huge blocks of stone as you take in captivating views back to the old town, out to sea and the iconic **lighthouse**.

Hania's massive fortifications, built by the Venetians to protect the city from marauding pirates and invading Turks, are impressive. Known as Topanas, this is one of Hania's most appealing neighbourhoods. Best preserved is the western wall, running from the **Firkas Fortress** to the **Siavo Bastion**. Follow lanes to the top of the bastions for sweeping views down into the moat, which was recently restored with a park along the base. The hulking Firkas Fortress is also home to the interesting **Maritime Museum of Crete**.

The collection of the **Archaeological Museum of Hania** is as striking as the new building. Treasures from across Crete are displayed in light-filled galleries, with signage offering details. Artefacts from Neolithic to Roman times fill the main floor.

Best Places to Eat in Hania

To Maridaki A modern seafood *mezedhopoleio* (restaurant specialising in mezedhes) that's usually packed. Excellent locally sourced fare.

Kouzina EPE This stylish cafe serves a creative mix of modern options and blackboard-listed daily specials.

Thalassino Ageri A delicious fish taverna among the vestiges of Hania's old tanneries near the new Archaeological Museum building.

Christostomos Tucked away from the crowds behind the harbour; popular with residents and visitors for its classic Cretan cuisine.

Marina Sailing Club Wonderful views and fewer crowds at the eastern end of the historic harbour near the breakwater.

31 Ancient KNOSSOS

PALACE | MINOANS | ART

Knossos was the capital of the mighty Minoan empire more than 4000 years ago. An extraordinary wealth of frescoes, sculptures, relics, jewellery and structures lay buried under the soil here until the site's excavation in the early 20th century. Combining a visit to this unmissable ancient marvel with a spin around the excellent archaeological museum in nearby Iraklio is highly recommended.

HERACLES KRITIKOS/SHUTTERSTOCK ©

How to

Getting here Knossos is only 5km south of Iraklio. It is served by city buses.

When to go From May to September Knossos is open into the evening. Dusk here is evocative. In the winter months, you may have vast swaths of the sight to yourself.

Top tip See original frescoes (many on-site ones are replicas) and other treasures plus a scale model of the palace at the Heraklion Archaeological Museum.

DZIEWUL/SHUTTERSTOCK ©

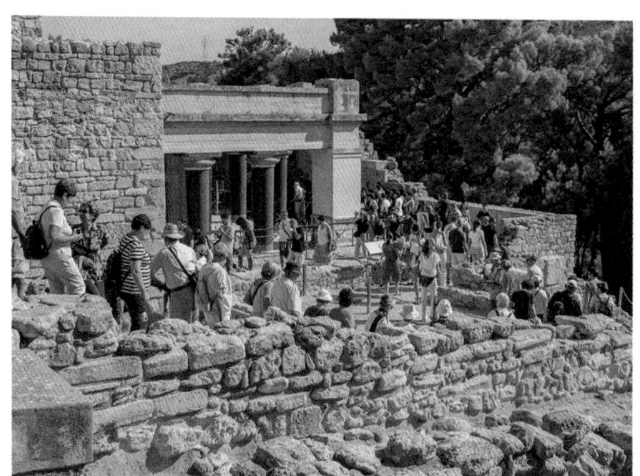

DIMAKIG/SHUTTERSTOCK ©

Far left Throne Room
Bottom left South Propylaion
Above left King's Megaron

A spin around the partially and imaginatively reconstructed Palace of Knossos delivers an eye-opening glimpse into the remarkably sophisticated society of the Minoans, who dominated the Mediterranean some 4000 years ago.

From the ticket booth, follow the marked trail to the **North Entrance** where the *Charging Bull* fresco gives you a first taste of Minoan artistry. Continue to the Central Court and join the queue to glimpse the mystical **Throne Room**, which probably hosted religious rituals. Turn right as you exit and follow the stairs up to the so-called Piano Nobile, where replicas of the palace's most famous artworks conveniently cluster in the **Fresco Gallery**. Circle back and descend to the **South Propylaion**, beautifully decorated with the *Cup Bearer* fresco.

Make your way back to the Central Court and head to the palace's eastern wing to admire the architecture of the **Grand Staircase** that led to what might have been the royal family's private quarters. For a closer look at some rooms, walk to the south end of the courtyard, stopping for a peek at the **Prince of the Lilies fresco**, and head down to the lower floor. A highlight here is the **Queen's Megaron**, playfully adorned with a fresco of frolicking dolphins. Stay on the lower level and make your way to the **West Magazines** with giant *pithoi*, huge clay jars used for storage.

Enjoying Knossos

To beat the crowds and avoid the heat, get to Knossos before 10am when tour buses start arriving, or later in the afternoon when it's cooler and the light is good for photos. Budget a couple of hours to do the place justice.

Optional guided tours last about 1½ hours and most are in English, though other languages are available too. You can arrange private or group tours.

Eating options in and around the site are uninspiring. Bring a picnic, or save your appetite – and thirst – for the many wineries in the nearby **Iraklio Wine Country**, where winemaking dates back to Minoan times.

32 Exploring GORGES

WILD | OUTDOORS | HIKING

There are scores of superb hikes in Crete, including many on the crenellated southern coast. Gorges abound here and offer fascinating glimpses into life through the aeons, with ancient churches, crude caves with the ghosts of hermits, often-lush foliage and stark, geologic beauty. The Samaria Gorge is the most famous of these walks, or you can try other excellent and less-crowded choices.

PROSLGN/SHUTTERSTOCK ©

How to

Getting here The gorge walks are one way, so you'll need to arrange transport in one direction to or from your car.

When to go In spring, the gorges are lined with wildflowers and green grasses, and in autumn the leaves change colours. In summer it can get very hot.

Top tip Bring plenty of water and wear sturdy shoes as the paths have many large and loose stones.

KVN1777/SHUTTERSTOCK ©

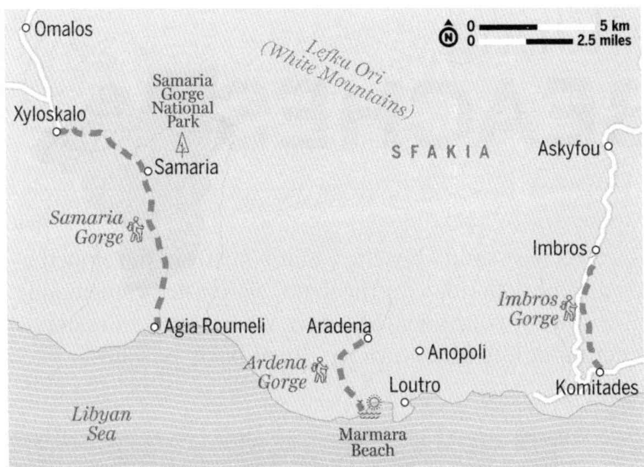

Top Samaria Gorge
Bottom Imbros Gorge

Samaria Gorge Often referred to as Crete's only national park, Samaria National Park is the well-organised home to its namesake gorge, one of the most popular sights on the island. From the park entrance in the hillside village of **Xyloskalo**, an 18km trail descends through sheer cliff faces down to the Mediterranean. Along the way you'll pass through 500m-high rock faces that are at times only 3m apart. The route is dotted with holy sites.

Imbros Gorge The 8km walk through Imbros Gorge is much recommended for its natural beauty and lack of crowds. An old mule path is bracketed by 300m-high walls lined with fig and almond trees, cypresses and oaks. At one point the sheer cliff faces are only 2m apart. Another highlight is an arch of stone over the path. The route begins in the tiny village of Imbros and finishes at **Komitades**.

Aradena Gorge The 3.5km trail into this gorge begins just before the rickety **Vardinogiannis Bridge**, which also draws bungee-jumpers. After the first 800m, the uncrowded trail reaches the early Byzantine **Church of Agios Ioannis**. Follow the route through the fairly lush landscape to the endpoint, idyllic **Marmara Beach**. This is one of the best of the isolated beaches on Crete's southwest coast and is lapped by water that seems an almost impossibly vibrant teal in colour.

Hiking Samaria Gorge

Day trips to the gorge are heavily marketed to tourists across Crete. All start at the park entrance and include pickups from major tourist areas such as Hania or from nearby coastal towns such as Sougia or Hora Sfakion, both about a 40-minute ferry ride from the walk's finish point at the car-free seaside village of **Agia Roumeli**.

The gorge is open for hiking from May to mid-October, although it may open earlier in April. Stay alert for *kri-kri*, a mountain goat that's native to Crete. At the trail's end, few can resist a dip in the water at Agia Roumeli.

33 Alluring BEACHES

SWIMMING | FUN | NATURE

Crete has some of Greece's best sandy beaches, many far from developed areas so you can truly enjoy a remote holiday on the sand. No matter your mood, there is a beach for you – if you want your own little cove where you can take it all off, you can, or join the action at one of the taverna-lined party beaches.

How to

Getting here The most popular of Crete's beaches are easily served by car or bus. For others, you'll need your own vehicle. Reaching even more isolated ones requires a 4WD.

When to go June to September are the best months as the water is warm.

Ferries Many beaches along the south coast are linked by scheduled ferries, which offer a relaxing way to travel and enjoy the beautiful scenery.

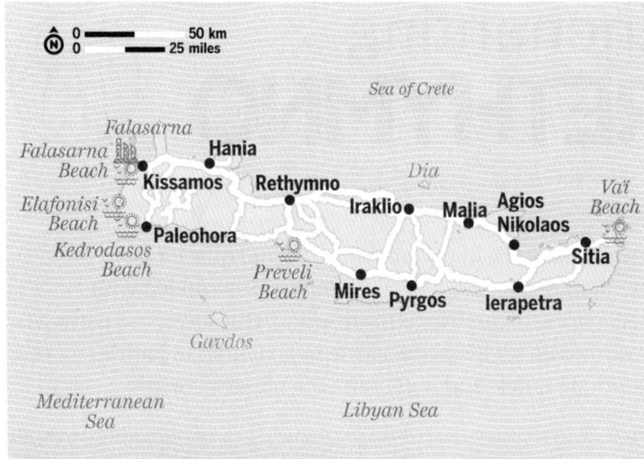

Top Falasarna Beach
Bottom Elafonisi Beach

Elafonisi Beach Sparkling white sand with a pinkish hue makes Elafonisi a standout in a nation of islands where pebbly, grey beaches are common. Its shallow, azure waters surround an islet just offshore that is an easy walk. Cliffs, dunes and semi-secluded coves are highlights here. Beat the summer crowds by walking 1km along the coastal trail east to **Kedrodasos Beach**. Otherwise, climb the dunes on the islet for panoramic views of this entire magical spot.

Falasarna Beach Sunsets dazzle throughout the year at this very long beach, which faces directly west across azure water. Waves here are regularly the largest in Crete as sets of rollers crash into the sand from the open Mediterranean, which draws people ready to ride them, whether on a board or freestyle. Tavernas, cafes, modest hotels and gear-rental stands line the shore in summer; olive trees and greenhouses form the backdrop. An easy 2km walk along a dirt path takes you to the site of **Ancient Falasarna**, which dates to the 4th century BCE.

Vaï Beach Try to catch falling dates from the largest natural palm forest in Europe at this beach at the far northeastern end of Crete. The beach at Vaï is small but perfectly framed by turquoise waters lapping at the edges of the inlet. Trails lead to cliffside walks, vista points and more secluded spots.

More Wonderful Beaches

Agios Pavlos For crowd-free suntanning, head to the massive sand dunes spilling into this isolated southern-coast beach.

Balos Go tropical on this sultry and incredibly photogenic lagoon-like sandy beach.

Chrissi Island Count shades of blue and green as you contemplate the shimmering waters lapping Chrissi (aka Gaïdouronisi Island).

Gavdos Island The southernmost spot in Europe exudes a sense of happy isolation and has wonderful, untrodden beaches.

Preveli Beach Crete's 'other' famous palm beach, at the confluence of river and sea amid cave-combed cliffs.

Xerokambos Find solitude and natural beauty along the dozen or so beaches stretching for 4.5km in this remote southeastern region.

34 Enchanting RETHYMNO

HISTORY | WALKING | FOOD

Wandering the labyrinthine lanes of Rethymno's historic old quarter is a highlight of Crete. Charismatic Renaissance-era Venetian buildings sprinkled with exotic features from the Turkish period are enlivened with wonderful surprises: perhaps a romantic flower-filled courtyard or an idyllic plaza, a cafe in an Ottoman bathhouse or a Venetian mansion turned boutique hotel. And don't miss the massive fortress.

MAIRUIO/SHUTTERSTOCK ©

How to

Getting around Rethymno is entirely walkable, and that is the best way to explore this age-old city. There are good bus connections to the airports in Iraklio and Hania.

When to go Many of the best tavernas, restaurants and shops close from November to March. Conversely, in winter you can savour Rethymno's charms without being jostled.

Avoid the crowds Quiet lanes worth a stroll include Minoos, Neophytou Patealarou, Patriarchou Grigoriou and Vivylaki.

LUCIAN BOLCA/SHUTTERSTOCK ©

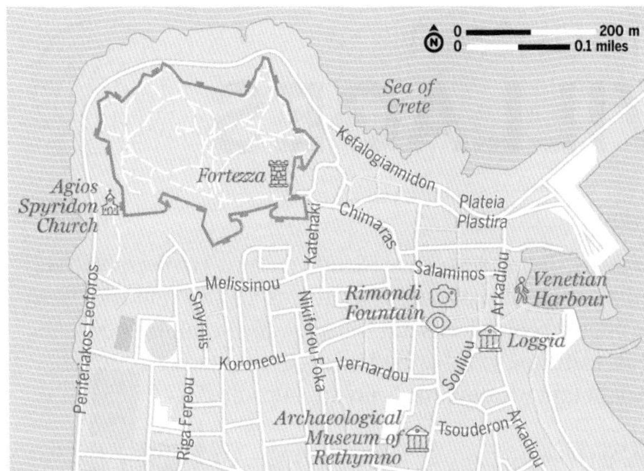

Top Venetian harbour
Bottom Fortezza

Can you say 'Rethymno' with a pirate voice? Try your best as you gaze out to sea from the 15th-century **Fortezza**, the vast fortress built to protect the port from marauding pirates and invading Turks. The old town's tangle of streets off the **Venetian harbour** are delightful. Although small enough not to get too lost, they still allow you to get swallowed up by the past – and you can always stop for a drink at an atmospheric cafe. Wander the maze of old stone lanes, which are shaded by canopies of flowers and accented by old buildings with wooden balconies and the occasional minaret.

Seek out the tiny **Agios Spyridon Church**, built into the cliff below the fortress. You'll be dazzled by the cacophony of gilded treasures, ancient icons and colourful artwork. Major Venetian sites include the **Loggia**, a restored 16th-century landmark that originally served as a meeting house for Venetian nobility. Just west, join the scores of selfie-takers posing in front of the ornate **Rimondi Fountain**. Originally, animals drank from the smaller of the three basins fed by water flowing from lions' heads.

At the **Archaeological Museum of Rethymno**, don't miss the bronze lamp from the 1st century BCE depicting Dionysus riding a panther, exquisite hand-painted Minoan ceramics and a 9000-year-old limestone deity statue.

Rethymno's Old Bakeries

Among the many fine restaurants in Rethymno are two bakeries that preserve old traditions.

Run by one of the last traditional filo masters, the eponymous **Yiorgos Hatziparaskos** bakery still makes superfine pastry by hand. Enter through a Venetian doorway and watch the spectacle when they whirl the dough into a giant bubble before stretching it over a huge table.

Hidden away in an alley, **Spanoioakis** bakery is famous for its bread shaped like dinosaurs and flamingos, as well as *kouloures* – a lacquered, intricately decorated (but inedible) bread. Each design is symbolic: pomegranates bring luck; trees, longevity; and rings, an eternal bond.

35 Mountain VILLAGES

COUNTRYSIDE | REMOTE | VIEWS

Crete's mountain villages are the cradles of the island's culture. Hardscrabble and self-reliance are two characteristics proudly embraced by Cretans and for centuries were essential for survival amid the craggy peaks. Today, the villages offer stunning views, an enthusiastic welcome and meals featuring wood-grilled meats in cosy tavernas. In the mountains of western Crete, you'll find winding roads linking top villages.

DIGITALPEARLS/SHUTTERSTOCK ©

How to

Getting here Some villages are along bus routes but there may be limited service, which makes village-hopping hard. Consider renting a vehicle for a day or two of exploration.

When to go May to September are the months with the best weather and the widest choices for eating and shopping. In winter you can join residents hunkered down near wood fires.

Join the crowd On Sundays, tavernas fill with festive families.

DZIEWUL/SHUTTERSTOCK ©

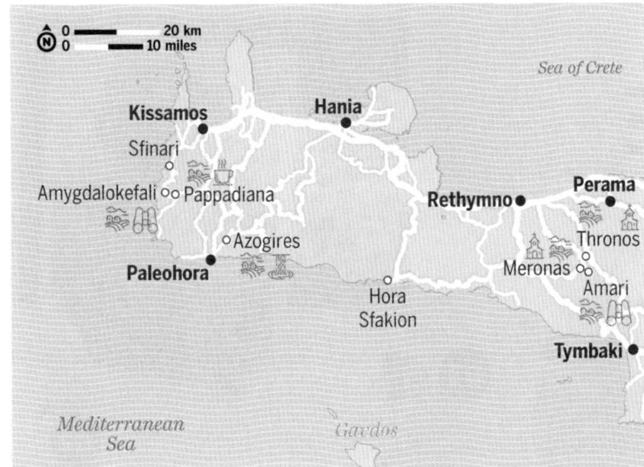

Top Rethymno
Bottom Kritsa

The **Amari Valley**, not far from Rethymno, is a quilt of tranquil villages punctuated by Byzantine churches and framed by olive groves and orchards amid mountainous grandeur. Highlights include **Meronas** and its 14th-century Church of Maria, with beautiful frescoes and lavish royal-blue altar vestments. **Thronos** is a tidy one-taverna kind of hamlet, perched on a hillside. The Agia Panagia (Church of the Assumption) boasts extraordinary, if faded, 14th-century frescoes. The valley's namesake, **Amari**, has an enchanting medley of Venetian buildings and a square framed with cafes and overflowing flowerpots. Climb the 19th-century bell tower to share beautiful views with the pigeons.

In the hills above Paleohora, you'll discover some of western Crete's most scenic and least visited mountain hamlets: the **Innahorion villages** (the name is derived from Enneia Horia, meaning 'nine villages'). Spread along the route connecting the main Paleohora road with the west coast and Falasarna, each of the villages beckons you with views, beauty and good food. This lush, quiet area is renowned for its chestnuts and olives and you won't want for opportunities to purchase olive oil, honey, dried herbs and raki.

Top Innahorion villages include **Azogires** and its sylvan valley with waterfalls and caves you can visit. **Elos** is the region's largest town and the centre of the chestnut trade. The hamlet of **Pappadiana** has a single cute cafe with good coffee. Enjoy superlative sea views at barely there **Amygdalokefali**.

Other Villages Not to Miss

Argyroupoli Devour trout while surrounded by rushing natural springs in this ancient mountain village.

Hora Sfakion This whimsical southern port boasts larger-than-life characters, a long, colourful history and delightful ferry rides.

Kritsa Clinging to the Dikti mountains, Kritsa offers fine shopping, an atmospheric old town and a church with amazing Byzantine frescoes.

Mohlos Minoan antiquity meets seashore vibes at this village with many fine tavernas.

Myrthios On clear days you can spot Africa from this whitewashed village high above the Libyan Sea.

Theriso Recharge your batteries at this historically significant mountain village in thick forest south of Hania.

Foods of CRETE

01 Rusks

Crunchy *paximadia* (rusks) are hard, dry crackers used in the famous *dakos*, a salad with tomatoes, olive oil and creamy cheese.

02 Kalitsounia

Cretan stuffed cheese pies start with hand-made filo-pastry dough, often formed into tiny cups. There are myriad variations.

03 Olive oil

Crete remains an important olive-growing area, producing the largest quantity of extra virgin olive oil in Greece. Many brands are acclaimed.

04 Gamopilafo

This rice dish is a deluxe risotto prepared in a rich meat broth and *stako-voutiro* (butter created from boiled fresh goat's milk).

05 Hohlioi (snails)

Collected after rainfall and prepared in dozens

of interesting ways: try *hohlioi bourbouristoi* (simmered in wine or vinegar and rosemary).

06 Horta

For centuries Cretans have been gathering and boiling *horta* (wild greens) for salads, pies and stews.

07 Sfakianes pites

From the Sfakia region, fine pancake-like sweets with a light cheese filling, served with honey and a dash of raki

08 Wood-grilled meats

Cretans have their own barbecue style called *ofto* or *antikristo*, in which chunks of meat are slow-roasted upright around hot coals.

09 Hirina apakia

It's a multiday process to create this delicious smoked pork. The marinated meat is smoked over a fire stoked with local herbs.

10 Cretan cheese

Many kinds of cheese are produced across the island, including *anthotiro* (buttery white cheese) and *yaourti*, a tangy sheep's-milk yoghurt..

Mysterious Minoans

AN ANCIENT CIVILISATION LONG BEFORE CLASSICAL GREECE

Much is not known about the Minoans, whose palaces and artefacts are found at archaeological sites and museums across Crete. What is known is that they had a rich culture as seen in surviving mosaics, sculptures, pottery and jewellery. Other evidence suggests that they believed in gender equality, peaceful relations and scientific achievement.

Pictured Frescoes, Palace of Knossos

A Sophisticated Culture

Speculation shrouds the Minoans – we don't even know what they called themselves, 'Minoan' being the term given by British archaeologist Sir Arthur Evans in honour of the possibly mythical King Minos.

Evidence uncovered in Crete's grand palaces indicates they were a peaceful, sophisticated, well-organised and prosperous civilisation with robust international trade, highly developed agriculture, splendid architecture and art, and seemingly equal status for men and women. Women apparently enjoyed a great degree of freedom and autonomy. Minoan art shows women participating in games, hunting, and public and religious festivals.

Their exquisite artistry in pottery and jewellery survives to this day. Richly coloured frescoes, such as those at Knossos, portray landscapes abundant in animals and birds, marine scenes teeming with fish and octopuses, and banquets, games and rituals.

Axes & Bulls

The double-axe symbol that appears in frescoes and on Knossos palace walls was a sacred symbol for the Minoans. Other religious symbols that frequently appear in Minoan art include the mythical gryphon and figures with a human body and an animal head. The Minoans appear to have worshipped the dead and believed in afterlife.

The bull was another potent Minoan symbol. The peculiar Minoan sport of bull-leaping, where acrobatic thrill-seekers seize the charging bull's horns and leap over its back, is depicted in frescoes, pottery and sculptures.

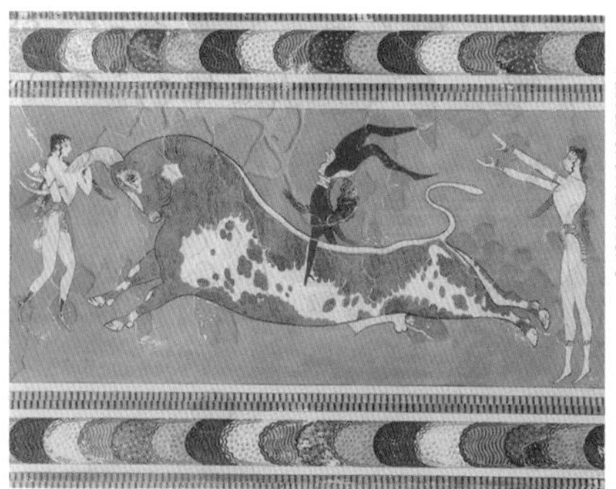
PECOLD/SHUTTERSTOCK ©

YURIIT/SHUTTERSTOCK ©

First in Pre-Greek Letters

In Crete, Minoan painting is virtually the only form of Greek painting to have survived. Large-scale sculptures have disappeared in natural disasters like the tsunami that swept from Thira (Santorini) in 1450 BCE. Minoan art inspired the invading Mycenaeans; its influence spread to Santorini and beyond.

> Minoan art shows women participating in games, hunting, and public and religious festivals.

At the same time, the Minoans' inscrutable written hieroglyph system, Linear A, provides another indication of a culture that was very advanced. The most significant example of this writing is on the 3600-year-old terracotta tablet known as the Phaestos Disk, which has been the object of much speculation since it was discovered in 1908. The disk, about 16cm in diameter, consists of an Early Minoan pictographic script made up of 242 'words' written in a continuous spiral. It has never been deciphered.

We know more about Linear B, a script written on clay tablets that lay undisturbed until they were unearthed at Knossos. The decipherment of this script by English architect Michael Ventris in 1952 provided the first tangible evidence that the Greek language had a recorded history longer than scholars had previously believed. The language was an archaic form of Greek 500 years older than the Ionic Greek of Homer. The Knossos clay tablets are mainly inventories and records of commercial transactions, dating from the 14th to the 13th centuries BCE. They give a glimpse of a fairly complex, well-organised civilisation.

Minos: Man or Myth?

Minos, the legendary ruler of Crete, was the son of Zeus and Europa and attained the Cretan throne, aided by Poseidon. Or maybe not.

Homer describes him and his land in the 'Odyssey': 'Out on the dark blue sea there lies a rich and lovely land called Crete that is densely populated and boasts 90 cities... One of the 90 cities is called Knossos and there for nine years, King Minos ruled and enjoyed the friendship of the mighty.'

His mythical heritage aside, whether Minos even existed is open to much debate and is yet another – and key – Minoan mystery.

Listings

BEST OF THE REST

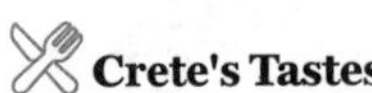

Crete's Tastes

Kalderimi €€

A traditional taverna in Topanas, Hania's most characterful neighbourhood, that's always busy. Here you'll find Cretan standards such as *hirina apakia* (marinated, smoked pork) cooked with a creative flair.

To Stachi €€

Stelios Michelakis and his family grow almost everything used in their excellent vegan and vegetarian taverna on their farm near Hania. He arrives each day at 5am to start baking the delectable whole-grain bread.

Monogram €

Grab a street-side table and watch Hania rush by. The beans here are sourced globally and then roasted locally in Iraklio. It's a buzzy, busy take on a classic Greek cafe.

Domenico €

In Hania's Topanas neighbourhood, artisans make your ice cream or gelato right in front of you. The results are an uncommonly creamy treat you can customise in myriad variations.

Taverna Knossos €€

Amid a sea of mediocrity lining Rethymno's old port is this absolute delight. The hard-working Stavroulaki family will feed you well – bounteous platters of fresh seafood come in waves from the kitchen.

Byraki €€

Tables filled with residents spill out into the street in Rethymno at this classic – and excellent – Cretan taverna. Expect great platters of food and be sure to order some of the local cheeses.

To Pigadi €€

On an attractive lane out of Rethymno's fray, this genteel taverna has a short menu of seasonal Cretan fare. As in the past, what you eat here depends on the seasons.

Meli €

Succumb to the lure of the gorgeous mountains of ice cream at this busy corner shop right by the Rimondi Fountain in Rethymno. The creamy goodness is made with goat's milk from the owner's family farm.

Peskesi €€

Culinary magic forged from family-farm ingredients and served amid relaxed sophistication in a candlelit Venetian mansion in Iraklio. Enjoy the intimate surroundings within the atmospheric stone walls.

Rakadiko Oinodeion €€

Tops among Sitia's waterfront tavernas, this rustic place offers local seasonal specials that shine. Many ingredients, including the oil, bread and raki, are produced by the owners.

Hiking in Crete

Local Goods

Philly

Say goodbye to anaemic pastels at this clothes shop with the motto 'Life is too short for boring clothes'. It's a fun and clever small boutique on a busy pedestrian street in Hania.

Sifis Stavroulakis

Beautiful naturalistic jewellery made in this Hania workshop takes on floral and human forms. The small shopfront is on a lane with other interesting higher-end stores.

Georgina Skalidi

This renowned Hania designer creates wonderful contemporary leather bags, jewellery and accessories. The scent of leather goods as you walk in borders on intoxicating.

Outdoor Thrills

Eco Events

This excellent Rethymno-based Cretan tour company specialises in small-group English-language tours that get you in touch with land, people and culture.

Mountaineering Club of Rethymno

An excellent resource for advice on treks in western Crete including up into the nearby peaks – Crete's highest. They also lead and organise climbing adventures.

Cretan Ski School

Offers equipment hire, lessons and guided trips to Mt Psiloritis, Crete's tallest peak. The island's soaring mountain ranges get a surprising amount of snow in winter.

Hotel Porto Loutro

In the southern Crete beach town of Loutro, this hotel rents canoes, sea kayaks and personal pedal boats for exploring the coast. They are available to guests and nonguests alike.

Gortyna

Chania Boat

Rents out small powerboats from Loutro which you can use to explore the ravishing coast. There's no licence needed to pilot your way to little coves with untrodden pockets of beach.

Odysseia Stables

See Crete on horseback: this top-rated facility high above Avdou is geared to skilled riders. It offers multiday treks to the Lasithi Plateau or across Mt Dikti.

Historical Vibes

Etz Hayyim Synagogue

Hania has Crete's only remaining synagogue, which was badly damaged in WWII and reopened only in 1999. It sports a *mikveh* (ritual bath), tombs of rabbis and a memorial to the local Jews killed by the Nazis.

Gortyna

This mesmerising archaeological site is about 23km northeast of Matala. It's been inhabited since the Neolithic Age but capped its career by becoming the capital of Roman Crete in the 1st century BCE.

Scan to find more things to do in Crete.

CYCLADES

BEACHES | RUINS | FOOD & WINE

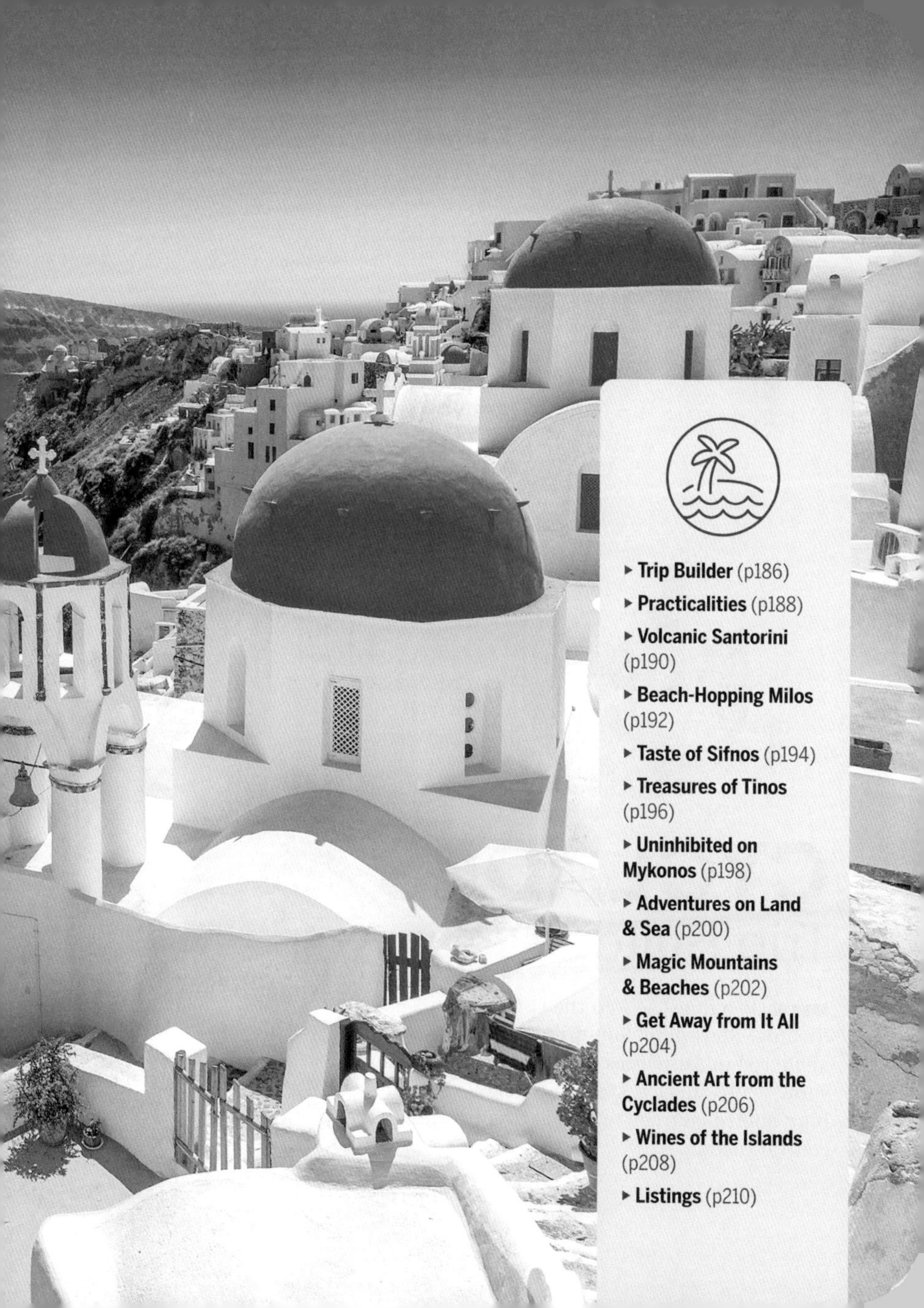

Tour marble villages and gorgeous dovecote valleys on **Tinos** (p196)
35mins from Mykonos

Admire natural beauty with delicious Cycladic cuisine on **Sifnos** (p194)
2½hrs from Piraeus

Sun yourself on the stone cliffs of volcanic **Milos** (p192)
2hrs from Santorini

CYCLADES
Trip Builder

On a quest to find the Greek islands of your dreams? Start here. Sun-drenched outcrops of rock, anchored in azure seas and peppered with vibrant snow-white villages, stellar archaeological sites and blue-domed churches – this is Greece straight from central casting.

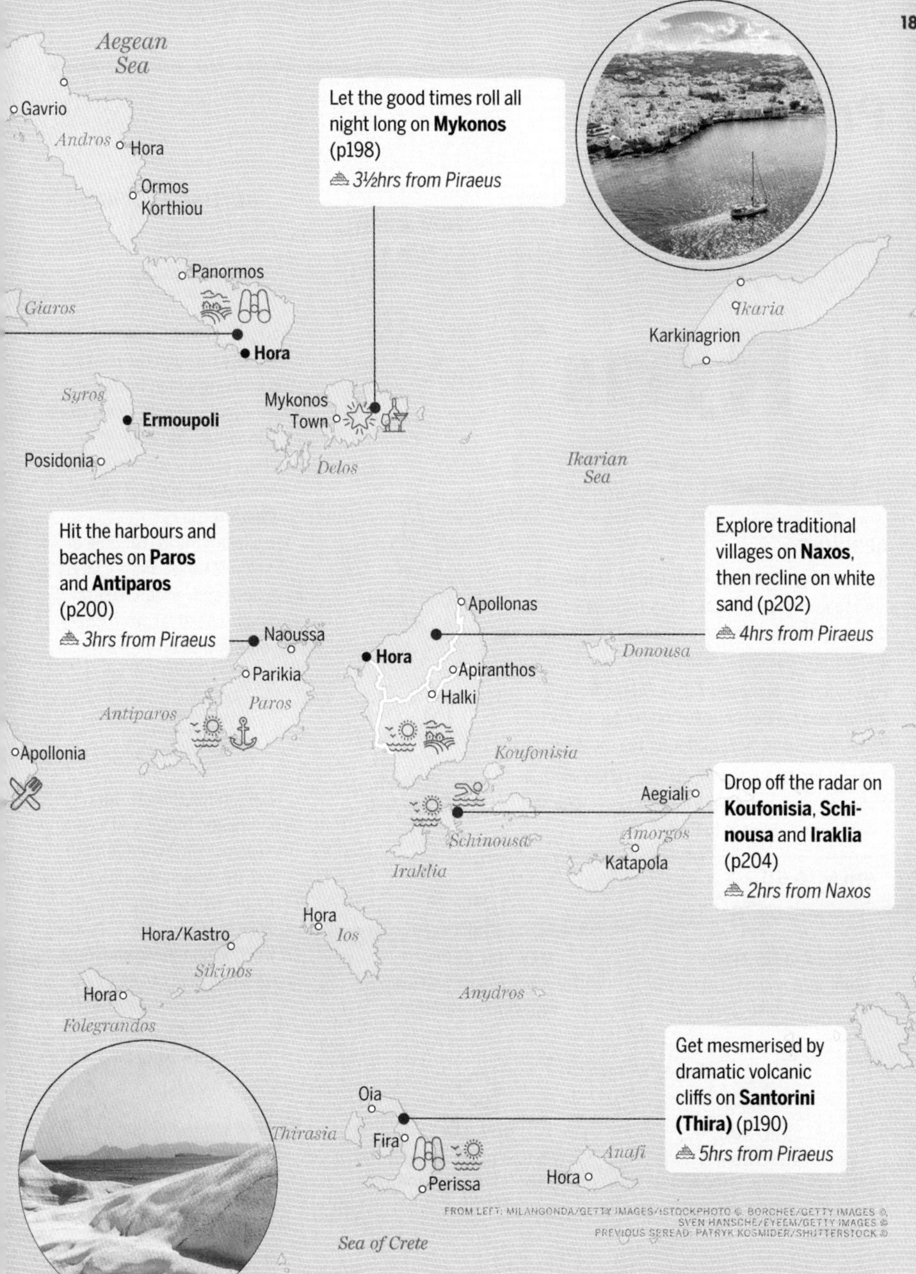
Let the good times roll all night long on **Mykonos** (p198)
3½hrs from Piraeus
Hit the harbours and beaches on **Paros** and **Antiparos** (p200)
3hrs from Piraeus
Explore traditional villages on **Naxos**, then recline on white sand (p202)
4hrs from Piraeus
Drop off the radar on **Koufonisia**, **Schinousa** and **Iraklia** (p204)
2hrs from Naxos
Get mesmerised by dramatic volcanic cliffs on **Santorini (Thira)** (p190)
5hrs from Piraeus
Aegean Sea
Gavrio
Andros
Hora
Ormos Korthiou
Panormos
Giaros
Hora
Ikaria
Karkinagrion
Syros
Ermoupoli
Posidonia
Mykonos Town
Delos
Ikarian Sea
Naoussa
Parikia
Paros
Antiparos
Apollonia
Apollonas
Hora
Apiranthos
Halki
Donousa
Koufonisia
Aegiali
Amorgos
Katapola
Schinousa
Iraklia
Hora
Ios
Hora/Kastro
Sikinos
Hora
Folegrandos
Anydros
Oia
Fira
Thirasia
Perissa
Anafi
Hora
Sea of Crete

Practicalities

MARKUS MAINKA/SHUTTERSTOCK ©

ARRIVING

Santorini or Mykonos Flights from Athens and European cities. Fly in and ferry to other islands. Be aware that ferries are packed in high season and some are pricey – book ahead.

Paros, Syros, Naxos or Milos Flights from Athens and connections to onward ferries, with Paros, Syros and Naxos offering the most choice.

Ferry ports All islands are served by ferries from one or more mainland ports: Piraeus, Rafina and Lavrio. Some connect to Crete.

HOW MUCH FOR A

Gyros €3

Craft beer €5

Sunbed €10 to €25

WHEN TO GO

FEB–APR
Cool, sunny days, perfect for hiking.

MAY–JUN, SEP–OCT
Gorgeous swims and walks, with gentler weather.

JUL–AUG
Peak high season: crowds, party life, baking temperatures.

NOV–JAN
Windswept winter with serenity, but many services close.

GETTING AROUND

Ferry The key to sculpting an itinerary through the islands is knowing which ferries go where – and when. Peak services run in July and August. In winter, services are reduced or nonexistent on some routes. Check ferries.gr, then see ferry locations in real time at vesselfinder.com. Many islands have both conventional (slower) and high-speed ferries – check duration when booking.

Car On the islands, cars, scooters and buzzing ATVs are the easiest way to get around and are reasonably priced outside high season, though larger islands have buses (super crowded in summer), and most have small boats to beaches.

Walking Towns and tiny islands are perfect for walking. All islands have hiking trails.

EATING & DRINKING

The Cyclades islands are home to excellent regional cuisines, and each boasts different traditions with local cheese, herbs and sweets. Some excel in everything, like Tinos or Amorgos. Don't miss the chance for a long seafront-taverna lunch – a parade of dips, salads and seafood. Fancier islands like Mykonos, Santorini, and increasingly Paros, Syros and Koufonisia, have sophisticated high-end restaurants. Sometimes the best food isn't in the most stupendous location, so delve into small villages and backstreets. Book ahead on crowded islands in high season.

Best cake Sifnos' *melopita* (honey-cinnamon custard cake) at To Steki (p210)

Must-try Shrimp *saganaki* with local cheese at Santorini's To Krinaki (p210)

CONNECT & FIND YOUR WAY

Wi-fi Free in most hotels and available in many restaurants.

Navigation Mobile signal gets spotty outside towns, and local print maps are of varying quality. It's easy to get lost on unmarked back roads and trails without a proper offline resource. Terrain (terrainmaps.gr) maps are invaluable for getting off the beaten track and exploring on foot or wheels.

ARRIVAL PICK-UP

Many hotels and rent-a-car outfits will send someone to pick you up from the ferry or airport. When booking, check if port/airport transfer is included.

WHERE TO STAY

Summer season is highest-priced and busiest – always book ahead. Shoulder season is about 20% less expensive, and in winter many lodgings on the islands close.

Island	Pro/Con
Santorini and Mykonos	Heart of the action (particularly Fira and Oia on the former and Mykonos Town on the latter), but pricey and crowded.
Paros and Naxos	Large, interesting islands with a broad range of lodgings. They get hectic in summer.
Amorgos, Small Cyclades, Serifos	Quiet islands with gorgeous nature. Sleepier outside high season when services close.
Tinos and Syros	Interesting small islands central for island-hopping, though they lack world-famous sights.

MONEY

Carry €100 or €200 for places that don't take cards. To save money, visit during low season (exact months are a bit different on each island) and stick to less touristy islands.

36 Volcanic SANTORINI

LANDSCAPE | WINE | RUINS

Approaching Santorini (also called Thira) from the water, it's hard not to be awed by the sheer cliffs soaring above a turquoise sea, by the fact that you're sailing in an immense crater of a drowned volcano and that high above, the main villages of Fira and Oia are a snowdrift of white Cycladic houses. The feeling is almost supernatural.

IHOR_TAILWIND/GETTY IMAGES/ISTOCKPHOTO ©

How to

Getting around Though having your own wheels is the easiest way to explore, traffic in high season (May to October) is a menace. One-way streets encircle Fira and Oia, and roads are jammed with racing transfer vans and inexperienced drivers on scooters and ATVs.

When to go Plan for the fact that Santorini is expensive and crowded. Visit in low season (November to April); avoid July and August.

Foodie tip Best small villages with excellent restaurants are Finikia, Pyrgos and Megalohori.

IVANMATEEV/GETTY IMAGES ©

Top Oia
Bottom Fira coast

Caldera rim Santorini's main town of **Fira** is a booming place where the caldera edge is layered with swish cave hotels, infinity pools and restaurants. On the caldera's northern tip **Oia** sparkles, built on a steep slope with many of its white dwellings hewn into the volcanic rock. The stunning walk from Fira to Oia (three hours, 9.1km) traces the rim of the caldera via Imerovigli and Skaros Rock. If you time it right, you can reach Oia for its world-famous sunset.

Pick the colour of your beach Two of the best qualities of Santorini's beaches are their dramatic cliffs and how the different volcanic sands and pebbles play on the water's colours. Choose between **Red (Kokkini) Beach** with its impressive red cliffs, the sheltered cove of **White (Aspri) Beach** – named for the colour of its cliffs, not its sand – or **Black (Mesa Pigadia) Beach**. Although, truth be told, the majority of Santorini's beaches are beautifully black.

Incredible ruins Vertiginously positioned on a mountaintop above Kamari and Perissa, the magnificently sited and elaborate town of **Ancient Thira** was first settled by the Dorians in the 9th century BCE and remains a massive maze of Hellenistic, Roman and Byzantine ruins. Nearby, explore the ancient Minoan city of **Ancient Akrotiri**, unearthed in 1967 from deep beneath volcanic ash from a catastrophic eruption in 1613 BCE.

Top Santorini Wineries

Estate Argyros Terrific, internationally renowned *asyrtiko*, Nykteri (*asyrtiko* made at night) and *mavrotragano*, plus exceptional Vinsanto (dessert wine) in a gorgeous vineyard with mountain and sea views.

Hatzidakis Winery Santorini's only organic winery, run by the family of a Cretan oenologist.

Art Space The island's smallest winery, combined with an interesting art gallery.

Gaia Winery Seafront with delish *asyrtiko* and reds from their other winery in Nemea.

Vassaltis Winery Modern winery with peaceful sea views.

37 Beach-Hopping MILOS

BEACHES | VILLAGES | ANCIENT ART

Volcanic Milos arches around a central caldera and is ringed with dramatic coastal landscapes of colourful, surreal rock formations. The island's dozens of beaches (supposedly the most of any Cycladic island) have something for any mood – or weather pattern. The built-up portion of Milos covers a small part of the island; Plaka is the crowning village, ideally suited for wandering on foot.

SVEN HANSCHE/SHUTTERSTOCK ©

How to

Getting here/around Ferry service is frequent and there's an airport. You'll need to rent a vehicle to visit most beaches; a 4WD or ATV is required to reach the rugged ones.

When to go Summer is best as the water is warmest.

Go really remote The tiny neighbouring island of Polyaigos is uninhabited. Its top beach, Ammura, is a semi-popular stop for day-trippers who luxuriate in the idyllic water.

KITE_RIN/SHUTTERSTOCK ©

Top Sarakiniko
Bottom Plaka

Splendid Beaches

Milos and its offshore islets have more than 70 beaches garnished with different-coloured sands and stone. It's always possible to find a sheltered beach, no matter which way the wind is blowing.

Prouvatas is bookended by glowering headlands and boasts a long swath of golden sand. One of Milos' best, it has a few tavernas and water-sports rentals.

Plathiena sits at the end of a valley beyond Plaka to the north. Pebble-strewn and sandy, the beach is exceptionally pretty, with craggy limestone formations at each end plus a summertime beach bar.

Firopotamos is quiet and framed by a little cove lined with craggy limestone cliffs and *syrmata* (traditional fishers' huts).

Sarakiniko features meringue-like rock formations and caves. The sandy beach is tiny but there's a deep channel that's perfect for swimming, and room to spread out on the rocks.

Mandrakia is a cute fishing harbour with small shingle beaches on either side. It also has one of the island's top lunch spots.

Timeless Villages

Plaka embodies the Cycladic ideal with its white houses and labyrinthine lanes perched along the edge of an escarpment. The courtyard of Panagia Korfiatissa church offers spectacular sunset views.

Klima is a waterfront fishing village that offers the best example of Milos' *syrmata*.

The Home of Venus de Milo

Clinging to a lonely patch of hillside amid olive trees, a large Roman-era theatre entertained the citizens of Ancient Melos from the 1st to the 4th century CE. It was rediscovered in 1735. Only 85 years later, a farmer stumbled upon a statue that was immediately spirited away by French archaeologists.

Taken to the Louvre and named *Venus de Milo,* this artefact remains a sensation. Meanwhile, you can see a Venus replica at Plaka's **Archaeological Museum of Melos**. A campaign to repatriate the statue (takeaphroditehome.gr) has the slogan: 'She's not missing her arms, she's missing her home.'

38 Taste of SIFNOS

WATERFRONTS | STROLLING | CUISINE

Sifnos is a feast, both literally and figuratively. Whitewashed villages, anchored by the capital Apollonia, sit like pearls on a string along the crest of the island. The changing light kisses the landscape which has beguiling vistas. Known first for food, Sifnos has excellent places to eat, which celebrate the island's bounty.

How to

Getting there/around Sifnos is a ferry hub. Roads stretch down to beachy bays, with Apollonia as the head. Distances are short.

Stay in the port The ferry port of Kamares is appealing beyond its utility. There are waterfront cafes, tavernas, shops, tiny churches and a beautiful large beach.

Go hiking Sifnos is laced by trails and the roads are (mostly) quiet enough to make walking a pleasure – you can get a feel for the fabric of the island.

Exceptional Kastro

Dramatically positioned on a crag with sheer drops to the crystalline waters below, Kastro is Sifnos' most atmospheric and magical settlement.

It's a sleepy place where cats snooze the day away on stoops. A handful of alleys curve around the hilltop perch, passing through tunnels formed by ancient houses and emerging onto terraces with stunning views of the coast and across the Aegean to Paros. A couple of tavernas have verdant views inland across terraced hillsides. Like a diamond on a ring, the **Church of the Seven Martyrs** sits on a rocky promontory surrounded by surging blue water right below Kastro.

Far left Church of the Seven Martyrs
Above Apollonia

Apollonia Labyrinthine and church-studded, the island's main town comes alive in high season with the well-dressed promenading along buzzing Odos Prokou, better known as the Steno (meaning 'narrow') because of its slenderness. From Apollonia, the string of white houses continues north into the conjoined village of **Ano Petali** and then to **Artemonas**, with its terraced olive groves, mansions and blue-domed churches. By day, there are upscale food vendors and stylish shops selling designer clothes and expensive handmade knick-knacks. By night, fine restaurants and bars come alive for a great nightlife. Away from the Steno bustle, follow your nose to traditional tavernas serving island specialities like *revithada,* the savoury chickpea stew for which every family has its own treasured recipe.

Faros The beach hamlet of Faros is an appealing traditional village, with a mix of fishing and pleasure boats in the harbour. The main beach is a mix of sand and pebbles atop which taverna tables and sunbathers compete for space. It's worth taking a short walk along a curving path past a clutch of tavernas to the west beach, which is serene. Only a short hike from here around a knoll is the beautiful, azure **Chrysopigi Beach**, home to two excellent tavernas.

Vathy On the southwest coast, this relaxed resort village is on an almost circular and sheltered bay of aquamarine beauty. The beach is wide and shaded in parts, although the string of slightly upscale cafes, tavernas and shops is built right up to the water's edge. This is a good town for fresh seafood.

39 Treasures OF TINOS

VILLAGES | FOOD | VISTAS

Tinos beguiles with a mix of tradition, intrigue, divinity and the region's best food. Within Greece, it's known for a Greek Orthodox pilgrimage site in the port and main town of Hora. Across Tinos, the countryside is a wonderland of natural beauty, dotted with more than 50 marble-ornamented villages found in hidden bays, on terraced hillsides and atop misty mountains.

How to

Getting there/around Tinos is a ferry hub. The closest airport is at nearby Mykonos. Buses from Hora serve the larger villages.

Sampling the food Local cooks, many running their own family tavernas, draw on the local produce (cheeses, sausages, tomatoes, wild artichokes, honey and more) for extraordinary culinary creations.

There she blows Tinos is known for its winds. Staying off exposed ridgelines is a good idea.

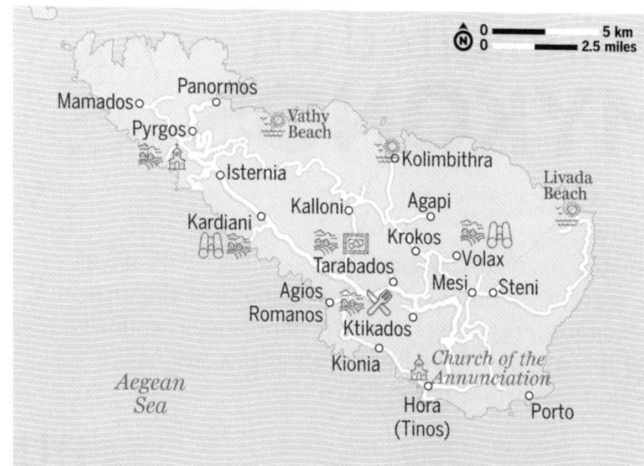

Top Volax
Bottom Pyrgos

The interior of Tinos is a glorious mix of broad terraced hillsides, mountaintops crowned with crags, and more than 50 unspoilt villages with fascinating architecture. From one whitewashed hamlet, others can be seen in the distance.

The centre of the island's marble industry is the intriguing, church-dotted village of **Pyrgos**, one of the prettiest in the Cyclades. Narrow lanes accented in marble wind towards a little square lined with cafes, which looks like a film set.

Just north of Hora, beautiful **Ktikados** perches in a hanging valley, with a good taverna and a skyline punctuated by a blue-domed church with an elegant campanile. **Kampos** sits atop a scenic hill surrounded by fields.

Don't miss **Tarabados**, a maze of small streets, blue-shuttered houses and marble sculptures. Excellent signage details local history. The surrounding breezy valleys are lined with dovecotes and watched over by Tinos' prominent landmark, the rocky peak of **Exobourgo**.

A minor detour takes you to ethereal **Agapi**, a pretty village set in a lush valley of dovecotes. It lives up to its name (meaning 'love' in Greek). Nearby, **Volax** sits at the heart of an amphitheatre of low hills festooned with hundreds of enormous and incongruous multicoloured boulders.

The main road runs high along the northwest coast and the views towards Syros are exhilarating. Lovely **Kardiani** perches on a steep cliff slope.

Making a Pilgrimage

The large **Church of the Annunciation** rising behind Hora's centre is one of the most significant Orthodox pilgrimage sites in Greece.

Built in 1830 using marble from the island's Panormos quarries, the church lies within a pleasant courtyard.

Its most important sacred object is the icon of Our Lady of Tinos, uncovered in 1823 in the ruins of a chapel beneath the current church after a nun, now St Pelagia, received visions from the Virgin instructing her where to find it.

The icon's image is now almost completely obscured by jewels.

40 Uninhibited on MYKONOS

BEACHES | BARS | PARTIES

Mykonos is one of the top party destinations on the planet. Yes, it's a playground for people who travel with entourages. But it's not just the dissolute mega-rich – much of the island's energy comes from its enormous popularity with gay men, who party with abandon. All visitors revel in the exquisite restaurants, rollicking bars and salubrious beach clubs.

TED HOROWITZ/GETTY IMAGES ©

How to

Getting there/around Ferries from across the Aegean call on Mykonos throughout the day. The airport is busy. Many people rent cars, but there's not far to drive. Buses and boats serve the party beaches.

When to go From May to September the island hops.

Get on Mykonos time The clichéd schedule for visitors is close to reality: breakfast at 4pm, lunch at 6.30pm, dinner at 11pm and party till dawn.

MEANMACHINE77/SHUTTERSTOCK ©

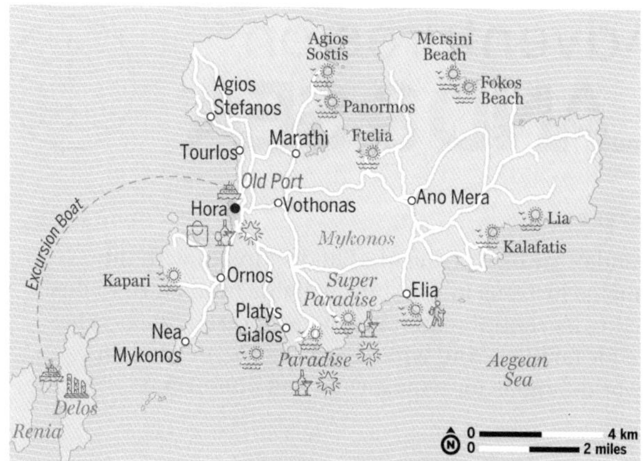

Hora (aka Mykonos town) is a maze of narrow lanes and whitewashed buildings, all watched over by the island's iconic windmills. Tiny flower-bedecked churches jostle with luxe boutiques for a 'Greek-island village by central casting' scenario. Vast numbers of humble visitors join the catwalk cast of wannabe influencers, celebrity-spotters, party boys and the dazed and hungover squeezing past the clubs, cafes and bars.

The beaches on Mykonos' south coast are among the most rollicking in the Mediterranean. Stylish clubs, all-day party bars, loungers jammed together and moods from snotty to promiscuous create an unmatched scene.

Platys Gialos is one of Mykonos' most popular beaches – you may need to step on someone to reach the water. It's ideal for making new friends. Tip: pay to park your car, as the tiny lanes are clogged with fuming visitors trying to find a free space.

Paradise is completely lined with hopping beach bars like Tropicana and tight rows of loungers and umbrellas. The partying barely pauses during the morning hours.

Super Paradise is flashy, trashy and great for people-watching. The action is split between the glitzy and expensive JackieO' Beach Club and the Super Paradise beach bar.

Elia is backed by a large resort, and rows of loungers jam the sand. It's especially popular with gay men. Head further west for the nudist area and an intimate cove.

Top Tavern in Hora
Bottom Elia

Unmissable Ancient Delos

The Cyclades fulfil their collective name (*kyklos* means 'circle') by encircling the sacred island of Delos. The mythical birthplace of twins Apollo and Artemis, splendid **Ancient Delos** was a shrine turned treasury and commercial centre.

This Unesco World Heritage Site is one of the most important archaeological sites in Greece. Cast your imagination wide to transform the sprawling ruin into the magnificent city it once was – it's not difficult to picture Ancient Delos in all its original splendour.

Just 5km long and 1300m wide, Delos offers a soothing contrast to Mykonos, from where it's easily reached on a short ferry ride.

41 Adventures on LAND & SEA

HARBOURS | BEACHES | WATERSPORTS

The large, fertile island of Paros is redolent of herbs, tinkles with the sound of goat bells and remains lustrous in the shifting lights from dawn to dusk. With a zippy ring road circling its central mountain and connecting the beaches and villages, it's a favourite for families. And with its brisk *meltemi* wind and a channel to Antiparos, it's world-famous for windsurfing and kitesurfing.

KITE_RIN/SHUTTERSTOCK ©

How to

Getting there/around Paros has an airport served by Athens and a well-connected ferry port. Smaller car ferries run from Paros to Antiparos. Realistically, it's important to have your own wheels on Paros.

What's on Paros has a rich cultural life year-round. Find out what's up at parosweb.com and friendsofparos.com.

Most famous residents Antiparos attracts the glitterati, perhaps lured by homeowners Tom Hanks and Rita Wilson? Or maybe it's just the beauty!

JEKATARINKA/SHUTTERSTOCK ©

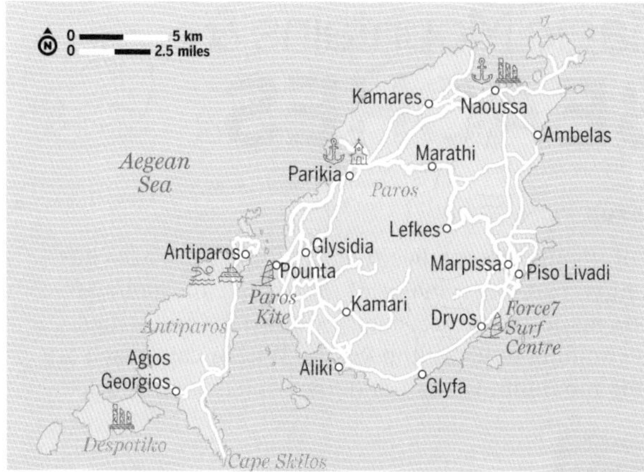

Pretty harbour towns For its petite size, **Parikia**, the port town where the ferries arrive, packs a wallop. Its labyrinthine Old Town contains the **Panagia Ekatontapyliani** (Our Lady of the Hundred Doors) church dating from 326 CE. It's one of the finest churches in the Cyclades, with superb columns of Parian marble and a carved iconostasis. The incredibly Insta-worthy village of **Naoussa** has gradually turned from a quiet fishing village into an increasingly stylish resort and visitor magnet. Boats bob in its harbour, perched on the shores of the large **Plastira Bay** and guarded by crumbling remains of a 15th-century Venetian *kastro* (castle). Both towns' charming whitewashed lanes are filled with boutiques, restaurants and sparkling chapels draped in blossoms.

Beaches, sea and ruins The beauty of Paros' ring road is that it takes you to most any beach you'd like. But don't forget the glorious, tiny **Antiparos** across the channel, where the quiet countryside is rimmed by luminescent cerulean waters. There, **Captain Sargos Boat Trips** goes to the archaeological site of **Despotiko** on its own uninhabited islet, including time to swim off the island's spectacular beach and cruise through sea caves.

Take to the air Paros' west coast, around Pounta, is the hub for top water sports: a long shallow-water shoreline and perfect side-shore wind conditions make it ideal for all skill levels of kiteboarder or windsurfer. **Paros Kite** or **Force7 Surf Centre** will outfit you with all you need.

Pictured Naoussa, Paros

Craft Beer on Paros & Beyond

56 Isles, Paros Sample crisp Aegean wit beer, Pilsner, IPA and lager made using local wheat and barley, at the taproom outside of Naoussa.

Ftelos Brewery, Santorini Swing in to Santorini's newest brewery for its range of beers named after the blue monkeys from the Akrotiri frescoes.

Mikònu Craft Beer, Mykonos This tiny brewery makes great IPAs, lagers and saisons, some barrel-aged.

Nissos Beer, Tinos A superb island to visit, it's also home to this brewery with top lager-style beers.

42 Magic Mountains & BEACHES

NATURE | VILLAGES | GRANDEUR

The largest and one of the most magnificent of the Cyclades, Naxos has wow factor from the moment you see the remains of the Temple of Apollo at the mouth of the harbour. Its main town backs a gorgeous waterfront with a web of steep cobbled alleys climbing to its hilltop *kastro*. Within easy reach are excellent beaches, fascinating mountain villages and inspiring ancient sites.

How to

Getting there/around
Naxos has an airport served by Athens and a well-connected ferry port. It's important to have your own wheels to explore outside Hora.

Summer festivals
Domus Festival and Naxos Festival hold cultural events in the *kastro*, Bazeos Tower and around the island.

Wildest artefacts
Naxian marble is famous, and three *kouroi* (giant statues of young men) can be found left where they fell in ancient marble quarries.

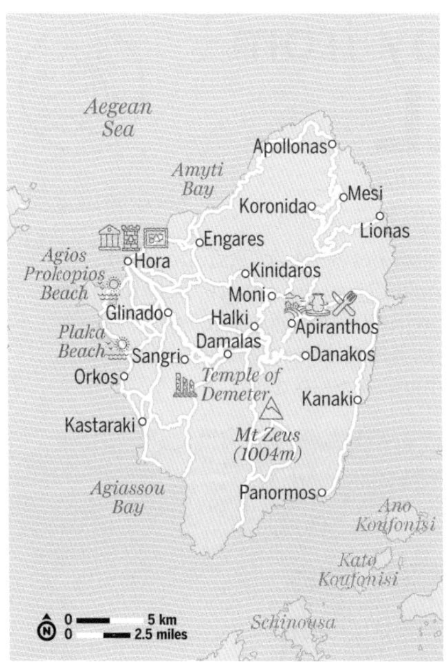

Top Temple of Apollo
Bottom Plaka Beach

Artistic Inspiration on Naxos

Archaeological Museum of Naxos In my early days on the island they would kick me out for returning day after day to look at the Cycladic-era figures.

Temple of Demeter When you walk the site, you feel the sheer beauty and power.

Bazeos Tower The best place for a summer programme of theatre, art and music.

The landscapes of Naxos and its villages I feel like I am inside the spaces, like they can gently hold me, not be outside of them looking in.

By Ingbert Brunk, *sculptor of Naxian marble (ingbert-brunk.de)*

Brilliant beaches Beaches south of **Agios Georgios** (Hora's town beach) get quieter the further you go – idyllic places for a chilled-out beach stay. The closest, beautiful **Agios Prokopios**, lies in a sheltered bay to the south of Cape Mougkri. Broad sandy beaches, some with blindingly white sand like **Glyfada**, continue as far as **Agiasos**, passing the turquoise waters of the long, dreamy **Plaka Beach.**

Fortified town The main town of **Hora (Naxos Town)** feels different from other Cycladic island capitals. It's bigger and busier, for starters. Spend the afternoon climbing to its fortified Venetian **Kastro**. This was the seat of power for Marco Sanudo, the 13th-century Venetian who founded the town and made Naxos the heart of the Duchy of the Aegean. Then, have sunset cocktails or dinner at **Avaton 1739** with sweeping views of town and sea.

Mountain villages Naxos' lovely inland Tragaea region is a vast plain of olive groves and unspoilt villages high in the mountains, crowned with Byzantine churches and ringed by crumbling Venetian towers. The Cyclades' highest peak, **Mt Zeus** (1004m; also known as Mt Zas), dominates. **Apiranthos** seems to grow out of the stony flanks of Mt Fanari (883m). The village is known for its crafts, best seen at the **Women's Association of Traditional Art** (paradosiakai fanta.gr), where they also sell homemade sweets. Apiranthos' excellent tavernas include **Lefteris** for meat dishes, **Amorginos** for traditional fare with views, and **Bakalogatos** for mezedhes.

43 Get Away from IT ALL

BEACHES | WALKS | PEACE

A band of small islands scatters the seas between Folegandros and Amorgos, along with dozens of islets and rocks. They are surprisingly distinct from one another in character and terrain, with Koufonisia welcoming rural-chic swimmers, quiet Schinousa appealing to beach lovers, and Iraklia luring folks looking to slip off the radar. This is where to go to relax.

SVEN HANSCHE/SHUTTERSTOCK ©

How to

Getting there/around In addition to occasional conventional and high-speed ferries, these islands are served by old-fashioned Small Cyclades Lines, great for open-deck island hopping. They are all easily walkable, and have taxis, buses or caïques.

When to go Outside the high-season months of July and August these islands get quiet, and services begin to close in September.

Fiercest wind The *meltemi* can howl from the north in summer throughout the Cyclades.

MILAN GONDA/SHUTTERSTOCK ©

Top Koufonisia
Bottom Iraklia

Glittering waters The smallest of the inhabited Cyclades, **Koufonisia** has slowly been transformed into a fashionable destination with prices to match, a beautiful place to unwind in contrast to the frenetic action of Mykonos and Santorini. Koufonisia's radiant white-sand beaches reflect through shockingly blue waters and include the main village's **Ammos Beach** and those along its southeast coast. A path continues to the north, skirting the headlands with dramatic, multihued rocky swimming coves, including the deep and clear **Piscina**, a swimming hole surrounded by rock and linked to the sea.

Beach bumming The undulating hills of small, laid-back **Schinousa** are a palimpsest of fields, ancient stone walls, Byzantine chapels and ruins of Venetian fortifications, reflecting the ebb and flow of many civilisations. During three centuries of Turkish rule, the island sheltered pirates from the Mani, but these days it attracts sunseekers looking for a slower pace of life. Walk its earthen roads to 16 exquisite beaches.

Drop out Sparsely inhabited (115 people!), **Iraklia** only shakes off its soporific air in July and August, when the cove-like harbour and village of **Agios Georgios** grows lively and yachts dot the island's sheltered **Livadi Bay**. Iraklia rewards hikers who explore its hills with secluded bays and thyme-scented solitude – there are five well-marked trails. In local restaurants, look out for Iraklian thyme honey, goat cheeses and fava.

Eat & Drink in the Small Cyclades

Mikres Cyclades, Koufonisia Elegantly showcases the best of Cycladic produce.

Capetan Nikolas, Koufonisia Cheerful seafood mainstay overlooking the harbour and sunset at Loutro.

Scholio, Koufonisia Cosy cavern of a bar and late-night hangout, with a long list of cocktails.

Loza, Schinousa For handmade pizza and traditional Greek dishes, plus delicate sweets.

Okto Adelphia, Schinousa Generous portions of local produce shine at this family-run upper-level terrace in Hora.

Araklia, Iraklia Sensational sea views and creative Cycladic fare in a lively atmosphere.

Surfin Bird, Iraklia Favourite chilled-out cocktail bar and accompanying restaurant overlooking mountains and Livadi Beach.

Ancient Art from THE CYCLADES

01 Akrotiri frescoes

Spectacular Minoan frescoes from the prehistoric settlement of Ancient Akrotiri on Santorini (Thira) were discovered protected under ashes from a 16th-century eruption.

02 Cycladic figurine

These mysterious minimalist marble statues dating from 3000 BCE to 2000 BCE inspired many 20th-century artists, such as Picasso and Modigliani.

03 Lions of Delos

The terrace facing the Sacred Lake at Ancient Delos was lined with nine to 19 (the number is unknown) stone lions, guarding the way.

04 Mosaic from the House of the Dolphins

One of Delos' grandest houses contained this well-preserved mosaic with youths riding dolphins in each corner.

05 Venus de Milo

That's Aphrodite to you! The island of Milos' most celebrated export, the *Venus de Milo* sculpture, is now far away in the Louvre.

06 Golden ibex

This glowing pure-gold ibex from Akrotiri was hand-crafted in the 17th century BCE and now sparkles at the Museum of Prehistoric Thera.

07 Kouros of Naxos

One of Naxos' three fallen *kouroi* – marble statues of youths left in quarries, damaged and discarded millennia ago.

08 Nike of Samothrace

Winged *Nike* was discovered on the north-eastern Aegean island of Samothraki, but she was crafted of Parian marble, like many masterpieces of her time.

09 Nike of Delos

A stylised contrast to her sister from Samothraki, the 570 BCE *Nike from Delos* was carved by a sculptor from Chios.

10 Mykonos vase

This giant 7th-century BCE pithos has one of the earliest depictions of the Trojan horse story from Homer's *Iliad*.

Wines of the Islands

ENJOY THE FRUITS OF AEGEAN VINEYARDS

Rich reds and bright whites, the wines of Greece have come a long way since they were quaffed on the knee of Dionysos. The Cyclades make some excellent wines, right up with those from other regions of Greece. Local cafes and tavernas always have a few examples ready to pour.

Left and right Santorini vineyards
Centre Chrysoloras Winery, Serifos

KYELLOW PHOTO/SHUTTERSTOCK ©

Santorini

Beyond caldera views, infinity pools and black-sand beaches, Santorini has become a magnet for oenophiles, drawn to the island by its reputation for excellent wine (p191). Santorini is blessed with a dry volcanic microclimate and wine culture here goes back millennia. The island's existing vines are Europe's oldest, impervious to the phylloxera bug that wiped out most of the continent's vines in the late 19th century. Grapes are grown close to the ground, in a *kouloura* (nest) of vines to make the most of the moisture and protect the grapes from fierce winds, while also inhibiting the spread of infestations and disease.

Santorini's most lauded wine is the crisp, dry white *asyrtiko*, as well as the amber-coloured, unfortified dessert wine known as Vinsanto (it must be made from at least 51% *asyrtiko*, plus *aidani* and *athiri* in order to qualify). Both wines are made from the heritage-protected, indigenous grape variety *asyrtiko*, as is Nykteri (*asyrtiko* made at night). *Asyrtiko* grapes are grown across the Cyclades, but the Santorini variety stands out in terms of unique flavour. You'll also come across *mavrotragano* (full-bodied red) and *mandilaria* (medium-bodied red).

Paros

Paros is a rich agricultural island, with much food – from olives to figs, citrus and potatoes – grown here, and the vineyards yield increasingly interesting wines.

Near Naoussa, pressing grapes since 1910, the Moraitis family has it down to a fine art. Sidle up to the Moraitis Winery bar for a taste. Their bestseller is the Paros White,

ALEXANDROS MICHAILIDIS/SHUTTERSTOCK ©

TRAMONT_ANA/SHUTTERSTOCK ©

made with the island's indigenous grape, *monemvasia,* also used to make the Malvasia dessert wine. They also have Moraitis Vinothéque in Naoussa proper.

The new kid on the block is Domaine Myrsini in the south of the island, where a Nantes native and her husband have just started pressing their own Parian wine. They can give tastings outside the harvest season (August), when they are busy pulling in the grapes.

> Santorini is blessed with a dry volcanic microclimate and wine culture here goes back millennia.

Other Islands

In the hills above Platys Gialos on arid and rocky Serifos, Chrysoloras Winery is now making some good organic whites. It uses grapes that are right at home in the Cyclades: *serifiotiko, mandilaria, monemvasia* and *asyrtiko*.

In Arnados on Tinos, Ballis Tinos Winery creates wines in a medieval style using grapes from the surrounding vineyards. Famous for all manner of food, Tinos is lusher than many Cycladic islands, so grapes that like it wet do well here.

On Naxos, visit Saint Anna Winery in a lush, olive-grove-draped valley with lovely historic walking paths between Ano and Kato Potamia villages.

Milos isn't known only for its ring of beaches – it also has a growing wine rep thanks to Kostantakis Cave Winery. A relative newcomer, it has rescued vineyards that had been neglected for 40 years. Its wines age in naturally formed caves near the beach town of Pollonia.

Greek Grape Varieties

Greece's wine industry benefits from some age-old indigenous varietals with unique character. The contemporary generation of winemakers is producing great, award-winning wines from Greece's premier wine regions, including the Cyclades.

Greek white varieties include *moschofilero*, *asyrtiko*, *athiri*, *roditis*, *robola* and *savatiano*. The most popular reds include *xinomavro*, *agiorgitiko* and *kotsifali*.

Retsina (white wine flavoured with the resin of pine trees) became popular in the 1960s and is what many visitors associate with Greek wine, given its prevalence in Greek restaurants worldwide. It's something of an acquired taste but some winemakers produce a smoother, modern version.

Listings

BEST OF THE REST

Seafront Tavernas

Armeni €€

With the seashore at your table, this gem of a taverna is worth the steep descent from Santorini's Oia to sup at the altar of seafood with a short, brilliantly executed menu.

Halaris Ouzerie €

Harbourfront in Paros' Piso Livadi, this seafood-taverna-cum-*ouzerie* is ideal for small plates of creative seafood and salads for the quintessential long lunch.

Captain Pipino's €

A highlight of a day at Antiparos' beaches is lunch at Captain Pipino's. You may need to wait for a table at this gloriously old-school fish taverna with panoramas of uninhabited Despotiko island.

To Steki €€

Excellent traditional taverna on Sifnos' Platys Gialos waterfront, with tables on a tree-shaded stone terrace.

Medusa Taverna €€

In the fishing harbour of Mandrakia on Milos, village ladies cook at this fabulous taverna. The views are killer, so get there early to be sure of getting a table.

Village Eats & Plateia Cafes

Symposium €

Parikia in Paros contains inviting village cafes, but none so much as Symposium. Under a massive bougainvillea, it serves delicious light meals with jazz and classical music.

Tereza €€

This renowned lunch stop is hidden amid the maze of lanes in pint-size Myrsini. Once a tiny old market, it now serves stupendous lunches.

To Krinaki €€

Slip away from Santorini's caldera edge to the traditional hamlet of Finikia, where chef Elvis sources and combines local produce to delicious effect at this sweet, small restaurant.

Doukato €€

Reserve a table at this always-jammed former monastery on Naxos, now a courtyard filled with happy eaters of specialities like *kalogeras* (beef, eggplant and cheese).

O Rokos Myrsini €€

Perfect taverna meals on a terrace amid trees in Volax on Tinos. Follow a cobblestoned lane to the entrance and enjoy fine hillside views.

Hidden Beaches

Pori Beach

Koufonisia's broad scoop of Pori Bay is a gorgeous swirl of blues and a favourite yachtie

Cove on Milos

anchorage. Alongside the Ksylompatis Sea Caves, it's around the corner from Piscina, a literal swimming hole in the cliffs.

Firiplaka

On Milos, Firiplaka has a stunning cliff-backed setting with a hodgepodge of dirt parking areas above a series of tiny coves. The larger main beach is covered by loungers from a stylish club.

Hawaii Beach

This wee baylet on Naxos' west coast is aptly named for its iridescent cerulean waters and is backed by tawny rock formations and cliffs.

Fokos Beach

This Mykonos beach is never busy and attracts a laid-back crowd all summer. A short jaunt around the headland to the east, Mersini is easily the quietest beach on Mykonos.

Active Outings

Atlantis Oia

Santorini's underwater topography is no less spectacular than the land above. Atlantis Oia, a member of Cousteau Divers with a stellar record in marine conservation, will take you there.

G3 Boats

In Paros, this outfit is run by affable Georgios, who will take you zooming across the water to Antiparos' sea caves, a deserted island with ancient ruins or even to Mykonos.

Naxos Kitelife

One of three excellent operators in the Naxos' windsurfing capital, Mikri Vigla, it will train or outfit you for kitesurfing and kite foiling.

Monasteries & Museums

Museum of Prehistoric Thera

This standout museum in Fira, Santorini, houses extraordinary finds excavated from

KAVALENKAVA/SHUTTERSTOCK ©

Panagia Paraportiani

Ancient Akrotiri. Examine the wealth of Minoan frescoes and the glowing gold ibex figurine, dating from the 17th century BCE.

Panagia Paraportiani

Mykonos' landmark whitewashed church looks like it's grown organically from the rock. Built between the 15th and 17th centuries, it's one of 70 Hora churches hiding in plain sight.

Museum of Marble Crafts

A short walk uphill from the village of Pyrgos on Tinos, this outstanding, modern complex creatively explains the island's centuries of marble quarrying and sculpting techniques.

Sanctuary of Poseidon & Amphitrite

On Tinos, this ancient site offers an engrossing look at the classical Greek era. From the 4th century BCE to the 3rd century CE, this was a major religious sanctuary.

Moni Chrysopigi

Perched on an islet off Sifnos and connected to the shore by a stone footbridge, this whitewashed monastery with divine sea views is considered the protector of the island.

Scan to find more things to do in the Cyclades.

DODECANESE

CULTURE | HISTORY | NATURE

Experience Dodecanese online

Experience your own vision in the **Cave of the Apocalypse** on Patmos (p232)
15mins from Skala

Enjoy the sweeping sea views from the **Pandeli Castle** on Leros (p230)
12mins from Leros port

Try out an ancient sponge-diving suit on **Kalymnos** (p224)
day trip from Pothia harbour

DODECANESE
Trip Builder

Often referred to as a bridge between Europe and the Middle East, the Dodecanese islands are scattered in the southeastern Aegean hugging the Turkish coast. This has contributed to their multifaceted past, visible in the islands' architecture and gastronomy, yet Greek traditions continue to thrive.

Discover Greek traditions still maintained in **Olymbos** mountain village (p220)
1½hrs from Pigadia port

TURKEY

Yenihisar (Didim)

See where Hippocrates taught medicine under the **Plane Tree** on Kos (p233)

7mins from Kos Town port

Yatağan

Yalikavak

Bodrum

Turgutreis

Pserimos

Mastihari

Kos Town

Kos

Kardamena

Spend the day on the Venetian-flavoured island of **Symi** (p228)

1hr from Rhodes

Marmaris

Datça

Mandraki

Gialos

Symi

Nisyros

Travel back to medieval times in **Rhodes Old Town** (p218)

20mins from Diagoras Airport

Kastellorizo (See Inset; 60km)

Tilos

Livadia

Swim and dolphin-spot at the uninhabited islands of **Makri**, **Stroggili** and **Alimia** (p222)

day trip from Skala Kamirou, Rhodes

Alimia

Skala Kamirou

Emborios

Halki

Rhodes

Laerma

Monolithos

Lindos

Kastellorizo

Karpathian Sea

Kattavia

See unique stone carvings and meet their creator on **Kastellorizo** (p226)

3½hrs from Rhodes

Argos

Saria

Diafani

Take in the breathtaking scenery from the **Acropolis of Lindos** on Rhodes (p232)

45mins from Rhodes Town

Karpathos

Pigadia

Practicalities

LAZAROS PAPANDREOU/SHUTTERSTOCK ©

ARRIVING

Airports The most well-known islands, Rhodes and Kos, have airports with flights from several European destinations plus the Greek mainland. Some smaller islands have domestic airports.

Boats Athens' Piraeus port serves the main islands by ferry. Journey times can be up to 12 hours; onward trips to smaller islands might require a change. Buy tickets online or at the port. Mamaris in Turkey has a catamaran service to Rhodes, while Bodrum in Turkey serves Kos.

HOW MUCH FOR A

Souvlaki from €3

Greek salad from €8

Mythos beer from €2.30

WHEN TO GO

DEC–FEB
Coldest and wettest months. Not much open, very quiet.

MAR–MAY
Starting to heat up; the outdoor cafes come alive.

JUN–AUG
Hottest months; very busy. *Meltemi* wind blows from July.

SEP–NOV
Best time. Warm days and seas; the crowds gone.

GETTING AROUND

Boat The best way to travel between all the Dodecanese islands is by ferry or catamaran. Tickets can be bought online from the main companies, or at the harbours. Note that ferry services can be pretty sporadic, especially in July and August when the *meltemi* wind blows heavily in the Aegean Sea.

Car The best way to see the islands once there is to hire a car. Public transport services can be few and far between. Driving is a great way to explore hidden coves and visit out-of-the-way places.

Air Some of the smaller islands have domestic airports, making connecting by plane possible.

EATING & DRINKING

Each island in the Dodecanese has its own specialities stemming from traditional practices and the rich cultural heritage that combined make a unique regional cuisine. Expect delicacies such as *pitaroudia* (chickpea fritters) found in Rhodes. Symi is rich in fish, especially squid which is served with wild greens. Karpathos, a more agricultural island, produces its own *makarounes* – homemade pasta served with sautéed onions and local *myzithra* (sheep's-milk cheese).

Must-try meze Haihoutes *kafeneio*, Kos island (p233)

Best ice cream Davinci Gelato, Rhodes Old Town (p219)

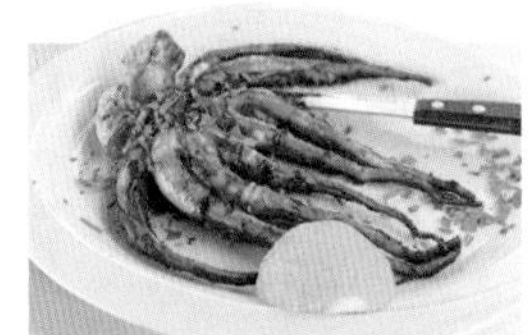

CONNECT & FIND YOUR WAY

Wi-fi All good hotels, cafes and restaurants offer free wi-fi. Some bigger islands have free wi-fi at ports and airports. As the islands are so close to Turkey, in roaming your phone might be prone to alternating between a Greek and Turkish mobile service.

Navigation Google Maps is useful when driving to remote beaches and villages or walking through the narrow streets of the old towns.

WHERE TO STAY

These islands are popular with tourists and offer a range of accommodation reflecting that; from island-hopping to staying put, there are options from budget to boutique. Prices are determined by season.

Island	Pro/Con
Rhodes & Kos	The two biggest islands both offer a choice of package-holiday hotels, cosy family-run establishments and boutique glory.
Symi	More romantic architecture makes it an attractive option for couples, with accommodation to reflect this.
Kalymnos	Most accommodation located at the port, with budget options found above tavernas.
Kastellorizo	Small island nearer Turkey and harder to reach, which makes it more pricey with mainly boutique options.

ANCIENT SITES

The Dodecanese offer a plethora of historic and archaeological sites to visit (some are even free) such as the Acropolis of Lindos on Rhodes or Asklepieion on Kos.

MONEY

Most places accept credit cards. Carry some euros with you to buy street food or for small souvenirs.

44 Knight's RESIDENCE

LUXURY | CULTURE | HISTORY

Ruled by the Knights of St John in the 14th century, medieval Rhodes Town has fortresses, gates and more than 200 labyrinthine streets and cobbled alleyways. The Old Town throngs with activity, making it an atmospheric, living Unesco World Heritage Site. Tucked down one of the twisting alleyways, Kókkini Porta Rossa is a former knight's residence offering a luxurious stay.

NEJDET DUZEN/SHUTTERSTOCK ©

How to

Getting here Fly into Rhodes or arrive by ferry. Kókkini Porta Rossa is located within the Old Town walls, about 120m behind St John's Gate. Taxis and rental cars drop you off just by the gate.

When to go The hotel usually opens its doors from April until October. The best times to visit are September and October, when the school holidays are over and it's still warm.

How much The cost varies over the year, from €375 a night. Check the website for deals (kokkini porta.com).

JAKUB RUTKIEWICZ/SHUTTERSTOCK ©

ENGINEERVOSHKIN/SHUTTERSTOCK ©

Far left Palace of the Grand Master
Bottom left Street of the Knights
Above left Rhodes Old Town

Knights' Quarter Essentially an occupying army, the Knights of St John (established during the Crusades) ruled the island from 1309 until 1522 and transformed the northern segment of the Old Town to create what's known today as the Knights' Quarter. Taking care to protect themselves from the local population as well as potential invaders, the knights erected mighty fortress-like mansions as well as a fortified palace.

Turbulent history The name Kókkini Porta Rossa ('red door') was inspired by St John's Gate, where the hotel is located. Also known as the Red Gate, it commemorates the knights who defended the city during the Ottoman siege. The once-derelict knight's residence with a small church opposite was restored by a family intent on showcasing Rhodes Town's past. The owners fell in love with its history and original inhabitants, so each individual suite is named after a former occupier to honour that heritage.

Sleep like a knight More than just a luxury place to stay within a unique setting of the Old Town walls, the residence presents the locals' view of Greece to visitors through history and culture. There are six suites, each one with distinct features – from a *hayat* (Turkish for 'living') and a covered wooden balcony overlooking the castle walls in one, to a small, walled private garden with an outdoor deep-soak tub in another, it's a step back in time.

Rhodes Town Gems

From Akandia Gate, turn right to find the 15th-century **Agios Panteleimon** church on Kisthiniou. It's one of the few that escaped conversion into a mosque during the Ottoman years. A walk up the **Street of the Knights** leads past seven medieval inns representing the countries the knights were from, ending at the **Palace of the Grand Master**. You must visit the **Walk Inn** on Plateia Dorieos. All the locals of the Old Town feel like one big family here, and Sokratous (the main shopping street) has a great ice-cream parlour, **Davinci Gelato**.

■ **By Lena Sidoroff,** *owner of Sidoroff Atelier in Rhodes Town*
@sidoroff_atelier_arts

45 Traditional VILLAGE

TRADITION | WALKING TOUR | FOOD

In the mountain village of Olymbos on Karpathos island, the women choose to maintain its heritage by wearing the vividly coloured dresses, stunning hand-spun jackets and floral headgear of its past. You can explore this place of proud traditions, pastel-hued architecture and spellbinding views with a walking tour, followed by the opportunity to cook with the locals.

NIBAPHOTO/SHUTTERSTOCK ©

How to

Getting here/around Karpathos has a domestic airport. Pigadia port is linked to Dodecanese islands and Piraeus. The nearest port to Olymbos is Diafani, serviced once weekly by ferry. Car hire is ideal, but be warned – Olymbos is reached via a hairpin road with sheer drops. Many visitors bus from Diafani instead.

When to go In summer, arrive in late afternoon or early morning to have the place to yourself.

Village music Keep an ear out for impromptu *mantinades* (improvised songs played on folk instruments).

MRGB/SHUTTERSTOCK ©

MATT MUNRO/LONELY PLANET ©

Far left Women in traditional dress for an Olymbos festival
Bottom left Centre of Olymbos
Above left The colourful houses of Olymbos

The second-largest island in the Dodecanese, Karpathos has wild mountains with cloud-wrapped villages, offering the opportunity to combine a beach and mountain holiday.

A historic village Founded in Byzantine times, Olymbos served as a refuge from invading pirates. Being so far from anywhere else on the island, and with poor infrastructure, for centuries the village was extremely isolated. Its inhabitants still speak a unique dialect (with traces of ancient Dorian Greek) and have their own traditional dress, crafts and music. In modern times the infrastructure improved, opening this remote hamlet to the outside world, yet the locals are proud of their heritage and still maintain their culture and cuisine.

Walking and culinary tour A great way to experience the best of Olymbos is with Evangelia (ecotourim-karpathos.com), a local who will meet you at the main entrance of the village and take you on an easy stroll to observe its architecture. It's not your imagined blue and white typical of many Greek islands – rather, the houses feature a variety of colours. There are also churches with many icons, windmills dotting the landscape and the remains of a castle. You'll learn about Olymbos' long history and why it likes to keep its traditions alive. Afterwards you have the opportunity to take part in cooking with the villagers. Make local bread and the traditional *makarounes* of Karpathos – pasta sprinkled with *myzithra* (cheese made from sheep's or goat's milk) and sautéed onions.

Karpathos' Pristine North

Karpathos is the ideal island for travellers who are looking for the authentic Greek spirit, as it's largely untouched by mass tourism.

Although it's hard to reach, don't let this put you off visiting the northern part of the island and especially the village of Olymbos, where the beautiful nature, the traditional flavours and the warm hospitality of the locals will turn your holiday into an unforgettable experience.

Spring is the best time to visit, with many wildflowers, wild herbs and vegetables growing in the fields. It's fun to pick these with our guests.

■ **By Evangelia Marina Agapiou,** *founder of Ecotourism Karpathos @karpathoseco tourism*

46 Islands & DOLPHINS

BOAT TRIP | MARINE LIFE | SNORKELLING

More than a boat tour, a unique marine-biology day cruise in the Dodecanese allows you to take in the rich marine life of the Aegean Sea in an educational yet fun way. Visiting three little-known, uninhabited islets west of Rhodes – Makri, Stroggili and Alimia – you'll get to swim in crystal-clear waters and possibly spot dolphins, seals and tuna.

JAROSLAV MORAVCIK/SHUTTERSTOCK ©

How to

Getting there The tour leaves from Skala Kamirou harbour in Rhodes; it's possible to get picked up from your accommodation. Note that a minimum of six people is required for the tour to run.

When to go September and October are the best months, as the waters have had all summer to heat up.

Try scuba For an extra cost, you can try scuba diving with an expert instructor – no previous experience necessary (blutopia.gr).

GIOVANNI RINALDI/SHUTTERSTOCK ©

Learn from an expert This full-day trip is run by a marine biologist who is proud of the marine life, flora and fauna of these waters and keen to enthuse others. The waters in this region are extremely clean, which has allowed the local ecosystem to flourish and encouraged large sea mammals such as dolphins, seals and tuna. Enjoy your time at sea, safe in the knowledge you're gaining environmental awareness first-hand.

Three unique Greek islands The tiny islands of **Makri**, **Stroggili** and **Alimia** are uninhabited and completely untouched by tourism – the perfect place to snorkel and dive among the marine life. Alimia, in particular, gives you the opportunity to not just have a swim but also explore the ruins of a once-flourishing old city, inhabited from antiquity until the 1970s. After your swim and exploration, enjoy snacks on board.

Visit an eco-island Round off the day with a visit to **Halki**. This former sponge-diving island with many colourful Italianate mansions was chosen as the first GR-eco Island by a national initiative. Green policies include renewable energy sources (allowing the island to be independent from the national grid) and electric public-service vehicles. Halki is also investing in strong 5G to attract digital nomads. Swim in **Cyclops Bay** and enjoy a seafood lunch at a taverna along the waterfront.

Top Halki
Bottom Alimia

The Good Harbour

Alimia island is only 8 sq km and 20 nautical miles from Rhodes. It has the ruins of an old city, inhabited up to 1970. You'll find four abandoned buildings originally used by the Italians during WWII, an old **Commander's House**, medieval castle and the **Agios Minas** church.

The **Agios Giorgos** monastery has been restored and is offered as a refuge for fishermen. Today only one man resides there, the person who helps with the upkeep of the church, plus his goats and sheep.

Alimia in ancient Greek means 'Good Harbour' because the island is completely protected against the winds. Due to this sheltered position, the old Fleet of Rhodes used to rest its ships there.

By Savvas Chatzinikolaou, *owner of Blutopia Marine Park*
@Blutopia_Rhodes

The Real Sponge DIVERS

TRADITION | BOAT TRIP | SPONGE DIVING

Since antiquity, Kalymnos was renowned as the centre of the Greek sponge-diving trade, which helped the island to prosper economically. Visit the unique sponge museum in the harbour that proudly showcases this heritage, and take a day trip at sea to snorkel and see a demonstration of how the *skafandro* (ancient diving suit with helmet) was once used.

MARCIN KRZYZAK/SHUTTERSTOCK ©

How to

Getting there Kalymnos is quite remote but has a small domestic airport. You can fly from Athens via Kos or Rhodes, or take the ferry from Piraeus (about 11 hours) or a shorter ferry from Kos or Rhodes.

When to go Summer is a good time for this activity, but busy. September is better as there are fewer crowds, yet the water is still warm.

Diving suit from antiquity This is a rare opportunity to see the original diving suit, and possibly even experience it yourself if you're a professional diver.

ZAFERKIZILKAYA/SHUTTERSTOCK ©

Far left Vintage diving suit
Bottom left Rabbitfish and sponges, Kalymnos
Above left Fisherman, Pothia

The waters of the southeastern Aegean Sea were perfect breeding grounds for the best sponges, helping cement Kalymnos as the centre of the Mediterranean sponge trade. The very first divers used the 'skin-diving' technique: sponges on the sea bed would be located from the surface by boat, then the diver would go naked into the sea clutching a *skandalopetra* – a flat stone weighing roughly 15kg to help them sink faster. They could dive to a depth of 30m, staying three to five minutes underwater to collect sponges with a special net.

The year 1865 saw the original diving suit introduced – the *skafandro,* covering the entire body and accompanied by a huge helmet. It looked like an astronaut's suit and allowed divers to go to greater depths such as 70m. This saw the industry really take off, as many fleets of ships would travel with several sponge divers on board. But undertaking many dives daily at such depths was dangerous, and many divers suffered terrible injuries before decompression sickness was understood. On the waterfront in Pothia, the **Nautical & Folklore Museum** focuses on sponge diving, with displays of the mighty stone weights used by ancient divers and haunting photos of the 20th-century divers in *skafandro* suits.

The *skafandro* is no longer used, but a boat trip with **Kalymnos Diving Club** (kalymnosdiving.com) or **Kalymnos Experience** (kalymnosexperience.gr) allows you to swim and even try out the original suit at an appropriate depth. It's also possible to snorkel, and you might get a chance to spot dolphins.

Diving Lessons

Sponge colonies across the Mediterranean have been devastated due to destructive diseases. While Kalymnos' sponge-fishing heyday is long past, it's one of the rare places where it's possible to see how the original suits were used.

The owner of Kalymnos Diving Club, **Dimitris Nystazos** is a diving instructor coming from a long family line of sponge fishers and is keen to impart his passion to guests. He is currently the only diver that demonstrates the use of the traditional *skafandro*. A certified instructor with professional diving experience, Dimitris has also taken part in endeavours such as surfacing sunken vessels and repairing parts of vessels underwater.

48 Unique Stone CARVINGS

ART | ROCK CARVINGS | SPIRITUALITY

As you sail into the harbour of the tiny Greek island of Kastellorizo, a stone's throw from the Turkish coast, you'll not only gasp at the colourful stately mansions seemingly rising from the sea – take a look to your right and you can't fail to notice the unique carvings in the rock face just past the Megisti Hotel.

FOXYS FOREST MANUFACTURE/SHUTTERSTOCK ©

How to

Getting there Tiny Kastellorizo (9 sq km) has an equally small domestic airport with flights from Athens via Kos and Rhodes. A ferry from Piraeus takes a long 21 hours; book a cabin.

When to go Any time of year is a good time to visit. The sculptures are on public land, and from April to October you might also find the artist himself on the island.

Look across to Turkey Kastellorizo is only 2km from the nearest Turkish port of Kaş, hence the presence of the Greek coast guard.

MILTON LOUIZ/SHUTTERSTOCK ©

NEJDET DUZEN/SHUTTERSTOCK ©

Far left Kastellorizo coast
Bottom left Blue Cave
Left Knights of St John Castle

Known locally as 'The Barefoot Sculptor', **Alexandros Zigouris** has been coming to Kastellorizo island for over 40 years. Originally from Preveza in mainland Greece, he first stepped foot here in 1979 during his travels. The locals welcomed him and he's been returning ever since during the summer, when the weather is warm enough for him to sleep outside in his tent. He prefers to walk barefoot and be in touch with the earth, literally.

Alexandros' artworks feature Greek gods, mythological figures and interpretation of phrases from Greek antiquity. He creates both 'mobile' sculptures, carved from marble, and 'immobile' works – those sculpted into the limestone rock just outside his workshop. It's the latter you'll spot on the right-hand side as the ferry glides into the port, or while you walk along the path at the harbour just past the Megisti Hotel. Free to visit, the workshop is in the old petrol warehouse at the entrance to the port, which was gifted to the artist by the municipality. It's a small whitewashed building, almost church-like in its appearance. Alexandros works only with hand tools – hammer, chisel and awl – which makes the intricacies of his work even more amazing, especially considering that he's self-taught.

It's an ongoing project that Alexandros continues to improve. You may get lucky if you visit in summer and see the artist at work. He welcomes visitors, but his creative work requires peace – be respectful of this.

Enjoying Kastellorizo

This far-flung island is insanely pretty. Sailing into its one village, past the ruined **Knights of St John Castle** (with splendid views of Turkey) and neoclassical houses huddled around the turquoise bay, is soul-enriching.

And while it may lack powder-fine beaches, there are bathing platforms with ladders into the ocean and satellite idylls reached by boat.

Venture up 400 zigzagging steps behind the village, and you'll be rewarded with a plateau, on which is a former monastery and the **Paleokastro** (old town and fortress).

Located on Kastellorizo's remote southeast shore, the extraordinary **Blue Cave** is famous for its mirror-like blue water. Take a water taxi from Kastellorizo; it's a 45-minute experience including the journey there and back.

49 Venetian-Style ISLAND GEM

DAY TRIP | BEACHES | MONASTERIES

Board the early-morning ferry from Rhodes and head out to the gorgeous Italianate Greek island of Symi. The neoclassical architecture comes into view upon entering the harbour, with houses seemingly tumbling from the hills into the sea, so grab your camera.

VALSIB/SHUTTERSTOCK ©

How to

Getting there/around Dodecanese Seaways (12ne.gr) operates day trips from Rhodes, or daily ferries if you want to stay the night. During the summer season, the beaches have water taxis connecting them.

When to go Summer is hot and crowded. September and October are less so, yet still warm enough to swim.

Saving water The water is shipped in, so be sure to use it sparingly. Don't drink tap water.

Magic Symi

People come to Symi for the crystal waters and stunning architecture. What brings them back is the small community. Strike up a conversation in any *kafeneio* (coffee house); people love to offer tips. Head to peaceful **Agios Emilianos** or magical **Roukoniotis** monasteries for take-your-breath-away moments.

■ **By Andrew Davies,** *owner of Old Markets on Symi @TheOldMarkets*

05 The island's houses and mansions are a riot of colour. Sunset in **Symi harbour** is the best time to see these colours come to life.

01 From the harbour to the hilltop village of Horio is a climb of 500 steps, known as the **Kali Strata**. Take your time and enjoy the wonderful sea views.

03 Tucked away up the Kali Strata, the quaint **Archaeological Museum** offers great insights into the island's rich past and its unique architectural style.

04 Symi isn't short of beautiful bays and coves. **Pedi Beach** is pebbly with umbrellas and sunbeds; a little further is quieter **Agios Nikolaos** with a small taverna.

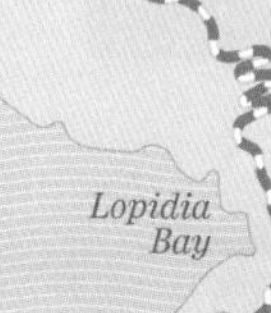

02 **Moni Taxiarhou Mihail Panormiti** (pictured left) is an 18th-century monastery in the village of Panormitis. It's worth visiting, even if locals think it's overrated.

Hondros
Platy
Oxia
Nimborios Gulf
Gialos
Horio
Pedi
Pedi Beach
Agios Nikolaos Beach
Symi
Gulf of Agios Vasilios
Lopidia Bay
Panormitis
Aegean Sea
Sesklion Islet
Strongylos
0 2 km
0 1 mile

CLOCKWISE FROM LEFT: THIRASIA/SHUTTERSTOCK ©, LALS STOCK/SHUTTERSTOCK ©, LUBOS K/SHUTTERSTOCK ©

Windmills & Castles of the DODECANESE

01 Windmills of Leros

Near the Pandeli Castle with sweeping sea views, these five restored windmills give a flavour of past island life. Now it's possible to stay in some.

02 Mandraki Harbour

These three famous 14th-century windmills, which also served as fortification towers, are the first you'll encounter as you enter Rhodes port.

03 Windmills of Patmos

Three island icons visible from the harbour and set on a hillside near Mili. One is now a museum, one generates electricity and the third, water.

04 Pandeli Castle, Leros

Known as the Castle of Our Lady after the Virgin Mary, this intact Byzantine castle is a trademark of Leros island and offers breath-taking sea views.

05 Windmills of Astypalea

Eight restored windmills, known as *xetrocharis,* sit above the town of Skala. Their sails and roof move, and they were once used for milling grain.

06 Palace of the Grand Master, Rhodes Town

An example of Gothic architecture, this 14th-century building underwent a massive restoration under Italian rule in 1937 and is a living museum with a huge courtyard.

07 Kastro, Astypalea

Sitting atop a hill of the old settlement of Hora, Astypalea's Venetian castle was built as a shelter against pirates and still stands guard over the island.

08 Neratzia Castle, Kos Town

This 14th-century castle, built by the Knights of St John, dominates the Kos harbour. Its name means 'bitter orange', referencing the trees that once grew in its vicinity.

09 Windmills of Olymbos, Karpathos

Probably the most iconic image of this remote mountain village – dozens are scattered around, some derelict, others restored into restaurants.

Listings

BEST OF THE REST

Historical Highlights

Acropolis of Lindos, Rhodes

Atop a steep cliff in the fishing village of Lindos (just over an hour's drive from Rhodes Old Town) sits the ancient Acropolis, dating back to the 4th century BCE. Wear sturdy shoes.

Asklepieion, Kos

This ancient healing centre and school, 3.5km from Kos Town, was built in the 3rd century BCE to honour Asclepius, the god of health and medicine.

Cave of the Apocalypse, Patmos

Enclosed within an 11th-century chapel, this is where St John is reputed to have rested his head and experienced the vision resulting in the Book of Revelations.

Church of Panagia tou Harou, Lipsi

The Church of the Virgin Mary of Death on this tiny island was built in 1600 by the monks from Patmos. Each year on 22 August, visitors flock to pay homage to its famous icon of the Virgin.

Pristine Beaches

St Paul's Bay, Rhodes

Spend a day on this quiet, sandy beach nestled in Lindos and home to the small St Paul's Chapel. With sunbeds and umbrellas, it's perfect for families.

Therma Loutra, Kos

Combine a swim in the clear waters at this black pebbly beach, famous for its volcanic rock, with a therapeutic natural spa in its open spring. It's near Kos Town.

Kyra Panagia, Karpathos

This secluded stretch of fine sand on Karpathos' east coast has blue waters rivalling those of the Caribbean. Also visit the church of the Virgin Mary that overlooks it.

Agia Marina, Symi

Symi is perhaps less known for its beaches but the sandy Agia Marina, accessible by water taxi from the harbour and watched over by a small church, is beautiful.

Eristos Beach, Tilos

With long pink-grey sand, Eristos is popular with locals and tourists. Swim over a reef to reach open water; the south end of the beach is nudist.

Natural Wonders

Nisyros Volcano

The whole island is a geological wonder, formed by several volcanic eruptions. Visit the hydrothermal, puffing crater named Stefanos at its centre, one of the largest in the world.

Nisyros Volcano

Petaloudes Valley, Rhodes

About 10km from Rhodes airport and you're in another world – a natural protected park of sweet gum trees, attracting thousands of tiger moths every May.

Harkadio Cave, Tilos

This tiny Dodecanese island had dwarf elephants roaming it in the Neolithic period. Head to this cave, southeast of Megalo Horio, to see their fossilised bones and other finds from this period.

Hippocrates' Plane Tree, Kos

Sit under the 2500-year-old plane tree where Hippocrates is said to have sat to teach medicine to his students and examine his patients. It's one of the oldest trees in Europe.

 Outdoor Activities

Kalymnos

The quality of the limestone rocks and sheer crags on this island make Kalymnos a favourite for many professional rock climbers, who come from all over the world.

Rhodes

Fox, deer and the spooky ruins of the abandoned summer residence of Mussolini await you on Mt Profitis Ilias (797m) in inland Rhodes. A great alternative to the beach.

Karpathos

Head to the southern side of Karpathos if you're an adrenaline junkie looking to wind- or kite-surf, and even to learn. The strong *meltemi* summer winds create the perfect conditions.

Symi

Walkers love Symi off-season for its unofficial paths, or *kalderimia* – old cobblestoned donkey tracks and goat paths going to several monasteries and Symi's highest point, Mt Vigla (616m).

Kalymnos

 Unique Villages

Agios Dimitrios, Kos

This eerie village in the Dikeos mountains, abandoned since the 1960s, has crumbling houses and a church. The dilapidated Haihoutes *kafeneio* now offers a substantial menu for visitors and walkers.

Panagia, Kasos

Panagia on tiny Kasos is a throwback, with stately homes and Byzantine churches. Visit for the celebration of the Virgin Mary on 15 August in the Church of Pera Panagia.

Lakki, Leros

For unique art deco and moderne Italian architecture, head to Lakki on Leros island. A legacy of Italian occupation, the *razionalismo* style stands in interesting contrast to the rest of the island.

Emborios, Halki

The only settlement on Halki, set at the foot of a mountain, this tiny port has a scattering of Venetian-style mansions in a horseshoe-shaped bay.

Scan to find more things to do in the Dodecanese.

50 Drinking Ouzo ON LESVOS

CULTURE | CUISINE | SOCIAL LIFE

While no drink is more synonymous with Greece than ouzo, on the northeastern Aegean island of Lesvos (Mytilini) it's much more – an expression of land, lifestyle and a rich cultural heritage that reflects a deep connection to Asia Minor.

NEJDET DUZEN/SHUTTERSTOCK ©

How to

Getting here/around Daily flights connect Mytilini Town with Athens. Ferries leave from Athens and the northern ports of Thessaloniki and Kavala. It's a large island; buses go to most places, but you might want a car to get around.

How much? Ouzo with a couple of simple mezedhes costs little more than a cocktail or two.

Pack some binoculars Between permanent avian residents and migrating visitors, more than 300 species can be spotted among Lesvos' diverse biotopes (lesvosbirds.gr).

YIANNISSCHEIDT/SHUTTERSTOCK ©

Ouzo & Lesvos

Ouzo may be ubiquitous all over Greece, but the North Aegean is its heartland. Lesvos has 17 distilleries and a total of 44 different labels, among them some of the most popular bottles in Greece and abroad. But its story goes much deeper than that: ouzo reveals the island's soul.

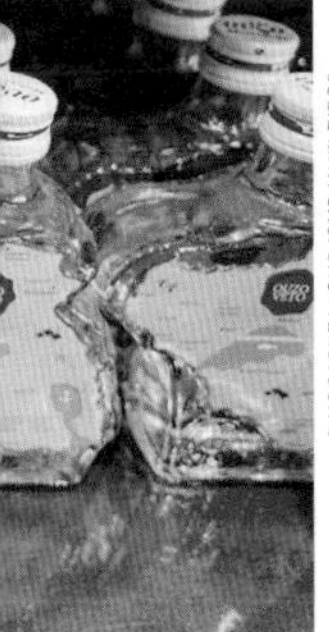

JULIE MAYFENG/SHUTTERSTOCK ©

Related to arak and raki, ouzo is part of the cultural heritage of Lesvos, an island populated by the descendants of Greek refugees from Asia Minor. It captures the scent of the island, with its signature note distilled from the famously fragrant wild anise that grows around **Lisvorio**. It also suits the island's palate; ouzo's delicate sweetness is the ideal counterpoint to the briny thrill of fresh fish and seafood. But most of all, the way locals enjoy ouzo on Lesvos is an expression of their

Bring Your Bathing Suit

Atmospheric Ottoman-era baths and toasty thermal springs offer another way to connect with the island. Of Lesvos' five springs, only **Therma Spa** at the Bay of Gera was open at the time of writing. The others will hopefully reopen soon.

Top left Mytilini Town
Top right Salted sardines from Lesvos
Bottom left Ouzo for sale, Mytilini Town

enviable talent for embracing the moment – a reason in itself to visit.

Ouzo, Mezedhes, Parea

Ouzo is a casual drink enjoyed with refined customs. There's always food – usually mezedhes (a selection of small dishes), but a handful of olives and some *ladotyri* (a sheep's-milk cheese ripened in oil) do very nicely. Much more importantly, ouzo is always enjoyed in the company of friends, known as the *parea*.

Ouzo glasses in the North Aegean are slender and tall, to encourage delicate sips. Adding water softens ouzo's bold flavours and keeps its effects at an enjoyable minimum, extending the pleasures of the moment. While drinking ouzo is a graceful ritual, sharing mezedhes is delightfully anarchic. Replacing a hierarchy of courses, mezedhes are shared communally from the centre of the table.

The ouzo experience centres on connecting the group: people serve their companions

Enjoying Ouzo like a Local

At the picturesque harbour of **Skamioudi**, near Lisvorio (where the anise for ouzo grows), fisherfolk bring in their catch from the Gulf of Kalloni. It's the perfect place for enjoying ouzo.

Add cold water – avoid ice – to your *kanonaki* (the special glasses we use for ouzo on Lesvos).

In cooler months, savour fresh mussels *(chavara)*, clams *(kidonia)* and scallops *(chtenia)*, grilled or raw. In summer, try sashimi, Aegean-style: *papalina* are delicate fresh sardines cured with local salt. Eat while drinking – small sips, small bites.

The essential ingredient: *parea*, or friends to share ouzo with. Toast with *'Eva!'*.

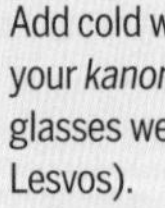

■ **Recommended by Maria Kaplanelli,** *Lesvos Food Fest coordinator @theotheraegean*

first, and everyone raises a glass together to enjoy the first sip. Light-hearted conversation, laughter and lots more toasting follow.

Experiencing the Amanedhes

Lesvos has an eastern soul. Ouzo is a taste of it, and the *amanedhes* its voice. *'Aman, aman!'* – an expression of anguish – lends the deeply emotive genre its name. A repeated rhythmic sequence creates a dreamy, timeless space. Then the song unfolds. Each fluid note slides into the next as they ascend; the vocals of the *amanedhes* share more with the call to prayer of the muezzin than with an aria. You don't need to understand Greek to relate to the depth of feeling; as ouzo brings the soul to fuller expression, so do the *amanedhes*. Its singers are increasingly rare. But with luck, you may find one in the cafes of **Mesotopos** or **Plomari**.

Celebrate Women, Celebrate Love

The works of Sappho, the lyric poet of Lesvos, so evocatively express a passion for women that she's honoured in the word 'lesbian'. In the beach town of **Skala Eresou**, today's lesbians – and indeed everyone – will find a warm welcome. The highlight is the **International Eressos Women's Festival** (womensfestival.eu), combining a spirit of pilgrimage and community with stellar DJs and various activities and events each September.

Far left Greek mezedhes
Below Lesvos street

By Amber Charmei
Amber's favourite aspect of life in Greece is the graceful way locals embrace the beauty of the moment; enjoying ouzo on Lesvos conveys it perfectly.

Practicalities

240

242

244

245

246

248

250

LANGUAGE

252

Right Athens at night

EASY STEPS FROM THE AIRPORT TO THE CITY CENTRE

Most travellers arriving in Greece come through Athens' Eleftherios Venizelos International Airport, located approximately 33km from the city centre (a 30-minute drive). The airport was renovated in 2021, and you'll find a variety of shops, restaurants, cafes and hotels. There are also currency exchange points, ATMs and car rental offices.

AT THE AIRPORT

GIANNIS PAPANIKOS/SHUTTERSTOCK ©

SIM CARDS
Although you can buy Vodafone SIM cards at the airport, they're double the cost of those in the city centre. Cosmote, Vodafone and WIND are the country's major operators; you'll find several branches in every city.

CURRENCY EXCHANGE
There are four Onexchange offices in the airport to change currency. Rates are more or less the same as those at places in the city centre; you can also exchange money in any bank branch.

WI-FI There's free, unlimited and open wi-fi at the airport, including at the taxi pick-up point. Just connect to ATH Free Wi-Fi.

ATMs There are many ATMs across arrivals and departures; all accept foreign Visa and Mastercard cards.

CHARGING STATIONS Charging stations are available at numerous points throughout the airport; they're free and work with EU plug types.

CUSTOMS REGULATIONS
Greece follows Schengen customs regulations. The maximum non-declared monetary allowance is €10,000. For duty-free goods from outside the EU, the maximum allowance per person is 1L of spirits or 2L of wine, and 200 cigarettes or 250g of tobacco.

GETTING TO THE CITY CENTRE

Metro Metro line 3 connects the airport to the city centre (Plateia Syntagmatos) half-hourly from 6.30am to 11.30pm. The journey takes 40 minutes and costs €10 (or €18 return). The station is located across from the airport and connected by a bridge.

Rental car There are two dozen companies with service desks in the arrivals hall. Be sure to book well advance for the best price.

Rideshare You can use either the Uber or TaxiBeat apps. There won't be any difference in cost, as this route is fixed price.

Bus There are four bus routes; tickets can be purchased outside the arrivals hall. Bus X95 takes you to the centre in about 60 minutes, and bus X96 takes you to Piraeus port. Tickets cost €6.

Taxi Queue outside the arrivals hall. Don't let your driver rip you off – airport taxis are a flat rate, with different costs during the day or at night (between midnight and 5am). To the centre it's €40/55, to Piraeus €50/70, and to Rafina port €30/40. You can book taxis in advance through welcomepickups.com. Note that not all taxis accept cards.

OTHER POINTS OF ENTRY

The other major mainland airport is Thessaloniki's Makedonia International Airport. Crete, Santorini, Rhodes, Kos, Corfu and Mykonos all have airports receiving international and chartered flights from Europe.

The majority of ferries for the Cyclades, Dodecanese, northeastern Aegean, Saronic Gulf islands and Crete leave from Greece's busiest port, Piraeus in Athens. Some Cycladic and Sporadic islands are serviced by the Rafina port. Igoumenitsa has boat services to Italy and some of the Ionian Islands, while Alexandroupoli and Kavala ports service some of the harder-to-reach northeastern Aegean Islands. Rhodes and Kos in the Dodecanese are connected by catamaran to Mamaris and Bodrum in Turkey respectively. For further information see openseas.gr.

There is a daily service connecting Thessaloniki with Sofia, although you'll have to transfer to a bus for the short section between Kulata on the Bulgarian side of the Greek border and Strimon on the Greek side.

From mid-June to mid-September there is also a train service between Belgrade and Thessaloniki via Skopje. In Belgrade you can connect to trains to other parts of Europe.

TRANSPORT TIPS TO HELP YOU GET AROUND

On the mainland and larger islands like Crete or Naxos, you'll definitely want a car. Car rentals and fuel are expensive (especially in summer) but nothing beats the freedom of going at your own pace. On smaller islands, you can get around by moped or motorcycle (you'll need a special licence). For all vehicle rental you need an International Driver's Licence.

BUS

The bus network is comprehensive. All long-distance buses, on the mainland and the islands, are operated by the regional collective known as KTEL (ktelbus.com). Fares are fixed by the government; bus travel is reasonably priced and has good safety records.

CAR

You can easily rent cars in towns across Greece; the largest selection is available at airports and ports. If you're planning on doing some off-road driving, it's best to rent a 4WD. If you're driving in the mountains during the winter, make sure the car has snow tyres.

CAR RENTAL COSTS

Car rental
€35–60 per day

Motorcycle rental
€25–50 per day

Petrol
€2 per litre

ROAD SAFETY

Greece has the highest level of traffic accidents in the EU. Drivers are aggressive, road signs are treated as suggestive rather than imperative, and people often drive over the speed (and alcohol) limit. Exercise extreme caution while driving, especially in the Peloponnese and on the islands. In places like Crete, don't cut off another driver with your rental car – this could be taken as an invitation to start a fight.

ROAD CONDITIONS The main highways in Greece are in good condition, but note that in major cities there are plenty of potholes. On smaller islands, expect dirt roads, and just about anywhere you go, there will be hairpin turns.

INSURANCE Make sure you have insurance that covers damages to vehicles and personal injury from your insurance company or credit-card company at home.

DRIVING ESSENTIALS

At a roundabout, cars entering have the right of way.

Speed limit: highways 100km to 120km; residential areas 50km unless otherwise noted.

On the islands, wildlife can jump onto the road, especially at night.

The blood alcohol limit is 0.05% (roughly two drinks).

Children under 12 years can't be in the front seat.

MOTORCYCLE Few images are more romantic than that of a couple zipping along a beach road at sunset on the back of a motorcycle. And while it's one of the most practical ways to get around the smaller islands, note that if you've never driven one before, a Greek island is not the best place to try. You'll need a motorcycle licence to rent any two-wheelers, including a low-CC moped.

FERRY Greece has an extensive ferry network – the only means of reaching many islands. Schedules are often delayed due to weather, and timetables change before each summer season; see ferryhopper.com or greekferries.gr.

PLANE The majority of domestic flights are serviced by Aegean Airlines, Olympic Air, Astra Airlines or Sky Express. Greece has 14 airports, seven of which are located on various islands, including Crete, Santorini and Mykonos.

KNOW YOUR CARBON FOOTPRINT A domestic flight from Athens to Thessaloniki emits 53kg of carbon dioxide per passenger. A train would emit 22kg for the same distance, per passenger.

There are a number of carbon calculators online. We use Resurgence at resurgence.org/resources/carbon-calculator.html.

ROAD DISTANCE CHART (KMS)

	Athens	Delphi	Epidavros	Ioannina	Kalamata	Kavala	Meteora	Thessaloniki	Volos
Delphi	185								
Epidavros	140	255							
Ioannina	445	315	380						
Kalamata	285	355	180	465					
Kavala	680	535	770	415	880				
Meteora	360	235	485	105	575	380			
Thessaloniki	515	380	620	360	715	155	225		
Volos	325	205	450	270	520	385	145	215	
Xanthi	705	580	820	430	930	55	430	205	410

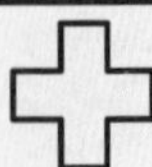

SAFE TRAVEL

Though generally a safe country, one of the biggest threats in Greece can be other people – whether that be drunk drivers, tourists trying to spike your drink, or men harassing you on the street.

EARTHQUAKES There's a lot of seismic activity in Greece, and earthquakes happen regularly across the mainland and some of the islands. Most are quite low on the Richter scale – just a small tremor you may not even notice – but occasionally, there are larger earthquakes that result in significant property destruction and some deaths.

WILDFIRES A sad but common experience of summer is at least one major wildfire. Extreme heat, climate change, poor government response and human activity have all contributed. They cause unimaginable destruction and can happen without any warning. Do your part to keep the environment safe – never litter, don't throw cigarette butts near wooded areas, and always properly damp out your campfire.

EXTREME WEATHER In the past years, weather has become increasingly extreme in Greece. Summers get hotter earlier and for longer, winters are colder and snowier than ever. Expect soaring temperatures and very little rainfall; be sure to keep hydrated and wear a sunhat during the peak of summer.

Spiked drinks There is a proliferation of both cheap, illegal alcohol and spiked drinks in Greece. In seedier bars, stick to beer (not hard alcohol) and never leave your glass unattended in crowded places.

ARON M/SHUTTERSTOCK ©

BLAZEJ LYJAK/SHUTTERSTOCK ©

Tap water On smaller islands, tap water is not drinkable, so you'll need to buy bottled water, drink boiled or bring your own filter.

INSURANCE
Emergency care is provided free of charge to everyone at public hospitals. For EU citizens, a European Health Insurance Card (EHIC) covers most medical care (not emergency repatriation or non-emergencies). Non-EU citizens can get travel insurance for private hospitals

PHARMACIES
A dime a dozen in Greece, and most pharmacists speak fluent English. Most medications are available over the counter and are much cheaper than elsewhere in Europe.

QUICK TIPS TO HELP YOU MANAGE YOUR MONEY

CREDIT CARDS Accepted in cities and most tourist places. Most businesses now have contactless and Apple Pay, but cash is still king – especially in taxis, outdoor markets and some cash-only spots. There are ATMs in all towns and on most islands (except for the smallest ones). Visa, Mastercard and American Express are accepted in nearly all ATMs.

PAYING THE BILL
Unless you're getting takeaway, it's common to pay at the table. If paying by card, you'll occasionally be asked to come up front.

TIPPING
While completely optional, it's always a nice idea to leave an extra euro or two on the table.

CURRENCY

Euro

HOW MUCH FOR A...

Gyros
€2.50

Freddo espresso
€1.90

Taverna meal for 2
€40

DISCOUNT OR TAX?

The VAT rate in Greece is 24%, and businesses are obliged to give you a receipt. However, in order to save taxes, some businesses will offer you a 24% 'discount' if you pay in cash. This just means you won't get a receipt, and the transaction is under the table. Though obviously not legal, it's a common practice.

BANKS & ATMs The major banks include Ethniki Trapeza, Piraeus Bank and Alpha Bank. You will find at least one branch and ATM in town; some smaller islands may only have a local ATM.

VAT REFUND
Those with permanent residency outside the European Union may claim a refund of the VAT on certain items purchased in Greece.

MONEY CHANGERS
Changing foreign currency is usually no problem at banks. ATMs will always prompt you to choose whether you want to be charged in euros or your home currency.

DISCOUNTS & SAVINGS

Most sights, activities and public-transport services are offered at reduced rates (or free of charge) to seniors, students, young children and families.

An Athens Museum Pass (€69) gets you entry into nine of Athens' top attractions, including the Acropolis, the Acropolis Museum and the Panathenaic Stadium.

RESPONSIBLE TRAVEL

Tips to leave a lighter footprint, support local and have a positive impact on local communities.

ON THE ROAD

Calculate your carbon There are a number of carbon calculators online; try resurgence.org/resources/carbon-calculator.html.

Choose more ecofriendly transport in cities Opt to walk or catch the bus for short distances as opposed to taking a private car.

Remember to save water Keep showers short and don't have a bath – on the islands, water is a precious commodity.

Consider opening the windows or turning on a fan Air-con is one of the leading causes of temperature changes in urban spaces in Greece.

Hold onto your rubbish (including cigarette butts) Until you find the nearest rubbish bin, whether you're at a campsite or on the beach.

Recycling It's basically nonexistent in Greece, so try to keep your single-use plastic to a minimum.

ALEXANDROS MICHAILIDIS/SHUTTERSTOCK ©

GIVE BACK

Support local businesses Greece suffered through a decade of economic crisis and austerity measures. It's always a good idea to spend money on locally owned businesses and leave tips in restaurants, cafes and taxis.

Help migrants and refugees Since 2015, a huge influx of refugees and migrants have arrived in Greece. You can volunteer with NGOs if you have the right skills, or donate money. Some NGOs on the ground are Humanity Crew, Za'atar, Second Tree and Lesvos Solidarity.

Donate for reforesting To help reforest Greece, donate to Plant Your Roots in Greece foundation, dedicated to reforesting burnt-down parts of the country.

Volunteer for wildlife conservation The Sea Turtle Protection Society of Greece operates a rescue centre in Glyfada near Athens, plus other projects around the country for which it's possible to volunteer.

DOS & DON'TS

Do learn a few words of Greek Even just a greeting in the local language will go a long way.

Don't be disrespectful in a church If entering one, keep your shoulders and knees covered and take off your hat.

Do eat up It's considered rude to refuse food (or a drink!)

LEAVE A SMALL FOOTPRINT

Pick a spot It's tempting to travel far and wide across Greece, but instead of island hopping, consider choosing one or two spots to visit and explore locally.

Go off-season Greece is inundated with tourists in high season, and it's creating a physical toll on both the landscape and people. Consider visiting in low season.

Don't clog the pipes Anywhere you go, make sure you throw toilet paper and any other products in the rubbish bin – never down the toilet!

SUPPORT LOCAL

Eat locally It's easy to do so in Greece – you can always find a green market or a local taverna for fresh produce and regional ingredients.

Spend consciously Purchase locally made souvenirs, crafts, food products and items from small brands as opposed to international chains.

CLIMATE CHANGE & TRAVEL

It's impossible to ignore the impact we have when travelling, and the importance of making changes where we can. Lonely Planet urges all travellers to engage with their travel carbon footprint. There are many carbon calculators online that allow travellers to estimate the carbon emissions generated by their journey; try resurgence.org/resources/carbon-calculator.html. Many airlines and booking sites offer travellers the option of offsetting the impact of greenhouse gas emissions by contributing to climate-friendly initiatives around the world. We continue to offset the carbon footprint of all Lonely Planet staff travel, while recognising this is a mitigation more than a solution.

RESOURCES

thehellenicinitiative.org
lesvossolidarity.org
zaatarngo.org
archelon.gr

UNIQUE & LOCAL WAYS TO STAY

Whether you're looking for a five-star resort perched on a cliff, a restored stone cottage in the mountains or a caravan by the sea, Greece has it all. With some of the most interesting architecture and stunning landscapes around, you'll be hard-pressed to get a bad night's sleep.

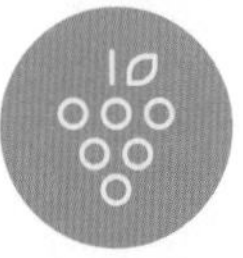

COST PER NIGHT AT A...

Campsite
€12

Luxury resort
€400

Apartment
€150

NATALIIA BUDIANSKA/SHUTTERSTOCK ©

CAMPING

There are dozens of campsites scattered across Greece, some of which happen to sit on some of the country's nicest coastline. There's parking for campers, space for tents (you can also rent), and some even have semi-permanent bungalows and small homes for rent. There are all sorts of services and amenities on site.

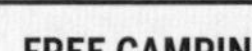

VILLAS

Greece has no shortage of villas for rent, and they make the ideal accommodation for larger groups of friends or families. Though some are more luxurious and expensive, you can find good deals through local realtors. Some owners may insist on a minimum stay of a week.

ALEXANDROS MICHAILIDIS/SHUTTERSTOCK ©

FREE CAMPING

While technically illegal, free camping (ie outside official campgrounds) is a lifestyle for many Greeks. There are still a few islands where it's possible to pitch a tent on the beach, kick back and enjoy the good life – especially in places like Anafi, Naxos and the smaller Cyclades.

CYCLADIC-STYLE ACCOMMODATION

One of the most emblematic images in Greece is a white cube of a structure with blue shutters and doors set against that sparkling Mediterranean sky. Apparently, painting these homes white and blue was actually a decree under the Metaxas dictatorship, but the stone structure underneath is authentically Greek. Cycladic-style architecture – which apparently inspired none other than Le Corbusier – can be found across the island chain of the same name, and makes for a particularly atmospheric architectural experience. Based on simple lines and natural materials, these buildings form an organic part of the landscape: it's a true wabi-sabi design. Thick stone walls, flat roofs and built-in, curved furniture round out the design.

Across the islands, you'll find hotels, villas and B&Bs that make use of this Cycladic style of architecture. On volcanic Santorini, you'll find these sorts of lodgings built into caves on the caldera, while on windy Mykonos, the entire island is covered in these sugar-cube constructions. The fanciest Cycladic-style hotels will have infinity pools and linen curtains, but you can also find simple stone homes that will fit a much more modest budget.

BOOKING

You'll want to book well in advance for the peak summer season (June to August), especially on the most popular islands. In the shoulder and low seasons, you can usually find good discounts on hotels, including the fancier ones.

Lonely Planet (lonelyplanet.com/greece/hotels) Find independent reviews, as well as recommendations on the best places to stay – and then book them online.

Hipaway Villas (hipawayvillas.com) For the most unique bohemian villas in Greece, perfect for groups or families.

My Greek Villa (mygreek-villa.com) Family and beach villas for rent, romantic getaways and more.

Campsaround (campsaround.com) Comprehensive map and booking site for campgrounds and hostels across the country.

Panhellenic Camping Association (greececamping.gr) A comprehensive list of campsite locations.

Greek Youth Hostel Organisation (higreece.gr) Covers 18 properties across the country including guesthouses and hotels as well as traditional hostels.

MOUNTAIN REFUGES

Around the mainland, Crete and Evia are all sorts of mountain refuges, from sparse huts with outdoor toilets to comfortable modern lodges. Run by the country's mountaineering and skiing clubs, they're an excellent (and cheap) way to sleep in nature.

ESSENTIAL NUTS-AND-BOLTS

HOSPITALITY
Greek culture is one of extreme hospitality. Paying for the bill, inviting you over for a meal, or insisting on giving you a free drink is common and should be accepted.

STRIKES
A frequent occurrence, strikes usually don't last more than a day but can seriously impact your travel. They are sometimes announced in advance in Greek media.

SMOKING
Most indoor places prohibit smoking (there are some exceptions) but it's permissible in outdoor areas.

FAST FACTS

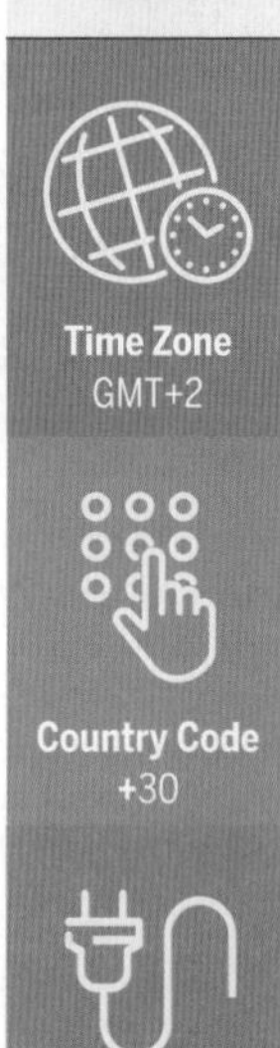

Time Zone
GMT+2

Country Code
+30

Electricity
220V/230V/50Hz

GOOD TO KNOW

Citizens from more than 90 countries don't need a visa (mfa.gr/en/visas).

A 24% VAT is added to all goods and services.

You'll pay a tourist tax of up to €4 per person/room in hotels.

To buy alcohol you must be 18 but there is no legal drinking age in private residences.

Stay on the right when driving, cycling and walking.

ACCESSIBLE TRAVEL

Greece is not very accessible. Footpaths are tiny, cars often park on them, and drivers barely stop for pedestrians. People with wheelchairs or strollers will find it frustrating to navigate Athens and Thessaloniki.

Hotels Some hotels and all all-inclusive resorts are wheelchair-accessible. Check disabledholidays.com to see which ones.

Public transport Metro stations have ramps and elevators; buses have wheelchair lifts.

Islands The most accessible are Corfu, Syros and Crete. Several beaches have the Seatrac (seatrack.gr) independent access system.

Ferries If you require special assistance getting onto the ferry, contact the ferry company 48 hours in advance to make arrangements.

Sights Not all archaeological sites are accessible, particularly the smaller ones in more rural places. The Acropolis has one wheelchair-accessible entrance.

GREETINGS
When meeting someone for the first time, it is customary to shake hands.

BREASTFEEDING
Though it's acceptable to breastfeed in public, few people do, so you may get a few stares.

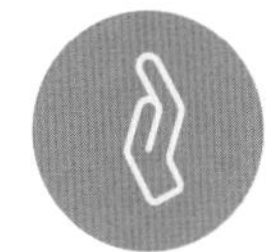

HAND GESTURES
Thrusting your hand palm-up in someone's face is considered an offensive gesture.

FAMILY TRAVEL

Restaurants and cafes Greeks love children, and will happily take care of your little ones. Highchairs are readily available, waiters will heat up a formula for you, and special food might magically appear at your table.

Transport Children under the age of four years travel for free on ferries, buses and the metro.

Sights and attractions Most sights and museums are free or half-price admission for kids and teens.

MAPS

Outside major cities it's not uncommon for Google Maps to get a little, well, fussy. Don't be afraid to ask locals for directions, and when all else fails, bust out that old paper map.

RELIGION

Most Greeks are Orthodox Christians, and the church still plays an important role in society – the church bells are an inescapable sound! Some 14% of Greeks are atheists, and there are a smaller number of Greeks who are Muslim or Jewish.

KOSTAS KOUTSAFTIKIS/SHUTTERSTOCK ©

LGBTIQ+ TRAVELLERS

Same-sex unions (but not marriages) Unions were legally recognised in Greece in 2015, and attitudes to the LGBTIQ+ community have grown more liberal across the country – but the Orthodox Church still has an outsized influence on the culture.

There's a huge gay scene In Athens and on islands including Mykonos. Each June, Athens hosts a huge pride parade that draws people from across Europe.

Lesvos, the birthplace of Sappho The western side of the island is popular with lesbians, and there's an international lesbian festival there every summer.

LANGUAGE

All Greek words of two or more syllables have an acute accent (´), which indicates where the stress falls. In our pronunciation guides, stressed syllables are in italics.

Masculine, feminine and neuter forms of words are included where necessary, separated with a slash and indicated with 'm', 'f' and 'n' respectively. Polite and informal options are indicated where relevant with 'pol' and 'inf'.

To enhance your trip with a phrasebook, visit **shop.lonelyplanet.com**.

BASICS

Hello.
Γειά σας./ Γειά σου. — *ya*·sas (pol)/ *ya*·su (inf)

Goodbye.
Αντίο. — an·*di*·o

Yes./No.
Ναι./Όχι. — ne/*o*·hi

Please.
Παρακαλώ. — pa·ra·ka·*lo*

Thank you.
Ευχαριστώ. — ef·ha·ri·*sto*

Excuse me.
Με συγχωρείτε. — me sing·kho·*ri*·te

Sorry.
Συγγνώμη. — sigh·*no*·mi

What's your name?
Πώς σας λένε; — pos sas *le*·ne

My name is ...
Με λένε ... — me *le*·ne ...

Do you speak English?
Μιλάτε αγγλικά; — mi·*la*·te an·gli·*ka*

I don't understand.
Δεν καταλαβαίνω. — dhen ka·ta·la·*ve*·no

TIME & NUMBERS

What time is it?	Τι ώρα είναι	ti o·ra *i*·ne
It's (two o'clock).	Είναι (δύο) η ώρα	*i*·ne (*dhi*·o) i o·ra
It's half past (10).	(Δέκα) και μισή.	(*dhe*·ka) ke mi·*si*

morning	πρωί	pro·*i*
afternoon	απόγευμα	a·*po*·yev·ma
evening	βράδυ	*vra*·dhi
yesterday	χθες	hthes
today	σήμερα	*si*·me·*ra*
tomorrow	αύριο	*av*·ri·o

1	ένας	e·nas (m)
	μία	*mi*·a (f)
	ένα	e·na (n)
2	δύο	*dhi*·o
3	τρεις	tris (m&f)
	τρία	*tri*·a (n)
4	τέσσερεις	*te*·se·ris (m&f)
	τέσσερα	*te*·se·ra (n)
5	πέντε	*pen*·de
10	δέκα	*dhe*·ka

EMERGENCIES

Help!	Βοήθεια!	vo·*i*·thya
Go away!	Φύγε!	*fi*·ye
Call the police!	Φωνάξτε την αστυνομία!	fo·*nak*·ste tin a·sti·no·*mi*·a
I'm lost.	Έχω χαθεί.	e·kho kha·*thi*

Index

H

I

K

L

M

000 Map pages

'Cruising to Tinos on the huge open deck of an old-style ferry at sunset while sipping a beer defines joy.'

RYAN VER BERKMOES

'I'm not usually into insects, but clearly it was a lucky day for me as the deaf and blind cave cricket, the dolichopoda, made a very rare appearance when I visited the cave network of Kastania. There's certainly more to see than stalactites and stalagmites!'

REBECCA HALL

'There's nothing quite like walking a village lane and meeting a chatty yia yia who's willing to speak with me in Greek and discuss the minutiae of the day.'

ALEXIS AVERBUCK

'Volos' tsipouradhiko ritual is the antidote to stress-filled urban banality. It represents the epitome of living spontaneously, as only Greeks know how.'

HELEN IATROU

FROM TOP: PIT STOCK/SHUTTERSTOCK ©, PHOTOS BRIANSCANTLEBURY/SHUTTERSTOCK ©

THIS BOOK

Design development Lauren Egan, Tina García, Fergal Condon

Content development Anne Mason

Cartography development Wayne Murphy, Katerina Pavkova

Production development Mario D'Arco, Dan Moore, Sandie Kestell, Virginia Moreno, Juan Winata

Series development leadership Liz Heynes, Darren O'Connell, Piers Pickard, Chris Zeiher

Commissioning editor Sandie Kestell

Editor Brana Vladisavljevic

Product editor Kirsten Rawlings

Cartographers Mark Griffiths, Alison Lyall

Book designer Aomi Ito

Assisting editors Kate Chapman, Andrea Dobbin, Gabrielle Stefanos

Cover researcher Fergal Condon

Thanks Gwen Cotter, John Taufa